Metaphors of Memory

The visitor is led into a darkened room. Through a window high in the wall behind him falls a narrow shaft of sunlight. The mirror reflects the light onto an octagonal wheel, with paintings of animal heads set on human shoulders. As a result of the revolutions of the wheel, the visitor sees his own image undergo one metamorphosis after another in the mirror. The aim of the designer of the device, the Jesuit Athanasius Kircher (1602–1680) was to conjure up with these transformations as many symbols and metaphors as possible for the observer: the optical reflections, he hoped, would move the observer to spiritual reflections on his own nature. In his own words: 'I myself have such a machine, which sends everyone into great raptures when they look into the mirror and instead of their normal countenance discern now the visage of a wolf, now that of a dog or some other animal.'

(Athanasius Kircher, *De Ars Magna Lucis et Umbrae*, Rome, 1646)

Metaphors of Memory
A HISTORY OF IDEAS ABOUT THE MIND

DOUWE DRAAISMA

Translated by Paul Vincent

CAMBRIDGE
UNIVERSITY PRESS

PUBLISHED BY THE PRESS SYNDICATE OF THE UNIVERSITY OF CAMBRIDGE
The Pitt Building, Trumpington Street, Cambridge CB2 1RP, United Kingdom

CAMBRIDGE UNIVERSITY PRESS
The Edinburgh Building, Cambridge, CB2 2RU, United Kingdom   www.cup.cam.ac.uk
40 West 20th Street, New York, NY 10011-4211, USA   www.cup.org
10 Stamford Road, Oakleigh, Melbourne 3166, Australia
Ruiz de Alarcón 13, 28014 Madrid, Spain

Originally published in Dutch as *De Metaforenmachine – een geschiedenis van het geheugen* by
Historische Uitgeverij 1995
and © Douwe Draaisma 1995, 2000

First published in English by Cambridge University Press 2000 as
Metaphors of Memory: A History of Ideas About the Mind

English translation © Cambridge University Press 2000

Printed in Great Britain at the University Press, Cambridge

This translation was supported by a grant from the Netherlands Organization for Scientific
Research

Typeface Swift 10/13 pt.   *System* QuarkXPress™   [SE]

A catalogue record for this book is available from the British Library

Library of Congress cataloguing in publication data

Draaisma, D.
[Metaforenmachine een geschiedenis van het geheugen. English]
Metaphors of memory: a history of ideas about the mind / Douwe Draaisma.
    p.   cm.
Includes bibliographical references and indexes.
ISBN 0 521 65024 0
1. Memory – History.   I. Title.
BF371.D6813   2000
153.1'2–dc21   99-088502

ISBN 0 521 65024 0 hardback

To Marius

Omnia in omnibus
Everything is contained in everything

Athanasius Kircher

What is truth?
A mobile army of metaphors

Friedrich Nietzsche

Contents

Illustrations

Acknowledgements

Many friends and colleagues have helped me to conceive and write this book; unfortunately one of them did not live to see its appearance. Pieter Vroon was the supervisor of the PhD thesis which developed into this book, he sadly passed away in January 1998. I regret his death, as he was a stimulating, witty and highly eccentric psychologist.

I would like to thank my colleagues in the Department for Theory and History of Psychology, University of Groningen, for letting me work quietly on the revision and translation of my book. Bert Roest was so kind to share some of his knowledge of medieval manuscripts with me. He was a valuable counsellor when I wrote the chapter on the metaphor of the book. Ann Boer, Else de Jonge and Anne Wolff of the Historische Uitgeverij Groningen have helped me in numerous ways. I am grateful to the Netherlands Organization for Scientific Research which offered a grant for the translation.

A good translation is little less than the re-creation of a book. I thank Paul Vincent for preserving so well the spirit and style of the Dutch edition.

Kurt Danziger, John North and Theo Verbeek have been valuable teachers to me (they still are); I highly appreciate their efforts in finding such a distinguished press for my manuscript. Sarah Caro and her dedicated staff have helped me overcome the thousand small and not so small problems which arise when one has to prepare a manuscript for a wider audience than peers and colleagues.

At the end I feel I should single out two persons. One of them is Patrick Everard of the Historische Uitgeverij. In the past decade Patrick has become both my publisher, coach and friend. His counselling encompasses the whole spectrum between the proper place for a comma and the vital choices in life; I owe him very much. The other one is Alison Gilderdale. She copy-edited my manuscript in such an elegant and dedicated way that it has been a delight to work with her.

Much of this book is about technologies for storing and distributing information and the way these technologies have shaped our ideas of memory. It is a strange thing to reflect that I will send off these acknowledgements in a few moments as an e-mail and will see it published, later this year, by the oldest press in the world.

Introduction

Leonhard Euler could boast one of the finest memories of the eighteenth century. Like many mathematical geniuses he was a child prodigy. The story goes that once, during a sleepless night, he calculated the first six powers of all numbers below a hundred and memorised the six hundred results in a mental table that he could read off days later. He also had an exceptionally retentive memory for the written word. Euler knew the entire *Iliad* by heart and could recite the text until the day he died. He could remember the first and last line of every page in the edition of the *Iliad* he had used at grammar school. Whatever he saw, read or heard seemed to stick immediately in his memory, from where it could be summoned up at will.[1]

Euler must have experienced this majestic memory as a life's task; he took pains to fill it with the best of science and art that was available. His erudition was legendary and embraced a knowledge of anatomy, physiology, botany, theology, chemistry, philosophy and Oriental languages. He demonstrated the same versatility in his own subject, where he is remembered for the many theorems and methods in number theory, algebra and geometry that bear his name. In the field of applied science Euler published on navigation and music, microscopes and telescopes, astronomy and geodesics, on statistics, magic squares and lotteries. By the time of his death, he had published 530 papers, mostly in the journals of scientific societies such as the Académie des Sciences and the Academies of Berlin and St Petersburg. After his death great bundles of papers containing unpublished treatises were found.

In 1768, following a rapid decline in his eyesight, Euler became totally blind. Thanks to his phenomenal memory and visual imagination this handicap had no effect at all on the nature and scope of his output. In the fifteen years up to his death in 1783 a further 355 papers appeared. In that period Euler worked jointly with his sons and a few pupils. Over the years a fixed pattern in their working methods evolved. In the middle of his study, we read in a biographical sketch,

> stood a large table covered with a sheet of slate, and on that slate, until he became totally blind, he detailed his calculations with a piece of chalk; he

also walked round it for hour after hour, reasoning, touching the table with his fingers for guidance, with the result that the edge eventually became completely shiny. Once the table was full, the general organisation of the paper was discussed and the master left it to a son or pupil to make the calculations and select examples; and usually the treatise was brought to him in outline the very next day. If this was approved, a fair copy was made and subsequently presented to the Academy.[2]

It is almost impossible to see a memory like Euler's as anything but a kind of natural history museum, as a collection of display cases, filled with precious items gathered in the course of a long, industrious life. But it is equally impossible to recall such a memory without being seized by a feeling of melancholy at the transience of it all. If we imagine the memory as a store of precious items, they are precious items that do not survive the death of the person and cannot be passed on. The memorised *Iliad*, those extensive tables of powers, the brilliant erudition, and all the other things that had been garnered in a well-spent scholarly life and carefully arranged into a collection, vanished into oblivion. However majestic a memory, however many splendid things fill it, death erases it all in a moment.

For Euler that moment came on 18 September 1783. On the morning of the day he died he had still managed

to sit and work on the laws according to which a hot-air balloon rises into the sky, which – of course – interested him, because on 15 June of that same year the Montgolfier brothers had made the first balloon ascent; and at lunch, at which his pupil and faithful helper Lexell was present, he had spoken of the calculation of the orbit of the planet Uranus, discovered by Herschel on 13 March 1781 . . .; after the meal, over a cup of tea, he was bantering a little with his favourite, i.e. mathematically most gifted, grandson, when suddenly the pipe fell from his hand, he collapsed and whispered, 'I'm dying', which was indeed the case.[3]

We have armed ourselves against the transience implicit in the mortality of memory by developing artificial memories. The oldest memory aid is writing, in ancient times on clay or wax tablets, in the Middle Ages on parchment and vellum, and later on paper. These same writing surfaces could also accommodate drawings of all kinds: hieroglyphics, diagrams, portraits. In 1839 an artificial memory for the direct recording of images, which rapidly became increasingly sophisticated, appeared in the shape of photography; from 1895, thanks to the invention of cinematography, moving images could also be captured. The preservation of sound, a centuries-old dream, became a reality through Edison's phonograph, patented in 1877. Nowadays numerous 'artificial' memories are available for what the eye and ear take in: cassette recorders, video, CDs, computer memories, holograms. Image and sound are transportable in space and time, they are repeatable, reproducible, on a scale that seemed inconceivable a century ago.

These artificial memories have not only supported, relieved and occasionally replaced natural memory, but they have also shaped our views of remembering and forgetting. Over the centuries memory aids provided the terms and concepts with which we have reflected on our own memory. We have 'impressions', as if memory were a block of sealing-wax into which a signet ring is pressed. Some events are 'etched' on our memory, as if the memory itself were a surface for engraving upon. What we wish to retain we have to 'imprint'; what we have forgotten is 'erased'. We say of people with an exceptionally powerful visual recall – for there have been Eulers in all ages – that they have a 'photographic memory'.

Everyday language relating to remembering and forgetting has a metaphorical cast. This applies even more to philosophical and psychological theories of memory. From Plato's wax tablet to the computers of our age memory-related language is shot through with metaphors. Our views of the operation of memory are fuelled by the procedures and techniques we have invented for the preservation and reproduction of information. This influence is so strong that in, say, nineteenth-century theories on the visual memory, one can trace exactly the succession of new optical processes: in 1839 the daguerreotype and the talbotype, shortly afterwards stereoscopy, then ambrotypes and colour photography, in 1878 'compound photography' and finally cinematography. Comparing the neuronal substratum of the visual memory to the structure of a hologram as some of our contemporary theoreticians do, fits into a venerable tradition which begins with the magic lanterns of the seventeenth century. The history of memory is a little like a tour of the depositories of a technology museum.[4]

But it is not only artificial memories that have served as metaphors. Anyone opening the index of this book at the entry 'memory', 'metaphors of', will find a long list. It includes the most varied storage spaces: for information, such as archives and libraries; for goods, such as wine cellars and warehouses; for animals, such as dovecotes and aviaries; for valuables, such as treasure chests and vaults; for coins, such as the leather purses or *sacculi* used by medieval moneychangers. Other metaphors are derived from the landscape: woods, fields and labyrinths. The hidden nature of memories is expressed in metaphors such as caves, grottoes, mineshafts, the depths of the sea. Buildings are also included in this imagery: palaces, abbeys, theatres. The memory has been seen as a magnet, stomach and a honeycomb, as a phosphorus ore, an Aeolian harp and a loom. Ever-changing images are projected onto our theories of memory, a succession of metaphors and metamorphoses, a true *omnia in omnibus*.

All these metaphors, whether taken from nature or technology, from organic or artificial processes, created their own perspective of memory. For Socrates, discussing the reliability of memories with Theaetetus, memory was like a wax tablet, whose wax was too soft and liquid, whereas Freud used a metaphor of a magic slate to suggest that even when there are no traces of memories on the

surface, there are bound to be deep layers of memories indelibly stored under-
neath. Reginald, the secretary to St Thomas Aquinas, saw his master's memory
as a sacred book, while the doctor–artist Carus described memory as a vast
labyrinth. These are not just shifts in emphasis; the history of memory, told in
metaphors, constantly shows us different kinds of memory.

Metaphors as literary–scientific constructs are also reflections of an age, a
culture, an ambience. Metaphors express the activities and preoccupations of
their authors. Without intending to, metaphors capture an intellectual climate
and themselves function as a form of memory. In 1682 Robert Hooke, a Fellow
of the Royal Society, in formulating his theory of memory, used the mechanical
analogies that were highly regarded in his circle. So through his metaphor of
the visual memory glow the experiments with the 'Bologna Stone' which
caused such a stir at the time – a phosphorescent substance which could store
light and afterwards, in the dark, emit it. In the 1970s in his theory of the visual
memory Karl Pribram, a neuro-psychologist, used the metaphor of the hologram, at the time the most advanced technique for storing and reproducing
light. Both processes, phosphorescence and holography, played a prominent
part in physical research into the manipulation of optical stimuli and found
their way almost automatically into psychological theories on the storage of
visual experience. In metaphors we find preserved what the author saw around
him when he was searching for powerful images for the hidden processes of the
memory. Metaphors are guide fossils, they help the reader to estimate the age
of the text in which he finds them.

At the end of the nineteenth century the professional study of memory passed
into the hands of psychologists. From the outset their research had an experimental and quantifying slant and in the past century clarified much about how
we remember and forget. The pioneer of this empirical research was Hermann
Ebbinghaus, who made the topic of memory accessible to experimental and
quantitative methods in his *Über das Gedächtnis* of 1885.[5] For many authors of
monographs on the psychology of memory, Ebbinghaus is the natural starting
point with many claiming that his work marked the real beginning of the
scientific study of memory.[6]

The reader will only meet Ebbinghaus half-way through this book, as one of
the many characters in a narrative which runs from Plato to today's designers
of neural networks. The abrupt transition which Ebbinghaus marked at the
methodological level, did not exist at the theoretical level. Thinking about processes in memory has been a constant and constituent part of philosophical
reflection; doctors in particular, but also theologians, physicists and writers
have contributed to theories of memory, and if one pays attention to the metaphors of memory, one is struck more by continuity and consensus than by
revolutions or a sudden start in 1885.

Memory, Socrates tells Theaetetus, was a gift from Mnemosyne, the mother of the Muses. Without memory no one could enjoy what her daughters produced: each sound would fade away without ever being included in a melody, every word in a poem would disappear before the rhyming word was heard. Psychology sometimes seems to suffer from a memory loss that borders on the pathological. Not only is the number of rediscoveries shamefully high, but valuable empirical and conceptual work carried out in older traditions has disturbingly little impact on present-day research. The result is that certain defects in theory formulation diagnosed as long ago as the nineteenth century, are repeatedly reintroduced into psychology. One might wish that psychology had a better memory. The obvious method for achieving this – Clio was after all a daughter of Mnemosyne – is historical research. The perspective chosen is that of the metaphors and graphic images projected by researchers through their theories. Of course one could write a history of memory equally well from other perspectives, and that would produce different histories. The perspective of metaphor is one of many.

Athanasius Kircher not only designed illusionist devices like the metaphor machine, but also made a thorough study of *anamorphosis*, the deliberate distortion of a representation, which requires special procedures to reverse. The clever Jesuit developed various 'mesoptical instruments' to construct such anamorphs.[7] Most anamorphs were painted or drawn, but they could also be executed on a grand scale, in the landscape for example, by laying out hedges in the form of a face. In that case the anamorph lay there like an illusion of clipped hedges in the garden, and could only be seen as a face from the point chosen by the constructor as the projection point, usually a window. Whether that face was an illusion or really existed, is a totally futile question: from every viewpoint except for that single one, one could only see a collection of hedges, laid out in no apparent order.

The anamorphic trick requires the spectator to be willing to adopt imaginatively the perspective which the designer had in mind when constructing it. Standing at that one window, his willingness will be rewarded by the fact that the hedges will form a face before his eyes.

Notes

1   H. de Vries, *Historische studiën*, Groningen/Batavia, 1934, pp. 220–58.
2   *Ibid.*, p. 254.
3   *Ibid.*, pp. 222–3.
4   Two previous short studies have appeared on metaphors of memory, both focusing on more recent psychology: J. C. Marshall & D. M. Fryer, '"Speak, memory!" An introduction to some historic studies of remembering and forgetting', in M. M. Gruneberg & P. E. Morris (eds.), *Aspects of Memory*, London 1978, pp. 1–25; H. Roediger, 'Memory metaphors in cognitive psychology', *Memory and Cognition*, 8 (1980), 231–46.

5   H. Ebbinghaus, *Über das Gedächtnis*, Leipzig, 1885.

6   The memory psychologist Baddeley begins his textbook with the assertion: 'Philosophers have speculated about memory for at least 2,000 years, but its scientific investigation only began about 100 years ago.' A. Baddeley, *Human Memory. Theory and Practice*, Hillsdale, NJ, 1990, p. 1.

7   A. Kircher, *De ars magna lucis et umbrae*, Rome, 1646.

1   The Mystic Writing-Pad

Whenever I distrust my memory, writes Freud in a note of 1925, I can resort to pen and paper.[1] Paper then becomes an external part of my memory and retains something which I would otherwise carry about with me invisibly. When I write on a sheet of paper, I am sure that I have an enduring 'remembrance', safe from the 'possible distortions to which it might have been subjected in my actual memory'.[2] The disadvantage is that I cannot undo my note when it is no longer needed and that the page becomes full. The writing surface is used up. Both shortcomings are absent in another method: slate and chalk. A slate can be constantly reused and hence has an unlimited capacity. But the disadvantage of the slate is that to jot down new notes you first have to rub out an old one. It therefore looks as though an unlimited capacity and enduring traces exclude each other among the aids that we use to replace our memory. Hence sheets of paper and slates lack precisely the quality that makes human memory so strangely efficient, says Freud, 'since our mental apparatus accomplishes precisely what they cannot: it has an unlimited receptive capacity for new perceptions and nevertheless lays down permanent, though not unalterable, memory-traces of them'.[3]

Subsequently Freud explains that as early as 1900 in *The Interpretation of Dreams*, he had voiced the suspicion that the unusual achievements of our psychical apparatus could be ascribed to the operation of two different systems. The first, the 'perception-consciousness', records perceptions without retaining a permanent trace of them. It is a *tabula rasa* in the face of every new experience. The second system, the 'mnemic system', lies behind the perceiving consciousness and retains the enduring traces of our perceptions. But how is one to imagine this combination of apparently incompatible functions?

Not so long ago, writes Freud, a device was put on the market under the name of *Wunderblock* or 'Mystic Writing-Pad'. It consists of a wax layer, covered by a sheet of wax paper and a transparent celluloid sheet. If one writes on the celluloid, one sees the text appear on the wax paper. If the text has to be erased one simply pulls the paper free of the wax layer and the Mystic Writing-Pad is again blank. But if one looks under the wax paper, one sees that at a deeper level an enduring trace has been preserved, the wax is now engraved with what was previously only visible on the wax paper. The outer sheets are again blank, as though they had never been written on, while on the inner one everything has been preserved. The Mystic Writing-Pad, concludes Freud,

> solves the problem of combining the two functions *by dividing them between two separate but related component parts or systems*. But this is precisely the way in which, according to the hypothesis which I mentioned just now, our mental apparatus performs its perceptual function. The layer which receives the stimuli – the system Pcpt.-Cs – forms no permanent traces, the foundations of memory come about in other, adjoining, systems.[4] [The italics are Freud's]

In Freud's view the shortcomings of the Mystic Writing-Pad are not important for the analogy, what matters are the points of agreement. We need not be worried by the fact that the Mystic Writing-Pad cannot 'reproduce' the vanished script from inside, something that our memory *is* capable of. What counts is the parallel that goes even further than the simple combination of functions. In the case of the Mystic Writing-Pad the script disappears whenever the paper is separated from the wax layer. In the perceptual apparatus the interruption of the stream of innervation, the course of the neuronal impulses, has the same effect: without innervation the stimulus is not conducted to the deeper level and perception remains insensitive. Innervation corresponds to the contact between the paper and the wax layer in the Mystic Writing-Pad: 'If we imagine one hand writing on the surface of the Mystic Writing-Pad, while another periodically raises its covering sheet from the wax slab, we shall have a concrete representation of the way in which I tried to picture the functioning of the perceptual apparatus of our mind.'[5]

Freud was a master of imagery, an aspect of his work that has contributed greatly to his prestige as a writer.[6] But for Freud – who in 1930 was awarded the Goethe Prize for Literature – those metaphors had more than just a decorative function. In a letter to Ferenczi he defined scientific creativity as the interplay between 'daringly playful fantasy and relentlessly realistic criticism'.[7] In that alternation metaphors, comparisons and analogies were both inevitable and desirable: 'In psychology we can describe only with the help of comparisons. This is nothing special, it is the same elsewhere. But we are forced to change these comparisons over and over again, for none of them can serve us for any length of time.'[8]

Freud was true to his own theory. In his work there are scores of metaphors and analogies deriving from the most diverse fields.[9] Mythology provided metaphors for the articulation of the complexes named after Electra and Œdipus. Military science provided the metaphors for the relationship between the *ego* and the unconscious. For example, Freud compared unconscious material which finds its way into the *ego* through a dream and there acts independently to an army of occupation which refuses to adapt to the laws of the land that it has invaded and promulgates new laws of its own. Sometimes the *ego* has to endure a siege by the *id* or psychoanalytic treatment is represented as a foreign intervention in a civil war. Other Freudian metaphors derive from physics and technology. The libido, for example, is a liquid which exercises a pressure and can overflow or drain away into a reservoir. There is a famous passage in which the *id* is compared to a pot full of seething excitement, a precarious balance of pressure and counter-pressure, fired up from below by urges and regulated from above by the compromises of the *ego*.[10] The second passion in Freud's life, archaeology, was also an inexhaustible source of metaphors. Just as an archaeologist tries to reconstruct the outlines and frescos of a vanished building from fragments of a wall and excavated shards, so the psychoanalyst has to draw his conclusions from his patients' fragments of memory and associations. When treating hysteria it was a case of working one's way layer by layer towards the trauma hidden beneath the hysteria. It was only when the traumatic memory had been thoroughly excavated and that erosion had taken hold of it that the symptoms could disappear. Wasn't it only after it had been excavated that the real destruction of Pompeii set in (figure 1)?

The metaphor must have been of great importance to Freud not only as a rhetorical instrument, but also as a heuristic aid in formulating a theory. What is the strange effectiveness of this tool based upon? A metaphor like that of the Mystic Writing-Pad is a 'verbal' phenomenon, but it also contains a reference to a concrete object and hence has a pictorial aspect. Like the Mystic Writing-Pad itself the metaphor is an instrument with two layers, a unification of word and image.

The metaphor as smoked glass. Three theories of metaphor

In the *Poetics* Aristotle defined the metaphor as 'the use of a strange name by the transfer from genus to species or from species to genus or from species to species or by comparison, that is: parallel'.[11] Present-day literary studies generally reserve the term metaphor for what Aristotle mentioned last, parallel, an analogous relationship between two objects, events or relationships. Aristotle's definition contains two terms which are still considered quintessential to metaphorical usage: the use of a 'strange name' and the 'transfer of meaning'. The first refers to the deviation from the usual context which can be pointed to in every metaphor. To give Aristotle's own example: the word 'evening' normally indicates a part of the day; therefore in the metaphor 'evening of one's life' the term 'evening' has become a 'strange name'. The concept of 'transfer' indicates that the connotations of the word in its usual context are transferred to the new, 'strange' context. That a river flows in one direction is an example of a

1. A cabinet in Freud's consulting room, next to the door to his study. According to Freud himself he read more about archaeology in his lifetime than about psychology. He was a passionate collector of ancient artifacts. On tables and in glass cases, both in his consulting room and in his study, there was a huge display of vases, bowls and pots, sphinxes and Buddhas, reliefs, statuettes and busts. In May 1938, a few days before the Gestapo forced Freud to leave for London, Eduard Engelman took photographs of all Freud's rooms in the flat at Berggasse 19 in Vienna. One can see from these photographs that Freud treated patients and studied in rooms that were half-way between a library and a museum of antiquities.

connotation which in the metaphor 'time is a river' is transferred to a new context. This quality of metaphor is recorded in its etymology: the Greek verb 'metapherein' means 'to transport', or 'transfer'.

That metaphors take words out of their usual context and transfer their meaning to a new context is about the only thing on which there is a consensus in literary studies. Precisely what the relationship is between two contexts, how metaphors are related to reality or whether all metaphors can be exchanged for literal descriptions, even whether literal descriptions exist at all – there is a fundamental lack of consensus on all these matters. The fact that Freud's Mystic Writing-Pad is sometimes called a metaphor and sometimes an analogy or a model, reflects the conceptual conflicts in this part of the linguistic world.

In his *Philosophy of Rhetoric* of 1936, Richards opened up a debate on the epistemological status of metaphor which continues to the present day.[12] He also introduced a terminology for the analysis of metaphors which is still in use. According to Richards's analysis a metaphor is the formulation of a relationship between two terms. One is the 'topic term', the term about which the metaphor is asserting something, the other is the 'vehicle term', the term which transfers that meaning from another context, Aristotle's 'strange name'. In 'Memory is like a dog that lies down where it pleases', a metaphor of the Dutch writer Cees Nooteboom, 'memory' is the topic term and 'a dog that lies down where it pleases' the vehicle term.[13] For the similarity which is suggested by metaphor, in this case a memory which will not be ordered about, Richards uses the term 'tenor'.

Leading on from the ideas of Richards, Max Black has presented three interpretations or perspectives, in which metaphors are conceived of successively in terms of substitution, comparison and interaction.[14] In the 'substitution' interpretation, the vehicle term is an intruder in the sentence: it worms its way into the place of the literal term and makes the sentence, at first sight, incomprehensible. In 'Romario is a puma' the 'puma' turns the sentence about the Brazilian footballer, read literally, into nonsense. Only with the realisation that 'puma' is substituted for dreaminess, alternating with explosions of power, suppleness and speed, does the sentence acquire meaning. Metaphors are strictly speaking superfluous. If they are tolerated it is for decorative reasons; in principle they could be replaced by a literal expression.

The problem with the substitution interpretation is that many metaphors, particularly in science, owe their existence precisely to the fact that they express what cannot be said literally – either not yet or in principle. It is said of certain cells in the immune system that they 'recognise' pathogens: biochemists are working hard to discover the mechanisms which enable immune cells to do this, but those efforts have not so far resulted in a theory where the metaphor 'recognise' can be replaced by a literal description. In practice, and also in this case, progressive theory leads to an increase in metaphors: for example the specification of 'recognition' at the molecular level has led to a 'lock-and-key' mechanism. The metaphor 'recognise' is therefore not so much decorative or superfluous, at this moment there is simply no other choice.

For psychological metaphors the objections to the substitution interpretation weigh even more heavily. Whereas in the case of physical processes like the interaction between immune cells and pathogens one can form some kind of idea about a literal description, the literal description of *mental* processes seems to be fundamentally excluded. What is the literal equivalent of 'search processes' in the memory? How do you literally describe a process such as 'storing'? If 'filtering of information' is a metaphor, what literal description does it replace? The problem with much figurative usage in psychology is that no literal alternative is available.

An identical problem arises with the second theory of the relationship between the terms of a metaphor: the metaphor as *comparison*. According to this interpretation a metaphor is the formulation of a similarity which the reader or listener must retrieve from the comparison between the metaphor's two terms. We know that time flows and we know that a river flows – in 'time is a river' flowing is therefore the parallel sought. In fact this view is a special case of substitution – Black also points this out – since it is assumed that the similarity between the two terms can be articulated in a literal description. For psychological metaphors this interpretation is as inadequate as that of substitution.

Black himself, following in the footsteps of Richards, argued for an interpretation of metaphor in terms of *interaction*. In a metaphor the topic term and vehicle term are linked by a set of associations and these associations are involved in an interaction. This reproduction creates a new meaning which is given neither in the one nor in the other term separately. In 'man is a wolf' for example, the associations of 'wolf' – cruel, treacherous, wild – are linked to the associations with 'man' and a new meaning of man as a wolf-like creature is created. Because this metaphor conversely gives the wolf something human, the interaction between both sets of associations are symmetrical, although in most metaphors the vehicle term will have a dominant influence. In the psychology of memory the computer metaphor is a convincing illustration of this interaction: the exchange of associations between computer and memory has not only made the memory more technical, but has made the computer more psychological.

Black has explained his position with the analogy of a visual filter. Anyone who looks up at the night sky through a piece of smoked glass with a few transparent strips across it, can see that the stars are in a straight line. In 'man is a wolf' the relevant associations of the vehicle term, cruel and wild, are the transparent parts, the irrelevant associations, hairy and fast moving, the black glass. In a formulation which evokes memories of the optical machinery of Athanasius Kircher, Black writes that in a metaphor the associations of one term are 'projected' over those of the other and so create a new pattern.

Although the filter analogy for metaphor has provoked quite a lot of criticism (rightly so: the dark glass may have an influence on what we see of the stars, but the stars change nothing about the glass), the interaction theory has been received enthusiastically. The idea that a metaphor creates a new meaning by eliminating some associations and accentuating others, links up with both older and more recent theories on the statics and dynamics of metaphors. So the core of the interaction theory had already been formulated by Richards in 1936: 'When we use a metaphor we have two thoughts active together and supported by a single word, or phrase, whose meaning is a resultant of their interaction.'[15] And this definition in its turn reminds us of the observation of Samuel Johnson that a metaphor 'gives you two ideas for one'. Present-day theorists like Martin and Harré write that the topic term and the vehicle term are each the centre of a 'semantic field' and that the interaction between these two fields enables us to produce and understand new insights.[16]

The interaction theory allows room for some marginal notes. The first is that the aspect of interaction will be more prominent the newer, more surprising and more original the metaphor is. Like all human creations metaphors are subject to wear and tear and the process of interaction between the two domains which is set in motion by a metaphor may become fainter and finally disappear. The phenomenon of the 'dead metaphor', the metaphor which has gradually become the literal expression, is the end result of this process. The metaphor 'go haywire', for example, derived from farming, has lost its graphic vitality as a description of human actions and has finally become ossified as a dead metaphor. (Ironically, such a metaphor has an amazing resurrection as soon as it is applied to a machine, as in 'the computer has gone haywire'.) Nietzsche compared the dead metaphor to a coin where the image of the head has worn away with use, a convincing analogy, because it is indeed the relief of the image which gradually becomes worn away and finally disappears completely from the expression. In this way the process of interaction also comes to a halt: the metaphor no longer gives 'two ideas for one' and has simply become a literal expression.

In the second place the interaction which is evoked by a metaphor will be more intense the more finely branched the networks of associations around both terms are. When both of the domains which are brought into contact in a metaphor are rich in associations, the mutual selection and organising of those associations will become all the more productive and it is more likely that the metaphor will produce new insights. Hooke's metaphor of the microcosm for the memory is – as will become apparent in a later chapter – an example of a metaphor in which the two terms were each linked with a detailed network of associations. In such a case a metaphor can have a considerable heuristic yield. The 'semantic fields' are in that case so fruitful that after the first harvest a second and a third may follow.

A third and final comment is that the interaction theory involves a move towards psychology. If the essence of metaphor is that associations from two domains come into interaction and that the product of that interaction is a new meaning, then that is a formulation in the categories of psychology. This poses the question of whether psychology is perhaps able to shed some light on the processes *behind* the use of metaphors. How does the interaction of associations operate? Exactly what processes are involved in the production and understanding of metaphors? What is the role of language, memory, or perception? What, in brief, has psychology to say about metaphors?

A brief psychology of metaphor

From the 1970s onwards psychological research into metaphors has grown rapidly. Important contributions have been made by such fields as linguistic and memory psychology. In developmental psychology, studies have been carried out into competence in the use of metaphors as a function of cognitive maturation. In some respects theories of 'imagery' attach to theories about metaphors. The same applies to research into non-verbal processes in thought, reasoning and creativity. In educational psychology experimental studies have been carried out into the value of metaphors as didactic tools. A slightly unexpected approach is that of neuro-psychology: the production and interpreting of metaphors has, like all psychological processes, a substratum in brain processes and for the last decade and a half, neuro-psychological research has produced some interesting results in this area.

An intriguing quality of metaphors is that they are a union of opposites: they combine concrete and abstract, visual and verbal, graphic and conceptual. In a metaphor, writes Beck, there is a reference to a set of concrete relations in one situation, in order to facilitate the recognition of an analogous set of relations in another situation.[17] The essence of the metaphor is in her view the use of a concrete image in order to be able to understand or formulate abstract relations. She distinguishes two levels of thought. One is sensory and perceptual and consists of relatively diffuse categories. The ease with which we can understand synaesthetic use of language ('a warm colour', 'a sharp sound') underlines the fluid boundaries of verbal designations at this level. The second level is that of verbal and semantic thought. The designations here are more precise and more abstract. In Beck's view, the metaphor is an intermediary between these two agencies – it belongs neither completely to one nor to the other level, it mediates between analogous and semantic forms of thought. The metaphor is a *go-between*.

One can find some support for this interpretation of metaphor in recent attempts to map the neurological location of figurative language use.[18] It has so far not been possible to locate the 'neurological co-ordinates of metaphor', to quote Danesi, to the nearest degree, but there are some findings which illustrate that the metaphor, as a combination of image and language, is also a *go-between* from the neurological point of view. Most of those findings have been collected through research into hemispheric specialisation.

In 1940 a *split-brain* operation was carried out for the first time in a number of epileptic patients. This involves the left-hand and right-hand side of the cortex being surgically divided by partially severing the corpus callosum, a thick bundle of nerve fibres at the bottom of the brain. This type of surgery alleviates epileptic fits, and the reason for this is not because the fits remain limited to one side alone, as was first thought, but because the frequency of fits is reduced. A number of researchers, including the pioneer of neuro-psychological research with *split-brain* patients, Roger Sperry, have subsequently set up an experimental programme to determine a psychological profile of both halves of the brain. The results put an end to the old image of the relationship between the left and right hemispheres. The old image was that of an unequal marriage: a dominant hemisphere, usually the left-hand one, which contained all language functions, assisted by a subordinate hemisphere which kept quiet and in which probably not much happened. The new view is that of equal part-ners, each with its own repertoire of specialisations. The left hemisphere has retained many of the language functions, such as the semantic, grammatical and phonological aspects of language. The verbal memory and abstract and analytical thought are also located on the left-hand side. The right hemisphere is associated with visual memory, spatial orientation and concrete and syn-thetic thought.[19] Various experiments suggest that this specialisation can also be identified in the processing of figurative language usage.

In a classic experiment Winner and Gardner presented their test subjects with a series of metaphors.[20] Each metaphor was linked with four pictures, from which the test subject had to choose the picture which best represented the meaning of the metaphor. Other pictures represented the literal meaning of the metaphor or the image used itself. In the case of the metaphor 'he was wearing a loud tie' the distracting images were a tie from which a noise came, an ordinary tie and a man who spoke loudly. The correct picture was a man with a brashly coloured tie. There were three groups of test subjects: aphasics (mostly patients with damage to the left hemisphere), patients with damage to the right hemisphere, and a control group of people without damage. Patients with brain damage to the left hemisphere as a rule chose the picture which corre-sponded with the meaning of the metaphor. But patients with damage to the right hemisphere chose the literal meaning as often as the figurative one, which suggests that they have difficulty in distinguishing the two types of meaning. In a similar study it emerged that patients with right-hemisphere damage have considerable problems in discovering and explaining the meaning of proverbs.[21] In view of the character of proverbs – a concrete image that has to be generalised into an abstract relationship – it is not surprising that interpreting proverbs can be disrupted by damage to the right hemisphere.

These results led to the cautious conclusion that in processing metaphors two different psychological processes are involved, each with its own neurolog-ical substratum. According to this view the correct interpretation of figurative language depends on the integration of a 'language-based' and an 'image-based' process. Right-hemisphere damage, it is argued, impairs the processing of visual 'image-based' aspects and hence the interpretation of the metaphor as a whole.

Through their combination of image and language, of graphic and abstract, metaphors are ideally suited to explaining and teaching theories. It would be appropriate to call this the 'Comenius function' of metaphors, after the seven-teenth-century Bohemian philosopher and pedagogue Johannes Amos Comenius who in 1657 in his *Didactica Magna* was the first to argue at length in favour of graphic education. First of all one can observe that metaphors are indeed used widely for that purpose, in both specialist and non-specialist publications. Curtis and Reigeluth checked a series of text books in the field of the sciences for the use of metaphors and analogies.[22] Their findings were sufficiently numerous to base a taxonomy on. In the case of a *structural* relationship the entities to which the topic and vehicle term refer have a similar structure, as in 'a cell is like a room, with a floor, a ceiling and walls'. In the case of a 'functional' relationship the two terms of the metaphor have their operation in common, as in 'feedback operates like a thermostat'. In most cases the topic term has an abstract character and the vehicle term refers to something concrete: 'The electrons in a grid behave like marbles on a drum skin.' In an analysis of articles in two Dutch popular scientific magazines, Woudstra found a total of 79 metaphors, predominantly of a functional kind (70%) in three issues of each magazine.[23] The proportion of functional metaphors increased as the context became more complicated. In all cases the vehicle term was concrete. In their much more extensive survey (26 books) Curtis and Reigeluth found a marked preponderance (82%) of metaphors in which the topic term was abstract and the vehicle term concrete.

The Comenius function of metaphors has been investigated experimentally as well as through the study of educational texts. Research by Reynolds and Schwartz suggests that metaphors contribute to the educational effectiveness of graphic presentation.[24] They presented their test subjects with eight short texts to be studied. Each text ended with a conclusion. In one condition the conclusion was phrased in a literal sentence, in the other condition, it was phrased in a metaphor. Reproduction of what had been read showed that metaphorically formulated conclusions had been retained better than literal conclusions. Moreover, test subjects in the case of the metaphor condition remembered more details from the preceding text. The authors think that metaphors enable one to set the process of reproduction in motion more easily and to pursue it for longer.

A finding such as this might be based on *dual coding*. On the basis of experimental and theoretical work, Paivio has suggested that in inventing and understanding metaphors two systems are involved which function autonomously, but can exchange information mutually.[25] One system is geared to linguistic information and makes use of verbal presentations which are processed sequentially. The other system processes information which relates to concrete objects and events and is represented in images which are in most cases visual in nature. Metaphors are the product of the co-operation between these two systems. Paivio specified various mechanisms which are intended to explain why the process of *dual coding* supports the communicative function of metaphors.

In the first place, the activity of two independent, but co-operating systems facilitates access to information in the long-term memory. If a metaphor activates *two* association processes, verbal and visual, it is more likely that the information will actually be found. Experiments have shown that the availability of non-verbal representations facilitates the reproduction of verbal material. Pictures are retained better than words, concrete words better than abstract words, and instructions to combine two separate words into an image of one's own invention leads to an improvement in verbal reproduction. The dual coding which is induced by metaphors is in this view a cognitive investment which pays off in the reproduction phase.

In the second place, the *image* in the metaphor allows for an efficient storage of information. The vehicle term refers to a concrete, vivid graphic image, the characteristics of which are stored as an integrated package or 'chunk' and can also be reproduced again as a coherent whole. With an image we immediately have a set of relationships. Unlike sequentially processed verbal information, these relationships are a simultaneous given. In the third place, the vehicle term can function as a *conceptual peg* on which the more abstract terms can be hung. In an experiment by Verbrugge and McCarrell the test subjects were presented with a series of metaphors.[26] Later they were asked to reproduce these. In one condition the vehicle term, containing the 'image' of the metaphor, was presented and the test subjects were asked to reproduce the metaphor as a whole (the complete metaphor). In the second condition, the experimenters presented the topic term, the 'subject' of the metaphor, as a clue. Comparison showed that the vehicle term was a more efficient clue than the topic term. Obviously the concrete image is able to attach more information to itself. Metaphor enables the memory function to fish with several hooks at once.

The metaphor as a heuristic tool

The cognitive characteristics of metaphors which have just been discussed can also be found in the phase which historians of science usually call the *context of discovery*. Jerome Bruner derived the impression from observation of himself and his colleagues 'that the forging of metaphoric hunch into testable hypothesis goes on all the time', but that researchers always tried to give their publications in the professional press an 'aseptic quality', cleansed of metaphorical impurities.[27] He added that in that way one is removing one of the most fruitful sources of ideas from view. In the natural sciences it has been extensively documented how concrete and graphic events or objects have provided the inspiration for new technical notions or hypotheses. A few examples will have to suffice. In 1866, three years before Mendeleyev compiled his periodic system of elements, the English chemist Newlands presented a specification of elements by using the analogy of a piano keyboard.[28] Newlands grouped the elements in series of eight and compared those series to octaves, because each eighth element was a repetition of the first. He called this the law of the octaves in chemistry. Thus, by projecting the semantic field of ordering notes onto the ordering of chemical elements he anticipated Mendeleyev's system. In the history of immunology, too, hypotheses can be pointed to which owe their existence to concrete relations in a completely different domain. The Russian biologist Metchnikoff investigated the behaviour of cells in the transparent larvae of starfish. When, more or less by chance, some wood shavings found their way into the vicinity of the larvae, he observed that the larvae wrapped themselves around the shavings and ingested them. This reminded him of the pus that forms when a splinter causes an infection, which in turn led to the discovery of the most important defence mechanism in the human immune system: the phagocytes (literally, 'eater cells'), white blood corpuscles which absorb and consume invading bacteria. One monograph on the history of immunology has the appropriate sub-title 'From Metaphor to Theory'.[29] Visual representations have also played a crucial role in the more theoretical parts of physics. It is known from his own statements that Einstein conceptualised his theory in the form of visual images which he manipulated in thought experiments.[30] For example, he imagined a journey on a ray of light. If he were to hold a mirror in front of him in such a situation, then he would not be able to see his own image in it, because light cannot go faster than the speed of light and hence cannot catch up with the mirror. Just like a vampire, writes Dreistadt, Einstein would look into an empty mirror and visualise the relativity of optical processes.[31] The representation in a concrete image which can be inspected and integrated as a whole in the case of Einstein preceded the conceptualisation in a formal theory.

The number of examples could easily be extended.[32] The invariable outcome is always that the relations in a semantic field which are accessible to the imagination are used to discover or make more precise relations in the research field. This form of heuristics can be divided into two types. *Theoretical* heuristics means that a metaphor introduces new theoretical notions, brings coherence to hypothetical processes or is able to resolve apparent contradictions between experimental results, while *empirical* heuristics describes the degree to which a metaphor produces new topics for research. Harvey's metaphor 'the heart is a pump' had powerful heuristic value in both theoretical and empirical respects. The pump metaphor provided theories on the operation of the heart with new concepts such as the '*circulation* of the blood', organised separate findings into a coherent representation and explained experimental results which in terms of an earlier metaphor – the movement of the blood seen as the movement of the tides – were an anomaly. The heuristic value of the pump metaphor was shown by experiments designed to answer questions such as: Does blood pressure relate to the distance from the pump? What is the speed of the circulation of the blood? Does restricting the flow in one channel increase the hydraulic pressure in other channels? These questions were all derived from associations related to the vehicle domain of the mechanical pump (figure 2).

But heuristics also has a downside. A meta-metaphor like 'filter' expresses the fact that metaphors make one part of the information more visible, but do so by eliminating the rest of the information. In the directing, filtering and selecting of attention there is the implication that the information which was originally present is reduced. This has negative effects in both theoretical and in empirical respects: theoretical notions which are not noticed, hypotheses which are neglected, relationships which are removed from view, research

2. This frontispiece to *Corporis humani disquisitio anatomica* (The Hague, 1651) by
    the English doctor Nathaniel Highmore, is an allegory on the empirical turn
    taken by anatomy. The goddess Anatomia is seated at the top in the centre
    on her throne. She has turned away from the bearded man on her left who
    is absorbed in philosophical reflection in a 'museum of contemplation', pre-
    ferring to give her attention to the Theatrum Autopsiae on her right. Here
    scientists are busily engaged in research. On the table lies a cadaver, under
    the gaze of a double row of onlookers. The anatomist has removed the heart
    (a section of the aorta is still dangling from it) and he raises it in devotion to
    the goddess. The centre of the picture is reserved for an irrigation pump, as
    a metaphor of a heart, which ever since Harvey's *De motu cordis* (1628) had
    pumped and caused the blood to circulate and irrigate the tissues of the
    body. The pump is operated by a hand that appears from the clouds. Even if
    the heart had become a mechanical instrument, it was still kept in motion
    from above.

topics which are ignored. This disadvantage has over the centuries fed suspicion and disdain towards metaphor in philosophy and science. For John Locke, metaphor was 'an instrument of error and deceit'. Francis Bacon classified the metaphor under the *idola fori*, the heresies which are the result of confused language use. As we will see in chapter 3, in Royal Society circles the deprecation even took the form of an explicit ban on imagery in scientific publications.

Freud's recommendation to alternate metaphors as often as possible is an attempt to benefit from the advantages of metaphors, while eliminating their disadvantages: if each filter makes a different aspect visible, it is only from a combination of metaphors that the most complete image of reality can be expected. Unfortunately this advice is not so easy to follow in recent memory psychology. As will be extensively documented below modern metaphors for memory like the computer or the hologram are so all-embracing that it would be better to speak of metaphoric *themes* than metaphors. They not only furnish metaphorical terms for separate functions, they also provide a background against which all those separate metaphors have meaning. The interpretation of specific computational and holographic metaphors presupposes the metaphor theme of which they are part. In this situation metaphors cannot be freely interchanged and that creates a completely different metaphorical dynamic than that outlined by Freud.

Freud's description of memory as a Mystic Writing-Pad was no more than a note, an essay of a mere five or six pages, but like a scale model it summarises a lot of what has already been discussed about metaphors. The topic terms in the note all refer to abstractions, such as 'perceptual consciousness', and 'memory system'. The vehicle terms are derived from the concrete, graphic apparatus, the Mystic Writing-Pad. In this way Freud, as Black would put it, projected the associations of one domain onto those of the other domain and so obtained Samuel Johnson's 'two ideas for one'. The effect is that some associations are eliminated, others accentuated. The metaphor of the Mystic Writing-Pad therefore functions as a filter. In the taxonomy of Curtis and Reigeluth the Mystic Writing-Pad would fall under the functional metaphors: the presupposed relationships between the mental systems correspond in function and operation to the various components of the Mystic Writing-Pad. What Freud intended with his metaphor was on his own testimony mainly at the level of explanation and clarification, the Comenius function of metaphors. To this end he explains as graphically as possible how a Mystic Writing-Pad is constructed. According to the *dual coding* of Paivio, both verbal and pictorial information is presented in this way and so the functional relationship between the various sheets of the Mystic Writing-Pad can be stored in the memory as an integrated whole. The vehicle term of the metaphor can subsequently function as a *conceptual peg* when the information has to be reproduced.

But besides this didactic or educative function the metaphor of the Mystic Writing-Pad also seems to have played a role in the development of Freud's ideas on the relationships within the 'mental apparatus'. He writes in the note that in *The Interpretation of Dreams* he had attributed the combination of a permanently available surface and a record of permanent traces to two different systems and that the existence of those two systems had been a 'hunch'. Once an artificial system was available that was actually able to unite both functions, Freud believed that this theory increased in plausibility. If one subjects the Mystic Writing-Pad to closer examination, he writes, 'it will be found that its construction shows a remarkable agreement with my hypothetical structure of our perceptual apparatus and that it can in fact provide both an ever-ready receptive surface and permanent traces of the notes that have been made upon it'.[33] The metaphor not only served to explain the theory: Freud also profited from the heuristic value of metaphor by linking a number of properties of the Mystic Writing-Pad with different qualities of the 'mental apparatus' *besides* the qualities which required clarification in the first instance. An example of this is the analogy between the erasure through the breaking of the contact between the paper sheet and the wax layer and the periodical interruption of innervation. It looks as though the combination of two different 'semantic fields' enables Freud to harvest more than what he was originally after. The metaphor of the Mystic Writing-Pad made his hypothesis more exact.

An appealing fantasy would be to transport Freud to the present day and ask ourselves what metaphor he would have used now in order to express the mysterious combination of permanent traces and an unlimited surface area for new notes. Possibly he would have turned to the Mystic Writing-Pad of our time, the computer, a quasi-'mental' device which can absorb, delete and reproduce information. In an analysis of Freud's comments on the 'mental apparatus', Erdelyi tried to group the metaphor of the Mystic Writing-Pad with more recent metaphors for the processing of information.[34] A simple programmable pocket calculator, Erdelyi argues, would be a better choice than the Mystic Writing-Pad. The information keyed in, which is visible in a window, can be stored, if required, in a back-up memory. That frees the window for the inclusion of new information, while the old information still remains available. In so doing, the calculator demonstrates the combination of functions which Freud pointed to as the essence of the Mystic Writing-Pad. Subsequently the calculator also has two functions which are lacking in the Mystic Writing-Pad. Writing, which once it has disappeared, as Freud pointed out himself, can no longer be reproduced by the Mystic Writing-Pad from within ('it would be a mystic pad indeed if, like our memory, it could accomplish that').[35] The calculator is able to do that. From the back-up memory the information can be brought back to the window. A second function which is lacking in the Mystic Writing-Pad is the possibility of changing permanent traces: what is written in the wax layer can be added to, not changed. The calculator does give us that option: the information in the back-up memory can be adapted at will, without first appearing again in the window.

But by turning the Mystic Writing-Pad into a 'pre-computer-information-processing-scheme' we are getting ahead of our story; the history of metaphors of memory begins with prosthetic memories considerably older than the Mystic Writing-Pad. The story should begin with the writing surface which in the days of Plato made the memory an instrument that absorbed impressions. This is the wax tablet.

Notes

1   S. Freud, 'A note upon the "mystic writing-pad"', in J. Strachey (ed.), *S. Freud, Collected Papers*, vol. v, New York, 1959, pp. 175–80. Originally published as 'Notiz über den "Wunderblock"', *Internationale Zeitschrift für ärztliche Psychoanalyse*, 11 (1925) 1, 1–5.

2   Freud, 'A note upon the "mystic writing-pad"', p. 175.

3   *Ibid.*, p. 176.

4   *Ibid.*, p. 179.

5   *Ibid.*, p. 180.

6   J. T. Edelson, 'Freud's use of metaphor', *Psychoanalytic Study of the Child*, 38 (1983), 17–59.

7   Quoted in D. E. Leary (ed.), *Metaphors in the History of Psychology*, Cambridge, MA, 1990, p. 43.

8   Quoted in B. Bettelheim, *Freud and Man's Soul*, New York, 1983, p. 37.

9   L. Breger, 'Some metaphorical types met with in psychoanalytic theory', *Psychoanalysis and Contemporary Thought*, 4 (1981), 107–40; H. Nash, 'Freud and metaphor', *Archives of General Psychiatry*, 7 (1962), 25–9.

10 G. H. E. Russelman, *Van James Watt tot Sigmund Freud. De opkomst van het stuwmodel van de zelfexpressie*, Deventer, 1983.

11 Aristotle, *Poetics*, 57b6.

12 I. A. Richards, *The Philosophy of Rhetoric*, Oxford, 1936.

13 Quoted from C. Nooteboom, *Rituals*, trans. Adrienne Dixon, Baton Rouge, Louisiana, 1983, p. 1. Strictly speaking, the figure of speech 'x is like y' is not a metaphor, but a simile.

14 M. Black, *Models and Metaphors*, Ithaca, 1962.

15 Richards, *Philosophy*, p. 93.

16 J. Martin and R. Harré, 'Metaphor in science', in D. S. Miall (ed.), *Metaphor: Problems and Perspectives*, Sussex, 1982, pp. 89–105.

17 G. F. Beck, 'The metaphor as a mediator between semantic and analogic modes of thought', *Current Anthropology*, 19 (1978), 1, 83–8.

18 M. Danesi, 'The neurological coordinates of metaphor', *Communication and Cognition*, 22 (1989) 1, 73–86.

19 S. P. Springer and G. Deutsch, *Left Brain, Right Brain*, New York, 1985.

20 E. Winner and H. Gardner, 'The comprehension of metaphor in brain-damaged patients', *Brain*, 100 (1977), 717–29.

21 D. B. Hier and J. Kaplan, 'Verbal comprehension deficits after right hemisphere damage', *Applied Psycholinguistics*, 1 (1980), 270–94.

22   R. V. Curtis and C. M. Reigeluth, 'The use of analogies in written text', *Instructional Science*, 13 (1984) 99–117.

23   E. Woudstra, 'Analogies in non-specialist journals', *Communication and Cognition*, 22 (1989) 1, 47–60.

24   R. E. Reynolds and R. M. Schwartz, 'Relation of metaphoric processing to comprehension and memory', *Journal of Educational Psychology*, 75 (1983) 3, 450–9.

25   A. Paivio, 'Psychological processes in the comprehension of metaphor', in A. Ortony (ed.), *Metaphor and Thought*, Cambridge, MA, 1979, pp. 150–71.

26   R. R. Verbrugge and N. S. McCarrell, 'Metaphoric comprehension: studies in reminding and resembling', *Cognitive Science*, 9 (1977) 494–533.

27   J. Bruner, *On Knowing*, New York, 1965, p. 5.

28   R. Dreistadt, 'An analysis of the use of analogies and metaphors in science', *Journal of Psychology*, (1968), 97–116.

29   A. I. Tauber and L. Chernyak, *Metchnikoff and the Origins of Immunology: From Metaphor to Theory*, New York, 1991.

30   G. Holton, *The Scientific Imagination: Case Studies*, Cambridge, MA, 1978.

31   Dreistadt, 'Analysis', 107.

32   E. S. Ferguson, 'The mind's eye: nonverbal thought in technology', *Science*, 197 (1977) 827–36.

33   Freud, 'A note upon the "mystic writing-pad"', p. 177.

34   M. H. Erdelyi, *Psychoanalysis: Freud's Cognitive Psychology*, New York, 1985, pp. 197–244.

35   Freud, 'A note upon the "mystic writing-pad"', p. 179.

2   *Memoria*: memory as writing

In the history of Western culture there has always been a close link between memory and writing. The Latin *memoria* had a double meaning: 'memory' and 'memoir'. Earlier, now obsolete, uses of the English noun 'memorial' included both '(a) memory' and 'written record'. This duality underlines the link between human memory and the means invented to record knowledge independently of that memory. From the very beginning, that is, from the wax tablet onwards, human remembering and forgetting has been described in terms derived from prosthetic memories.

Like a seal in wax

The classic passage on the metaphor of the wax tablet is found in Plato's *Theaetetus*.[1] In this dialogue on knowledge and truth Socrates, as usual mainly conversing with himself, asks the youth Theaetetus to imagine 'that our minds contain a wax block, which may vary in size, cleanliness and consistency in different individuals, but in some people is just right'.[2] This wax tablet is a gift of Mnemosyne, the mother of the Muses, says Socrates.

> and whenever we want to remember something we've seen or heard or conceived on our own, we subject the block to the perception or the idea and stamp the impression into it, as if we were making marks with signet-rings. We remember and know anything imprinted, as long as the impression remains in the block; but we forget and do not know anything which is erased or cannot be imprinted.[3]

At the time of Plato, wax tablets had already been in use for several centuries. They consisted of two or more narrow boards tied together. When coated with wax, they could be used for notes or sketches.[4] Unlike clay tablets – which became hard – wax tablets could be erased and reused. In Plato's Academy pupils probably carried similar tablets around and it must have been a very natural figure of speech to represent memory as a writing surface, whose quality varied with the composition of the wax. When someone has a good memory, when their mental wax 'is deep, plentiful, smooth and worked to the right consistency', they will find it easy to absorb memories and retain them for a long time.[5] This 'impressionability', a term which harks back to the wax tablet, is lacking in those who have to make do with wax that is too soft. They quickly forget their impressions and thoughts; such people, according to Socrates, have 'good learning ability' but are forgetful.[6] If the wax is hard and stony, the impressions will not be deep enough. Good judgement is based on the correct link between the original and the memory image, a relationship like that of a seal to its imprint.

The wax tablet was to return at greater length in Aristotle's theory of memory. In *De memoria et reminiscentia*, he writes that experience, absorbed by the senses, leaves an 'image', an *eikon* in our memory, 'just as persons do who make an impression with a seal'.[7] In the event of illness no clear image can be stamped on the memory, 'just as no impression would be formed if the movement of the seal were to impinge on running water'.[8] That is why young children and old people have poor memories: '. . . they are in a state of flux, the former because of their growth, the latter, owing to their decay. In like manner, also, both those who are too quick and those who are too slow have bad memories. The former are too soft, the latter too hard, so that in the case of the former the presented image does not remain in the soul, while on the latter it is not imprinted at all.'[9]

In Aristotle's highly sensual psychology the memory contains images of what has entered via the senses. More than Plato, Aristotle stresses the physiological aspect of memory. One could say that Aristotle gives the metaphor of the wax tablet, which in Plato is still a playful image, a more literal meaning. Something is literally stamped into the body, an impression with physiological features, a material trace. These physical traces, as Ackrill puts it, 'usually remain submerged, ineffective, unnoticed', but can be recalled as images.[10] Hypotheses on the physical substratum of memory traces had already been put forward by the pre-Socratic philosophers. Parmenides suggests that a pattern of light and heat, dark and cold corresponds with every memory and that any disturbance of this pattern erases the memory. Diogenes of Apollonia assumes that memories are contained in a particular section of the body's airways; he took as evidence the fact that people breathe a sigh of relief when what they have been trying to recall finally occurs to them.

In Aristotle's day the *pneuma* was the central concept in physics, and Aristotle's theory on the physical substratum of the memory trace fits in with it: memory is the gradually weakening motion with which the *pneuma* transports sense impressions through the body. The provisional destination of this transportation is the heart, the seat of the emotions.[11] Whatever must be 'taken to heart' is stored in the centre of the cardiovascular system.[12] After storage in the heart the higher impressions – those of sight, hearing and smell – are transported to the brain by the *pneuma*.

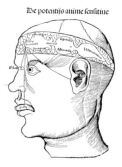

3. Gregor Reisch, prior of the Carthusian monastery in Freiburg, included a
    drawing of the human mind in his *Margarita philosophica* (Basle, 1503). This
    late-medieval diagram shows the influence of both Aristotle and Galen: the
    powers of the 'sensitive soul' (Aristotle) are housed in the ventricles (Galen).
    Sensory images are collected in the *sensus communis* which are in the two
    adjacent ventricles at the front of the brain (usually represented as a single
    cavity). These images allow the soul to be capable of *phantasia* and *imagina-
    tiva*. The images flow through a small aperture into the second ventricle,
    where *cogitativa* and *estimativa* are based. The third ventricle, at the back of
    the head and furthest from the senses, contains *memorativa*.

In later physiological theories the *pneuma* was to give way to the *spiritus animales*, a volatile substance, which (in the view of the Graeco-Roman physician
Galen) was stored in the brain cavities or ventricles. The rearmost ventrical was
reserved for memory; whatever needed to be retained was kept – literally – at
the back of the mind[13] (figure 3). This was a plausible location for a memory that
co-ordinated what the senses gathered, and remained unchallenged for over
fifteen hundred years.

After Plato and Aristotle, the metaphor of a wax-coated surface on which one
could write or make impressions developed into a *topos* in the literature on
memory. Cicero explained in his *De oratore* that just as writing consists of signs
and of the material on which those signs are written, so memory, like a wax
tablet, comprises both a space, a surface and the symbols written on it. And the
Ad Herennium, a treatise on memory techniques, tells us that the practised
speaker can place images in the 'background' and retrieve them at will; this
background is like a wax tablet or a sheet of papyrus, retention is like writing,
remembering is like rereading what has been written.[14] So the image remained
the same, though the writing surface varied. Long after the wax tablet had
given way to the codex and the codex had in turn been replaced by parchment
and later by paper, 'imprinting' and 'impression' remained intact as images for
the retention of information. In the thirteenth century Thomas Aquinas wrote
that a memory is a reduction of the original perception, just as wax adopts the
image of the seal but one cannot see from the impression whether gold or

bronze was used to make the impression.[15] As late as the end of the nineteenth century theories of auditive memory featured the wax layer as a receptive surface: acoustic memories were supposed to etch themselves into the memory just as a phonograph needle cuts a path across a wax cylinder (see chapter 4). In this way a metaphor that was over two thousand years old found a use in a field completely unconnected with reading and writing. This typifies the archetypal nature of the metaphor. Once stamped on theories of memory, the image could no longer be erased.

An inner place that is not a place

The wax tablet is not the only image that originates in the *Theaetetus*. After Socrates has defined 'recognition' as the search for correspondence between a perception and impressions already present in the memory, he begins questioning Theaetetus about the difference between *having* and *possessing* knowledge. This distinction, Socrates feels, requires a different metaphor:

> Earlier we constructed a kind of block of wax in our minds; now let's equip each mind with an aviary for all sorts of birds, some in exclusive flocks, some in small groups, and some flying alone, here, there and everywhere among all the rest.[16]

In this memory-as-an-aviary (other translations give 'birdcage' or 'dovecote') knowledge may be present in two ways: possessing knowledge means having the bird in your aviary, having knowledge means having the bird in your hand; it is the difference between potentially and actually remembering. While we are children, the aviary is virtually empty, but through education we add one bird after another to our collection. When we make mistakes it is because we grab hold of the wrong bird: 'as one might get hold of a wood-pigeon instead of a regular pigeon'.[17]

The physical image of the memory as a dovecote or aviary represents retention of information as the preservation of an experience in an enclosed space. A person wishing to remember something re-enters that space and tries to recover what has been kept. Like the wax tablet, the metaphor of the storage space has become an archetype in the literature on memory, which has had scores of variants from the Greeks to present-day theories. Even today we speak of 'storage time' and 'storage capacity' and 'search processes' are conducted in the memory.

No writer in antiquity used storage metaphors more gracefully than Augustine. In Book x of the *Confessions*, he writes of the buildings, storehouses, caves and treasure chambers of memory – images, as he himself admits, that give at most an approximate vision of memory.[18] With Augustine the reader never forgets for a moment the tension he feels between memory and the words that can be found for it. Memories, he writes, 'are retained in the great storehouse of the memory, which in some indescribable way secretes them in its folds'.[19] Metaphors, at once inadequate and indispensable, recreate memory in a quasi-space, 'an inner place – though it is wrong to speak of it as a place'.[20] What we remember is retrieved from a 'wonderful system of compartments'.[21] Augustine's descriptions of memory derive their charm from the high – and justified – level of wonderment, as in this celebrated passage:

> Yet men go out and gaze in astonishment at high mountains, the huge waves of the sea, the broad reaches of rivers, the ocean that encircles the world, or the stars in their courses. But they pay no attention to themselves. They do not marvel at the thought that while I have been mentioning all these things, I have not been looking at them with my eyes, and that I could not even speak of mountains or waves, rivers or stars, which are things that I have seen, or of the ocean, which I only know on the evidence of others, unless I could see them in my mind's eye, in my memory, and with the same vast spaces between them that would be there if I were looking at them in the world outside myself.[22]

Augustine's metaphors reduce these vast spaces to the human proportions of a palace, a treasure house or a cavern. What comes in through the gates, doors and passages of the senses is deposited and stored, images with images, sounds with sounds, smells with smells. In memory the images re-emerge, sensorily separate from each other, as separate as when they entered. When I reflect upon colours, Augustine argues, 'sounds do not break in and confuse the images of colour, which reached me through the eye. Yet my memory holds sounds as well, though it stores them separately.'[23]

The metaphor of the storehouse raises the question of how something can be found in the memory which has not entered through the doors of the senses. Why is it that we find abstractions in our memories, mathematical concepts, laws, numbers? Mathematical lines, Augustine points out, cannot have been conveyed to me by means of the senses. Even the lines drawn by architects, 'sometimes as fine as the thread spun by spiders', do not resemble the lines in my memory, for these 'are not images of things which the eye of my body has reported to me'.[24] Likewise, other abstractions have no sensory origin: 'For I can run through all the organs of sense, which are the body's gateways to the mind, but I cannot find any by which these facts could have entered. My eyes tell me "If they have any colour, we reported them." My ears say "If they have sound, it was we who gave notice of them." My nose says "If they have any smell, it was through me that they passed into the mind." '[25] Aristotle's representations of the memory as an assembly point of sensory copies offers no help here, but is rather the root of the problem. Therefore Augustine resorts to a Platonic solution: laws and abstractions are present in our memories from birth, hidden deep within 'its deeper recesses'.[26] It is the art of science and philosophy to drive this knowledge from its hiding places so that it can be 'recognised'. Whenever I had insights, writes Augustine, 'it was my own mind which recognised them and admitted that they were true. I entrusted them to my own mind as though it were a place of storage from which I could produce them at will.'[27] It is probably no coincidence that this turn of phrase evokes memories of Plato's aviary and the difference between possessing and having knowledge. In order to have what is contained in the memory in front of one as knowledge, one must gather together what has, so to speak, been dispersed. This is also why, Augustine believes, Latin uses *cogitare* (lit. 'to collect', 'to gather') for 'to think'.

Still, in Book x Augustine constantly returns to the Aristotelian representation of memory as a sensory impression.[28] And problems constantly arise. For example, he comes up against the problem of how we can think of 'forgetting' without assuming that the concept of 'forgetting' is present in our memory. How did it get there if forgetting is precisely the absence of memory? In other words, how can we store the fact that something is absent? This is a perplexing question. When I reflect on my own memory, Augustine wrote, I have a mental image of remembering in my memory.

> But when I remember forgetfulness, two things are present, memory, by which I remember it, and forgetfulness, which is what I remember. Yet what is forgetfulness but absence of memory? When it is present, I cannot remember. Then how can it be present in such a way that I can remember it? If it is true that what we remember we retain in our memory, and if it is also true that unless we remembered forgetfulness, we could not possibly recognise the meaning of the word when we heard it, then it is true that forgetfulness is retained in the memory. It follows that the very thing which by its presence causes us to forget must be present if we are to remember it.[29]

Augustine then opts for the solution that we do not remember forgetting itself, but an *image*, a representation of forgetting. But he immediately realises that this presents new difficulties, because we can only keep an image of something in our memory, if we have first seen something. My memories of Carthage, writes Augustine, were stamped in my soul like an image when I was actually able to take in that city through my senses. But how can one 'take in' forgetting through one's senses? If memory contains an 'image' of forgetting, forgetting must have once been actually present. But in that case how, Augustine wonders, was forgetting able to 'inscribe its image on the memory when its presence is enough to delete what is already noted there'?[30]

Augustine concluded his treatise on forgetting with the sigh that memory had remained unfathomable for him: 'O Lord, I am working hard in the field, and the field of my labours is my own self. I have become a problem to myself, like land which a farmer works only with difficulty and at the cost of much sweat.'[31] It may have consoled him that a variant of his problem – the 'knowing-not' phenomenon – remains unsolved in modern psychology. This refers to the fact that we know unimaginably quickly that we do *not* know something. In terms of the metaphor of the storehouse this is an anomaly: establishing that a particular item, say a name, is not there would require a search of the whole inventory, while the reproduction of something that *is* present, which makes a further search redundant, should take less time. Measured reaction times show that in reality the reverse is true. This reminds us involuntarily of one of Augustine's exclamations of awe: 'I am lost in wonder when I consider this problem. It bewilders me.'[32]

Augustine took his metaphors from what he saw around him: the fields and caves near Carthage, buildings and palaces, treasure houses and aviaries. In this way the imaginary space of memory became a reflection of the outside world, *his* outside world, an impression of external reality on what was internal. Other writers, living in different places, in different ages, left the mark of *their* worlds on the metaphors for memory. In antiquity and in the Middle Ages the memory as a storehouse was a *topos*, but one with constantly changing imagery.[33] In the third century BC the Stoic Zeno of Citium described memory as a 'thesaurismos phantasion', a store for representations. This 'thesaurus' later came to refer to a treasure house and also to a reinforced chest or locker for keeping valuables in: the three Magi produced their gold, frankincense and myrrh from their 'thesauri'.[34] Cassiodorus, founder of the monastery of Vivarium, saw memory, in rather more down-to-earth terms, as a collection of pigeonholes and cages, enclosed spaces where perceptions could be accommodated after sorting. Without the ordering process of sifting and selection, the memory would remain a *silva*, an impenetrable forest. The same notion of ordering is expressed in the metaphor of memory as a *sacculus* or purse. Such a *sacculus* was not a simple bag, but a carefully compartmentalised leather purse, with separate sections for the various types of coinage. In the twelfth century, Hugo of St Victor compared the practised memory to the *sacculus* of a money-changer: whatever one wishes to memorise must be carefully stored. The forming of memories was like the minting of coins: as with Augustine's signet ring the impression corresponded to the image of the stamp. Order in memory, wrote Hugo, facilitates retrieval, just as an experienced moneychanger's hand slips into the right compartment at the nod of his client.

The cell, originally a stable or stall for domestic animals, later a room in a monastery, was also used as a metaphor for memory. When Chaucer has a monk say that he has at least a hundred tragedies in his 'celle', that refers to what has been recorded in the privacy of his memory. In classical Latin 'cellae' were the niches in a dovecote. When later papyrus scrolls were kept on shelves divided into niches by vertical partitions, the associations with Plato's dovecote were obvious. The bird, swift and elusive, was a favourite image for the soul and the fact that memories were stored in 'cellae' which could house both birds and papyrus scrolls links the storage and writing metaphors.

This brings us back to the representation of memory as a writing surface. In the Middle Ages the memory was to change from a wax tablet into a codex, then into a book, and finally into a library.

The book as memory, the memory as book

In her introduction to *The Book of Memory*, Mary Carruthers juxtaposes two of the greatest intellects in history, Thomas Aquinas and Albert Einstein.[35] Or rather, she quotes two writers very close to Thomas and Einstein respectively, who try to sum up in retrospect the source of their greatness. What links the two descriptions is an intense admiration, but that admiration focuses on qualities which, as a pattern, are virtually each other's opposites. What is praised in Einstein is his originality and creativity. Einstein, we read, had 'tremendous imagination', let intuition take him into 'unexplored regions', steered clear of convention and in his desire for independence preferred to take 'lonely pathways'. The revolution he brought about was due to his ability to avoid the paths that others had trod.

Shortly after the death of Thomas Aquinas in 1274 the hearings began which were the customary first step in the procedure of canonisation. The praise showered on Thomas in the testimony of the fellow-members of his order were completely different in character from that lavished on Einstein seven centuries later. Thomas also possessed a luminous and original intellect, but he is praised first and foremost for his *memory*. We are told how he had made a compilation of commentaries on the four gospels for Pope Urban IV and had relied on his memory for texts that he had written and memorised during his time in other monasteries. His memory was extraordinarily rich and retentive: 'whatever he had once read and grasped he never forgot'. His pupils testified to the fact that Thomas would sometimes dictate to three or four secretaries at once, on different subjects, from memory, effortlessly: 'he seemed simply to let his memory pour out its treasures'. When confronted with a difficulty he turned inward in prayer, after which he returned to the writing table and 'was accustomed to find that his thought had become so clear that it seemed to show him inwardly, as in a book, the words he needed'. With this prodigious memory, which seemed incapable of forgetting, 'it was as if knowledge were ever increasing in his soul, as page is added to page in the writing of a book'.

What strikes Carruthers in these two descriptions is a contrast that can be summarised, in medieval fashion, as that between *imaginatio* and *memoria*. Einstein's genius is attributed to intuition and imaginative power, qualities that allowed him to break free of what had been thought before him. Thomas's genius in contrast seemed to be based on a majestic memory in which knowledge was garnered in a slow and cumulative process. In the thirteenth century compared with our own age, it seems that people had a completely different attitude to the value of memory as an instrument of thought. There has been a complete reversal in attitudes: whereas in the Middle Ages *memoria* was seen as the soul's highest ability and hence as located deep in the brain, in the third ventricle, in our age the greatest value is attached to the *imagination*, the capacity that medieval commentators situated in the foremost ventricle, immediately behind the senses.[36]

But equally important – and parallel to Carruthers's commentary – is the persistence with which witnesses return to the book as an image for Thomas's memory.[37] Naturally the members of his order knew Thomas as a man of books, reading, writing, dictating, as a scholar for whom each meal was an annoying interruption of his studies in his cell, the library or the scriptorium. Yet one suspects that the stubbornness of book metaphors was more than simply an elegant attempt to describe someone in terms of the world in which he moved. Calling Thomas's memory a book was equally an expression of the high regard in which the book was held in the Middle Ages. It was books which enabled the peripatetic Thomas to fill his memory with what previous generations of thinkers had produced; it was books which gave the dictating Thomas the opportunity to set down what his own judgement had to add. Books stood at the beginning and end of his memory. The fact that this memory finally itself became a metaphorical book, constantly filling and enriching itself, 'as page is added to page', was a tribute not only to Thomas, but also to the book.

Even without its association with Holy Scripture, the Book of Books, the prestige of the book in the Middle Ages is only too easy to understand. In an age where personal life was precarious and uncertain and it was the exception to live to experience the birth of one's grandchildren, the book embraced the experience of scores of generations. What had been entrusted to parchment, whatever had been transferred from the memory of an individual human being into the domain of the written word, escaped transience. Whatever had been set down in a book could be consulted by others, it became public, it could be passed on, transported, translated, exchanged, copied, disseminated, the text had in a sense been made secure.

One can also see the importance of conservation from medieval manuscripts and incunabula. Scribes and copyists in their scriptoria tried to achieve a harmony of content and execution, that is: sacred texts, recorded in a book made to last for eternity. The care with which books were manufactured, the marginal decorations, the quality of the parchment, everything was designed to contribute to this same impression: here lies a written memory, of a more permanent kind than is afforded human beings. That impression is not without foundation if one reflects that many of the monasteries where books were produced, with their walls many feet thick, no longer exist, having fallen into decline during the Reformation, burned to the ground or demolished, while the books, apparently so much more vulnerable, survive unharmed in libraries.

The dissemination of the book meant not only an expansion of the written word but also an expansion of the image. For a long time the view persisted that medieval laymen had to rely on visual representations, such as images of saints, paintings, frescoes and allegorical prints, and that cathedrals were Bibles of stone and glass for the illiterate, but this interpretation fails to explain the abundance of 'picturae' in books specially aimed at a select circle of scholars.[38] Miniatures and marginal drawings were more than a simple alternative for words; they were intended to do what is implicit in the etymology of 'illustration', illuminate the text, so that it could find its way more easily into memory. When in AD 600 Bishop Serenus of Marseilles had all the images in his church destroyed, for fear that his congregation would lapse into idolatry, Gregory the Great reminded him that the memory had two main gates, hearing and sight, and that access to the memory could therefore be gained in two ways – by word and image. Hence, in Gregory's view, churches and books should in fact be decorated with images and paintings of saints.

Nevertheless it would be a mistake to think that in antiquity and in the Middle Ages the book came to be regarded as an *alternative* to human memory, as a means of unburdening by recording in writing what would otherwise have to be memorised. In the monastic tradition, the book was intended as an *aid* to memory, its purpose was precisely to facilitate memorising. Carruthers has argued that this way of treating the written word differs from the present relationship between writing and memory. Whereas in our age we say to ourselves, 'I must remember this until I can write it down', our medieval ancestors thought, 'I must write this down so that I can remember it better.' When on the borderline of antiquity and the Middle Ages, St Jerome tells himself, 'By careful reading and daily meditation my heart should build a library for Christ', it is in his heart, the centre of the individual experience of faith, in which he gathers knowledge, not in the book or in the monastery library.[39] What was written in books must eventually find its way into the personal memory. This relationship between writing and memory is perhaps expressed most beautifully in Gregory the Great's story about Abbot Equitius. This Equitius was in the habit of travelling around with leather *sacculi* slung from his left and right sides, filled with sacred codices. He would stop anyone he met, writes Gregory, and then produce a codex and 'would tap the fountain of Scripture and water the meadows of their memories'.[40] Once again: this stream flowed from codex to memory, not the other way round.

As a rule, what was recorded in codices or books was of religious origin. Psalms, gospels, liturgies – whatever was worth preserving in a written memory, coincided with what issued from the Scriptures. As a result the book, being read or written, became the fixed attribute of prophets and evangelists, Church Fathers and saints in Christian iconography.[41]

The monastic custom of listening to readings at meals, quenching one's thirst from the Scriptures, taking nourishment from God's Word, led automatically to the metaphor of the memory as stomach. Partaking of God's Word like food had its origins in the Old Testament. In his vision revealing his vocation the prophet Ezekiel saw the Lord holding out a hand with a scroll for him to eat.

And he spread it before me; and it was written within and without: and there was written therein lamentations, and mourning, and woe. Moreover, he said unto me, Son of man, eat that thou findest; eat this roll, and go speak unto the house of Israel. So I opened my mouth, and he caused me to eat that roll. And he said unto me, Son of man, cause thy belly to eat, and fill thy bowels with this roll that I give thee. Then I did eat it; and it was in my mouth as honey for sweetness.[42]

Readings at meals were part of a tradition in which words were not only tasted but chewed upon: many medieval manuscripts contain initials which are being gnawed, chewed or bitten, as if to urge the reader on to sink his teeth into the text.[43] Study must be taken in portions, over-eating was harmful to good digestion. Meditating on what one had read by recalling it, was like rumination.

In the twelfth and thirteenth centuries a scholastic tradition gradually evolved alongside the monastic one. The increasingly prominent position of theological studies, no longer in monasteries but at the first universities, gave the book a new status.[44] An academic course in theology could not offer the life-long acquaintance with texts (read aloud) that was possible in a monastery: time was limited and during lectures several copies of the same book were required for students. In the thirteenth century, thanks to smaller script and thinner parchment, the Bible became a portable, single-volume book, which enabled travelling students and lecturers to take their own copy with them. In theological studies the need arose for compendia, reference works and collections of commentaries. In about 1250 the concordance to the Bible appeared, followed by indexes to the works of the Church Fathers, books which were not intended for reading, but for looking things up in. This new function – as an aid to accessing the external memory – required a new kind of presentation and classification. After the concordance the first books appeared with a list of contents and an alphabetical subject index. Finding specific passages was made easier by section headings, key words in the margin, red and blue initials, cross-referencing, references to quotations, proper names in red ink to catch the eye. In textbooks a new order was created, and to an increasing extent with an alphabetical arrangement of entries.

The advantages of *statim invenire*, being able to find something on the spot, was at odds with the conventions of the monastic tradition. In a universe ordered by the coherence of hierarchy and chronology, alphabetical order could scarcely be regarded as an order at all. The alphabet conflicted with the familiar principles of harmony and coherence. The rise of the book that was consulted instead of read proceeded in fits and starts and did not immediately displace the monastic approach to books. The book as a storehouse of information was restricted to a limited circle of scholars. Included in individual collections, collected in chests and cupboards, books for study formed still-life-like groups in formal portraits of theologians, which towards the end of the Middle Ages gradually moved from the background to the foreground.

4.   In 1440 a book of hours was made in Utrecht for Catherine of Cleves. It con-
      sisted of eight parts, one for each 'hour' of the liturgical day. According to
      Mary Carruthers (see note 4), the marginal decorations refer to the meta-
      phors of memory. The birdcages may be an allusion of Plato's metaphor of
      an aviary or pigeonloft for the memory.

In the margins of the traditional book, geared to the personal memory, there
were no directives such as those which characterised the scholastic tradition,
instead, there were allusions to the retention of what one had read. In books of
hours miniaturists drew coins or jewels or other valuables that could be saved.
Flowers and beehives are also found: what was reading if not collecting nectar
from flowers to be stored in the honeycombs of our memory? Equally popular
were hunting scenes, referring to a metaphor of Quintilian's: in a trained
memory the capacity to remember is like a hunter familiar with the habits of
game who knows exactly where to find his prey.[45] In the Middle Ages Albertus
Magnus used the same metaphor: 'Remembering is nothing but tracking down
what is concealed in the memory.'[46] Traces are 'vestigia', (foot)prints; remembering is a process of *investigatio*. A book of hours produced in Utrecht in 1440
for Catherine of Cleves, duchess of Gelderland, contains a series of marginal
decorations, visual metaphors for the memory to which the text had to be committed (figures 4 and 5).

Books of hours like this appeared at a time when the regard in which books
were held was at its peak, at the beginning of the fifteenth century. But even
before the invention of printing, in around 1440, there were the first signs of a
sea change. In order to meet the increasing demand, outside church and
monastery, books of lesser quality and less exalted content, produced by second-
rate copyists, were put on the market. As early as the end of the fifteenth
century, some fifty years after the invention of printing, the collecting of books

5. Carruthers interprets this marginal motif as the *catena* or chain, a succession of associations, in which one image pulls the other along with it like a fish on a hook. Since each fish bites the tail of the fish in front, only a few hooks need attaching to the text to draw up the whole chain of various fish from the depths.

in a private library is ridiculed as human vanity. In the very first chapter of *Das Narrenschiff* of 1494, by Sebastian Brant, we see a conceited, bespectacled scholar, the type that is found to this day in cartoons, surrounded by what the caption describes as 'useless books' (figure 6). The reverence for the written word, which in the Middle Ages was given such intense iconographical expression, began to wane, a development perhaps not caused but certainly accelerated by the invention of printing and the increased proportion of secular literature. The century from 1500 to 1600 saw a doubling of the population, but a fourteen-fold increase in book production. From being something unique, the book became a mass-produced item. Large print runs became common, from the mid-fifteenth century onwards and books were more often printed on paper rather than parchment. Slowly but surely, books turned from a rarity into an everyday practical tool, which like other utilitarian objects had a limited lifespan.

By the beginning of the seventeenth century the decline in prestige was complete. 'As already, we shall have a vast chaos and confusion of books, we are oppressed with them, our eyes ache with reading, our fingers with turning',

Sen vordantȝ ǥat man mir gefán
Danñ jcǥ on nutȝ viľ Bûcǥer ǥán
Sie jcǥ nit ľyß/ vnd nyt verſtan

Von vnnutȝê buchern

Sas jcǥ ſytȝ vornan jn dem ſcǥyff
Sas ǥat worľicǥ eyn ſundren gryff
On vrſacǥ iſt das nit getǥan
Dff myn ľiBry icǥ mycǥ verſan

6.   In Sebastian Brant's, *Das Narrenschiff* (Basle, 1494), the fool poses as a scholar among 'useless books'.

wrote Robert Burton in his *Anatomy of Melancholy* (1621). As a result the book gradually acquired a different metaphorical meaning. Books were no longer associated with permanance, with a memory that keeps transience at bay, but with the finite, the vanity and futility of earthly things. Books became a *vanitas* symbol.[47] In the new genre of the *Still Life with Books* the decline in prestige is visible in the way books are depicted: often books are worn out, the leather bindings are creased and have shrunk and can no longer protect the paper, a worn-out goose quill or an hourglass accentuate the transience of the book.

Scores of seventeenth-century still lifes feature chaotic piles of books, like displays of fruit, flowers or game, as a *topos* of transience. Skulls were placed among the books, hourglasses, snuffed-out candles, wine glasses that have been knocked over, but also lutes and violins, because music, in those days, was still the most transitory of all the arts. Surrounded by everything that was transient and inconstant, the book appeared as the opposite of what it had symbolised in antiquity and in the Middle Ages.

Only one book escaped this reversal (figure 7). At the beginning of the eighteenth century the Dutch Pietist poet Jan Luyken wrote the lines:

7. Mathias Holtzwart's depiction of the book as an emblem of constancy and protection against the vicissitudes of fate.

Eén Boek, gedrukt in 't Hert als was
Is meer als duizend in de kas[t]

(One Book, printed in the Heart's own wax
Is worth a thousand in the stacks)[48]

Thus Plato's wax and Aristotle's heart were combined with Dutch piety and the Book of Books at least remained linked with memory.

Ars memoriae: the palaces of memory

We live in an age of external memories. Erudition gradually gives way as a prerequisite for expertise to something like 'potential erudition': the capacity to orientate oneself, at short notice and as the occasion requires, in information that has been recorded externally. Access to these artificial memories is still partly by traditional means such as registers, bibliographies and indexes, at least in disciplines where books are the principal external memory, but increasingly through automated search procedures. The pinnacle of this new erudition is the electronic search through a database. For many people, their computer's hard disk has become an extension of their memory, just as glasses are for their eyes.

The culture of external memories means not only a shift from inside to outside, but also from oral to written. Nowhere is the shift as visible as in politics and law, two subjects with an oral origin and rich oratorical traditions. Nowadays they both belong to an almost purely written culture. What in parliamentary circles is called a 'debate' is in fact a series of readings, occasionally interrupted by adjournments during which parliamentarians are handed new written material by staff. The same applies to the law. Speeches for the prosecution and the defence as an aid to the public administration of justice are becoming an anachronism: most matters could almost be dealt with by fax or e-mail, with the public sections on the internet.

Once the human memory was the greatest information-carrier. In the largely oral culture of the Greeks, wax or clay tablets were little more than memory aids. Most of what one wanted to say in a speech still had to be committed to memory. A good, well-stocked memory was a piece of professional equipment that required maintenance and dedication. Just like our external memories, it had to be updated, added to and indexed at set intervals: an invisible, but painstaking process of management, for which all kinds of techniques existed. Just as we have to follow technical procedures to access external memories, so the Greeks had strategies for accessing the inner recesses of memory, 'mnemonics'. This originally purely practical activity developed into an art of memory, the *ars memoriae*.[49]

The invention of mnemonics is credited to Simonides of Keos. Simonides had been invited to recite a poem at a banquet in honour of a certain Scopas. Shortly after his performance he was called outside. While he was away the roof of the hall collapsed. The guests were crushed under the rubble and mutilated beyond recognition. Simonides remembered where everyone had been reclining and so was able to direct the families to their dead. According to Cicero, who included this story in his *De oratore*, Simonides inferred from this

> that persons desiring to train this faculty (of memory) must select places and form mental images of the things they wish to remember and store those images in the places, so that the order of the places will preserve the order of the things, and the images of the things will denote the things themselves, and we shall employ the places and images respectively as a wax writing-tablet and the letters written on it.[50]

Mnemonics was based on a procedure that turned the memory into an imaginary space, with a clear, accessible organisation, which could be filled with 'images' one wanted to retain.[51] Those using this method would picture a building, a house, temple or palace. A sign or logo was devised for each subject to be memorised which was left in strategic places during an imaginary walk through the corridors and rooms. At the appropriate time the walk was repeated and the visual representations recalled the topics.[52] A lawyer beginning his speech for the prosecution, says the *Ad Herennium*, recalls his prepared house and opens the door of the first room.[53] He sees someone lying on a bed. Beside the bed stands a man with a cup in his right hand and wax tablets in his left. A ram's testicles dangle from his little finger. Immediately the indictment against his client comes clearly to mind: the man on the bed is a victim of poison, the cup still contains some of the poison. The tablets indicate his motive, an inheritance. The testicles lead him via 'testes' and 'testimony' to the witnesses.[54]

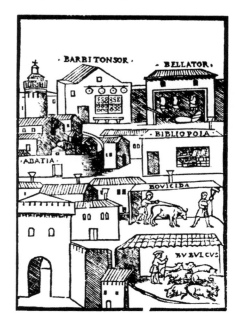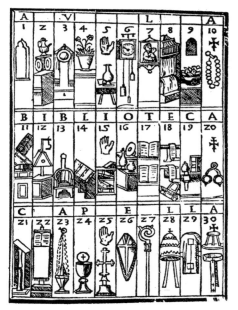

8a and 8b.   In the Christian use of mnemonics the classical palaces of memory were replaced by abbeys and cathedrals. In figure 8a an abbey with its out-buildings provides the backdrop for *loci*. Figure 8b is a list of images serving to memorise religious material, such as psalms or liturgical formula. For purposes of classification a hand was drawn on every fifth item and a cross on every tenth one. In addition, the objects were linked to each other by the place where they belonged: main hall, library or chapel. The illustrations were included in a treatise on mnemonics written by J. Romberch, *Gongestorium Artificiose Memorie* (Venice, 1533).

In order not to burden the memory unnecessarily most treatises recommended choosing buildings for the 'places' that actually existed and with which one was familiar. As a result mnemonics became architecture's mirror, with Classical, Gothic and Renaissance periods. And because the 'images' were derived from what people saw around them, the memory systems also give us an impression of contemporary attitudes and material circumstances. Some memory systems contain items which otherwise would have long ago vanished without trace. All that is known of some poems, is a line included as an example in a memory treatise, preserved like an insect in amber.

The capture of Rome by the Vandals brought an end to classical mnemonics. Only one treatise on memory, the *Ad Herennium*, reached the medieval script-oria more or less intact. And even there the art was not safe in its Classical form. All mnemonic systems underwent a thoroughgoing process of Christianisation. The palaces of memory were replaced by abbeys and cathedrals (figures 8a and 8b). In a veritable iconoclastic fury the classical images were destroyed, and were replaced in the alcoves by such virtues as Chastity and Moderation, with their own specific attributes. The *ars memoriae* became part of the *ars predicandi*, and the memory the instrument for keeping in mind liturgies and saints, heaven, hell and purgatory. It is no coincidence that mnemonics was practised mainly by the preaching orders.

Ironically enough, the mnemonic system that most worried the Church in the Italian Renaissance was the brainchild of a former Dominican monk, Giordano Bruno. Bruno had fled his order in 1576 and travelling through England, France and Germany had become a leading figure in the intellectual underground of the time. He was the high priest of Hermetics, the sixteenth-century New Age movement, a magical blend of a few parts natural science to many parts Cabbalistics, astrology, alchemy, necromancy and fire divination. Hermetics originated from the *Corpus hermeticum*, a collection of Greek texts from AD 100 to 300. In the fourth century the myth arose that the *Corpus Hermeticum* was based on the work of Hermes Trismegistus, an Egyptian priest, and hence had a pre-Christian origin. During the Renaissance, Hermeticism merged with Neo-Platonism and an intense revival ensued, with Bruno as its main representative.

The mnemonic system of this strange *magister* consisted of revolving wheels on which everything that existed was recorded. From the furthest solar systems to every last element, from the signs of the Zodiac to ores and minerals, from geometry and music to inventions like pottery and the making of fire, from the phases of the moon to instruments like pincers and combs – the whole universe, from infinitely small to infinitely large, revolved in Bruno's wheels.

Despite Bruno's commentary, his mnemonic system is one of the most impenetrable products of the *ars memoriae*. Even the ingenious Yates, who breaks 'seals' and 'seals of seals', is forced to leave much unexplained. It would appear that not enough of the prevailing occult mode of thought can be reconstructed for the modern reader. Large parts of Bruno's design remain hermetically sealed, inaccessible to those uninitiated in magic and sorcery. That very inaccessibility may help to explain the enduring attraction of Hermeticism. The Hermetic undercurrent retains its power far beyond the beginning of the seventeenth-century scientific revolution, constantly provoking new interpretations. The last great monument in this tradition was Fludd's theatre of memory.

Fludd's theatre of memory

The Englishman Robert Fludd (1574–1637) deserves our particular attention not only because his *ars memoriae* repeats – as in the final movement of a symphony – the principal themes from antiquity and the Middle Ages, but because his representation of the human mind as a microcosm exerted an influence on later, more mechanistically inclined theories of memory. Robert Hooke, the main protagonist of the next chapter, was influenced by Hermeticism in his youth. Fludd links the Middle Ages and the modern age.[55]

9. Leading on from classical and medieval traditions, the Hermeticist Robert
    Fludd saw the human mind as consisting of three sections, which are
    depicted here in relation to their correspondence with three 'worlds'. The
    mundus sensibilis unites whatever enters via the senses and just like the
    mundus imaginabilis, it is linked to the foremost ventricle. The second ven-
    tricle is the seat of the *cogitativa* and *aestimatio*. This most central and highest
    ventricle is linked to the *mundus intellectualis*, the God-related principle of
    rational thought. One finds the *memorativa* and *motiva* in the last ventricle.
    Motiva governs the body's motor system and for this reason it has a direct
    connection to the spinal cord. Each ventricle houses two faculties. Wherever
    the two overlap, one finds the words *hic anima est*, 'here is the soul'.

Fludd's mnemonic system is permeated with the harmony between the
macrocosm of the celestial bodies and the microcosm of the human mind. An
engraving from his *Utriusque Cosmi . . . Historia* (1619), in which the three psychic
spheres of perception, imagination and reason are depicted as the reflection of
the planets' orbits, remains famous to these days (figure 9). Fludd expressed this
same notion of harmony between 'above' and 'below' in two engravings accompanying his mnemonic system. The first is a depiction of the Zodiac, the second
a theatre, as a metaphor of memory. The engravings are on facing pages. When
the book is closed the astrological firmament covers the theatre of memory like
a canopy.

Yates believes that Fludd's theatre is modelled on an Elizabethan 'public
theatre', a large wooden structure, with a stage at ground-floor level, flanked by
galleries for the audience, and an upper storey where sieges could be enacted
(figure 10). The central part of the stage could be covered. The underside of this
ceiling, 'the firmament', was painted with depictions of the heavens. Fludd distinguished an *ars rotunda* and an *ars quadrata*. The 'round art' was concerned

10.   Engraving of the theatre as an artificial memory in Fludd's *ars memoriae*.

with non-corporeal representations like virtues, spirits and angels, the 'square art' with material things. In the orbits of the planets of the Zodiac, Fludd placed the square and round theatres which had to store the mnemonic images. By 'theatre', Fludd meant what would today be called the stage, the place where the actual performance takes place. In the foreground of the theatre are five columns. The outer columns are round, the centre one is hexagonal and those in between are square. Each column has its own colour. The columns and doors together provide ten *loci*. In the depictions of this theatre and of two other 'secondary' ones, the stages are empty and deserted, an effect that is all the more surreal if one considers that in the accompanying text Fludd invokes scenes intended to etch themselves in the memory with their vividness (Medea killing her brother by the red door, Medea collecting magic herbs, etc.). The material to be memorised consisted of lists of names and objects, mythological figures, tables of virtues and sins, to be accommodated on one of the stages, hanging from columns or nailed to a door.

Fludd was a declared opponent of fictional, invented 'places' as memory *loci*. Yates even suggests that Fludd was not depicting an arbitrary theatre, but the Globe Theatre, the permanent base of the company to which Shakespeare belonged, where the latter's plays were performed. The first Globe had burned down in 1613, but a second theatre rose from the foundations of the first, and is assumed to have been a faithful replica. However, no one knows exactly what the two theatres looked like. In 1644 the new Globe was also destroyed. Modern reconstructions are based on indirect evidence such as drawings of other theatres and stage directions. It is conceivable that Fludd left us an accurate representation of this legendary theatre, which Yates rightly considers a 'breathtaking possibility'. The hypothesis that a theatre long since razed to the ground, of which no plans or sketches exist, of which not a splinter remains, has an astral pendant in an occult mnemonic system and that we can wander round it three or four centuries later, has sufficient aesthetic appeal to push questions of authenticity into the background for a moment. Some hypotheses are too beautiful to be untrue. So in an unexpected way Fludd's theatre illustrates the conservation value of mnemonic systems. For that matter, all those imaginary palaces, abbeys and theatres contain not only items lodged by their designers, but also all kinds of things that have found their way in more or less by chance, just as in a burial chamber deep within a pyramid one finds not only mummies and sarcophagi thousands of years old, but also, among the bandages, the pollen and the air of those times.

Of all the mnemonic systems in the long tradition of the art of memory Fludd's is the most exuberant, to the point of theatricality. All that is visible to a modern audience on the stage of his artificial memory are ghosts, memories of a submerged world of Rosicrucians, Paracelsians, Cabbalists and mystics. Most of what Fludd presented is no longer fathomable for us. The *loci* he chose, the images he used, the geometrical relationship between columns and stage, door and gates, the representations on the canvas firmament above the actors – all of this was once undoubtedly inspired by meaning and reference, but three or four centuries on, too many keys have been lost for us to make reliable interpretations (figure 11). Some compartments in his theatre of memory will remain hermetically sealed.

The persistence of writing

Each mnemonic system produced by the *ars memoriae* is a further attempt to represent the inner space of the memory as an actual space. With the instructions for storing and retrieving the material to be memorised, the memory changed into a mnemonic storage depot, a warehouse, the metaphor which later became the 'storehouse of memory' in Locke, and eventually turned up as 'long-term store' in modern psychology. Presented in this way, it looks as if the metaphor of the storehouse has gone its own way, separately from the writing metaphor, which preceded it from the *Theaetetus* onwards. That impression is deceptive. In fact, variants of the storehouse metaphor have on the contrary underlined the persistence of the writing metaphor. Not only were written texts often kept in storage containers – the *cellae* with their scrolls of papyrus, the *sacculi* full of codices – but the imaginary spaces of mnemonics were also filled with writing. In all classical mnemonic treatises the 'positioning' of the memory images is represented as writing on a surface, be it a wax tablet or a sheet of papyrus. Reproduction during a speech was compared to the reading of a text. The same relationships prevailed in the 'spaces' Augustine wrote of. They might be 'inaccessible' and 'not expressible in words', but writing and reading was certainly going on in them. In the passages on forgetting, Augustine wondered how forgetting could 'write' its image in the memory, if through its very presence it 'erases' everything 'noted down'.

In this way fragments of the writing metaphor appear unexpectedly in metaphors from a completely different field. This situation is not symmetrical. Metaphors involving script, although spatial, do not represent the memory as

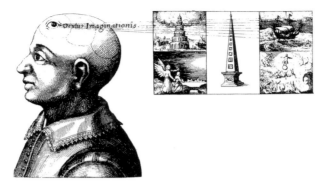

11. On the title page of the chapter devoted to mnemonics, Fludd's tripartite division of the human mind returns in the stylised depiction of the ventricles. From the front ventricle the 'eye of the imagination' views five 'memory places'; in the centre there is an obelisk, perhaps an allusion to the (supposed) Egyptian origin of Hermeticism, on the left there is the Tower of Babel and Tobias and the Angel; on the right one can see a ship in a storm and a depiction of the Last Judgement showing people about to be swallowed up into hell. The latter seems to be a medieval remnant of the reminder of hell. Fludd did not explain his choice of images, but they certainly meet the mnemonic requirement of being striking and memorable.

a store. Perhaps the explanation for this asymmetry must be sought in an essential difference between writing and storing: the former presupposes a process of abstraction, the latter does not. In writing, a *version* of experience is set down, a representation, the result of sifting and perspective. What has been written is not interchangeable with what has been experienced, it is based on distance and articulation. Stores, on the other hand, house the goods themselves. They have been assembled, brought in and ordered, but their storage lacks the character of representation that is the essence of writing. For memory that contains not the experience itself, but its record, writing is a more persuasive metaphor than the storehouse.

The strange appeal of this metaphor, which derives from the first external memory produced by our culture, can also be felt in more recent metaphors. Freud's Mystic Writing-Pad, with its wax layer, sheet of waxed paper and celluloid cover sheet, is a variant of the writing metaphor, just as the term 'engram' for the memory trace also refers to writing. In the description of computer memories, working with magnetic tapes, ample use is made of writing metaphors. Computer memories, says Bolter, are 'fully automated writing pads upon which a processor can engrave electronic messages and later read them back'.[56] In order to be stored in a computer's memory, data must first be 'read in' and on reproduction 'read out'. Storing new information in the place occupied by old information is called 'overwriting'. Data have to be 'machine-readable'. Information can be 'written across' from back-up memory to the hard disk, even if the information has nothing to do with text and the operations of the computer have little to do with reading. Hence the twofold meaning of *memoria* is preserved in the most advanced artificial memory we possess at present. The metaphor of writing shows the stubbornness of a palimpsest: apparently completely scratched out, but on closer inspection still vaguely legible among the words written later.

Notes

1 Quoted from Plato, *Theaetetus*, trans. with an essay by R. A. H. Waterfield, Harmondsworth, 1987.
2 Plato, *Theaetetus*, p. 99.
3 *Ibid.*, pp. 99–100.
4 M. Carruthers, *The Book of Memory. A Study of Memory in Medieval Culture*, Cambridge, 1990, p. 22.
5 Plato, *Theaetetus*, p. 104.
6 *Ibid.*, p. 105.
7 Quoted from *The Works of Aristotle*, Oxford, 1951, vol. III, *De memoria et reminiscentia*, I, p. 450a, 25.
8 *Ibid.*, p. 450a, 32.
9 *Ibid.*, p. 450b, 1–10.
10 J. L. Ackrill, *Aristotle the Philosopher*, Oxford, 1981, p. 67.
11 In the Hebrew tradition too, the heart was the seat of the memory. In Proverbs 3:1–3 we are exhorted to 'let thine heart keep my commandments . . . bind them about thy neck; write them upon the table of thine heart'. Not only commandments, but sins too may be indelibly imprinted in the heart: 'The sin of Judah is written with a pen of iron, and with the point of a diamond: it is graven upon the table of their heart, and upon the horns of your altars' (Jeremiah 17:1).
12 The theory of the heart as the seat of memory has left etymological traces: the Latin verb *recordari* ('to remember'), refers to the heart, as do such phrases as 'by heart' and 'par cœur' designating information that can be reproduced from the memory.
13 E. Clarke and K. Dewhurst, *An Illustrated History of Brain Function*, Oxford, 1972, p. 5.
14 Carruthers, *Book of Memory*, p. 28.
15 *Ibid.*, p. 55.
16 Plato, *Theaetetus*, p. 109.
17 *Ibid.*, p. 112.
18 Quoted from St Augustine, *Confessions*, trans. with an introduction by R. S. Spine-Coffin, Penguin Classics, Harmondsworth, 1961.
19 St Augustine, *Confessions*, p. 215.
20 *Ibid.*, p. 217.
21 *Ibid.*
22 *Ibid.*, p. 216.
23 *Ibid.*, p. 215.

24 *Ibid.*, p. 219.

25 *Ibid.*, p. 217.

26 *Ibid.*, p. 218.

27 *Ibid.*

28 J. Coleman, *Ancient and Medieval Memories. Studies in the Reconstruction of the Past*, Cambridge, 1992, p. 95.

29 St Augustine, *Confessions*, p. 222.

30 *Ibid.*, p. 223.

31 *Ibid.*

32 *Ibid.*, p. 216.

33 Carruthers, *Book of Memory*, pp. 33–45.

34 Matthew 2:11.

35 Carruthers, *Book of Memory*, pp. 2–6.

36 This location did not mean that *imaginatio* was guided by the vicissitudes of experience: *imaginatio* was rather the capacity to process sensory representations in such a way that they could be subjected to the judgement (*cogitatio* and *estimatio*).

37 Other witnesses also used book metaphors. Reginald, one of Thomas's permanent secretaries, stated that the former's dictation was so clear that 'it was as if the master was reading aloud from a book under his eyes' (Carruthers, *Book of Memory*, p. 5).

38 Carruthers, *ibid.*, p. 221.

39 *Ibid.*, p. 33.

40 *Ibid.*, p. 39.

41 J. Becker, 'Das Buch im Stilleben – Das Stilleben im Buch', *Das Stilleben in Europa*, catalogue, Münster/Baden-Baden, 1979, p. 450.

42 Ezekiel 2:10–3:3. These references are taken from an essay by Wiel Kusters on parallels between reading and eating, *Honingraten. De smaak van het lezen*, Maastricht, 1994.

43 M. Camille, *Image on the Edge. The Margins of Medieval Art*, Cambridge, MA, 1992, p. 64.

44 R. H. Rouse and M. A. Rouse, '*Statim invenire*. Schools, preachers, and the new attitude to the page', in R. L. Benson and G. Constable (eds.), *Renaissance and Renewal in the Twelfth Century*, Cambridge, MA, 1982, pp. 201–25.

45 Carruthers, *Book of Memory*, p. 247.

46 *Ibid.*

47 N. Schneider, *Stilleben. Realität und Symbolik der Dinge*, Köln, 1989, pp. 189–90.

48 Becker, 'Buch', p. 464.

49 On the history of mnemonics, see F. A. Yates, *The Art of Memory*, London, 1966 (ed. 1984). An older source is J. C. von Aretin, *Systematische Anleitung zur Theorie und Praxis der Mnemonik nebst Grundlagen zur Geschichte und Kritik dieser Wissenschaft*, Sulzbach, 1810.

50 Quoted in Yates, *Art of Memory*, p. 2.

51 The three sources for Classical mnemonics were Cicero's *De oratore*, Quintilian's *Institutio oratoria* and *Ad Herennium*. The last of these texts was written between 86 and 82 BC by an unknown teacher of rhetoric.

52 The 'places', *topoi*, later came to mean the subjects (or 'topics') themselves.

53   The sequence of places can still be recognised in the phrase: 'In the first place
. . . in the second place . . .'

54   Yates, *Art of Memory*, p. 11.

55   On Fludd's life and work, see W. H. Huffman, *Robert Fludd and the End of the
Renaissance*, London, 1988. On the esoteric slant of Fludd's writing, see J.
Godwin, *Robert Fludd. Hermetic Philosopher and Surveyor of Two Worlds*, Boulder,
CO, 1979.

56   J. D. Bolter, *Turing's Man. Western Culture in the Computer Age*, London, 1984, p.
157.

3   The splendour of the Bologna Stone

On Saturday 15 September 1677, after supper, the German alchemist Johann Daniel Crafft called at Robert Boyle's quarters in Pall Mall. Crafft announced that he had brought a strange new substance to England, which he offered to demonstrate to Boyle and his fellow-members of the Royal Society. Curious as to what this substance might be, Boyle assembled several Fellows in his chamber and invited Crafft to begin his demonstration. In a short account Boyle described some of the spectacular phenomena they witnessed that evening.[1]

First Crafft (or 'the Artist', as Boyle calls him) opened a large box and took out several glass vessels. The largest of these contained about two spoonfuls of liquid, looking like 'muddy water made a little reddish with brick-dust'. Next he retrieved some glass tubes and phials, all containing small quantities of liquids, and a glass bottle with a lump of matter in it, not exceeding 'the kernel of a Hasel Nut in bigness'. This, Boyle gathered from Crafft's demeanour, was the critical substance. Amidst 'the confused curiosity of so many spectators in a narrow compass', Boyle could only catch a glimpse of it. When Crafft's preparations were complete, he asked for the shutters to be closed and the candles removed'.

In the darkness, the company noted how the liquid that had at first looked like muddy water now faintly illuminated the glass sphere, 'not unlike a Cannon bullet taken red hot out of the fire'. When Boyle shook the glass, the swirling liquid seemed to flash before his eyes. The small glass tubes had turned into luminous cylinders. The lump of matter in the glass bottle shone even more brightly. Crafft broke a minute part of it into tiny fragments and scattered them over the carpet. To Boyle's delight the crumbs started to glow, twinkling like stars for a good while 'without doing any harm (that we took notice of) to the Turky Carpet they lay on'.

But even more extraordinary phenomena were to follow.

Crafft asked Boyle to give him his hand. The alchemist gently rubbed some of the matter on the back of Boyle's hand and cuff. Although Boyle had no sensation of either oiliness or roughness on his skin, his hand glowed intensely as if assisted by his body heat. When he blew on it, the light seemed to extinguish, but soon recovered its luminescence. Equally spectacular was Crafft's demonstration of writing in the dark. He took some of the substance on the tip of his finger and started writing on a sheet of paper that was handed to him. After a short while there appeared, in capital letters, across the full width of the paper, the word DOMINI, so bright that one could discern the fingers holding the sheet of paper. It was a fascinating sight, Boyle wrote, 'having in it a mixture of strangeness, beauty and frightfulness'.

With these demonstrations the experiments concluded: ''twas grown late, which made Mr. *Kraft*, who had a great way to go home, take leave of the Company after he had received our deserved thanks for the new and instructive Phaenomena, wherewith he had so delightfully entertained us'.[2]

Phosphorus and memory

Boyle wrote this 'memorial' at the request of his assistant Hooke, who had himself been present at the demonstration. As Curator of Experiments to the Royal Society, Robert Hooke (1635–1703) was a central figure in the physics of his day. He decided to include the account of Crafft's demonstration in a series of reports on the most recent experiments and findings concerning phosphorescent substances. In Italy, Germany and England a frantic search was underway for processes capable of producing phosphorescent materials, and scientific societies kept each other informed of progress through correspondence and the exchange of samples. Crafft's process was based on the lengthy distillation of large quantities of human urine and had been originally discovered by the German alchemist, Brand, who had sold his formula to Crafft. Another phosphorescent substance that cropped up regularly in Hooke's reports was the Bologna Stone, the luminescent stone or *lapis illuminabilis*, a mineral found in the vicinity of Bologna in Italy, which when ignited produced a substance (barium sulphide) that glowed in the dark. A third process had been discovered by the German alchemist Balduin (or Baldwin), who dissolved calcium in nitrous acid and distilled the resulting solution.

Seventeenth-century researchers were fascinated by the ethereal light emitted by phosphorescent substances.[3] The substances themselves derived from the alchemical tradition and explanations of their luminescent quality generally had a mystical flavour. It was assumed that phosphorescent substances were linked through 'sympathy' to the sun. Baldwin, for instance, wrote to Henry Oldenburg, Secretary to the Royal Society, that there resided in his piece of artificial phosphorus an 'innate and invisible philosophical fire, attracting by magical means the visible fire of the sun and emitting and throwing out in the dark its splendour in return'.[4] For Leibniz, who in his youth had belonged to an alchemical society, the soft glow of phosphorus was the symbol of the soul at peace with itself.[5] For over a century after the discovery of the first processes phosphorus was presented as a magic phenomenon. In 1771 Joseph Wright of

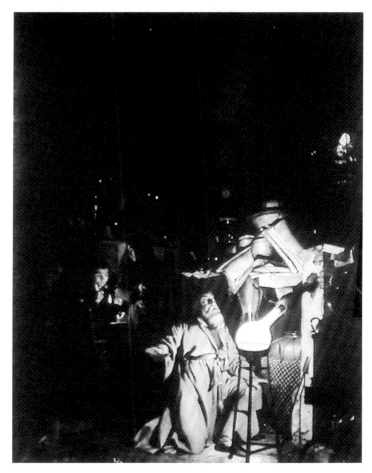

12.   *The Alchymist in Search of the Philosopher's Stone Discovers Phosphorus* (Joseph
Wright of Derby, 1771; possibly reworked in 1795). The painting hangs in the
Derby Museum and Art Gallery. (B. Nicolson, *Joseph Wright of Derby. Painter of
Light,* London, 1968.)

Derby painted *The Alchymist in Search of the Philosopher's Stone Discovers Phosphorus*
as a holy scene: amid the darkness of a Gothic vault the mysterious light of the
phosphorus glows in a retort, observed by an alchemist who has fallen to his
knees in reverence (figure 12).

The flashes of light in Dr Crafft's tubes, the tiny stars on the Turkish carpet,
Boyle's luminous hand, the glowing DOMINI – all this must have continued to
glow in Robert Hooke's imagination long after the event. Five years later, in
1682, phosphorescence reappeared in his work, in an unexpected place: in a
treatise on human memory. On 21 June of that year Hooke gave a lecture to the

Royal Society, the text of which was subsequently published under the title *An Hypothetical Explication of Memory: how the Organs made use of by the Mind in its Operation may be Mechanically understood*.[6] In it, Hooke maintained that purely material explanations may be given for all memory processes. In a passage on visual memory he mentioned the findings of phosphorus research and subsequently adduced the glow of phosphorus as a metaphor for the brain's capacity to absorb and store light impressions. The miraculous powers latent in phosphorus were reflected in the imagery used by Hooke to describe the operation of the visual memory.

In Hooke's view every sense is linked with a special substance in the brain suited to the retention and reproduction of impressions reaching the brain via that sense. According to this principle, there must also be a substance in the human brain capable of preserving light impressions by purely physical means. In order to lend plausibility to this hypothesis Hooke refers to phosphorescent substances like those of Baldwin and the luminescent stones of Bologna. He argues that if these substances have the capacity to receive the impressions of light, retain them and emit them in the dark, why should one not just as easily find a substance in the brain capable of preserving light stimuli and hence forming the physical residue of our visual memories. This may be explained, Hooke added,

> by the Matter of the Phosphorous made of the *Bolonian Stone*,[7] or that found out by *Baldwinus* made of Chalk and Niter; which Matters are so made and adapted by the Chymical Preparations of them by the force of Fire and Mixtures made in their Processes, that they, so soon as exposed to the Impressions of Light, receive and retain those Impressions, though for no long time, yet enough to shew us a Specimen of a certain Qualification not to be found in most other Bodies, which may yet possibly be done much more powerfully and effectually by the Chymistry of Nature in the Digestions and Preparations made in the wonderful Elaboratory of the Animal Body; where all things are ordered and adapted by the All wise Creator, for the Work to be done.

The structure of the argument is clear. If it is possible to produce a substance chemically that can retain light and emit it again, it is also possible for brain matter to absorb and reproduce light impressions in a purely physical way. The metaphor has a nice inner logic: the light in the Bologna stone pointed to a material property which the human brain – thanks to the 'Chymistry of Nature' – possessed in a perfect form.

At the same time this phosphorus metaphor illuminates the scientific milieu in which Hooke operated. In 1681, a year before his lecture, Hooke had been sent the report *Il Fosforo or a Preparation of the Bolognian Stone, whereby it shines in the dark* by the Academy of Physics and Mathematics in Rome.[8] He himself, together with Boyle, had conducted experiments with the 'Pneumatick Engine' or vacuum pump, which showed that phosphorus continued to shine even in a vacuum. Obviously the light was not a product of combustion. Whereas light is normally accompanied by heat, as in the case of red-hot iron, phosphorescent substances remained cool. Demonstrations featuring phosphorus were considered ideally suited for a wider public rather than just the research community: such as acquaintances, servants, women, children.[9] Not only did this help raise funds for the acquisition of the precious raw material, but the experiments also played a part in creating a public scientific culture. Demonstrations like those of Crafft, Hooke and Boyle and the semi-public experiments that followed them were a step in the direction of the openness which the Royal Society promoted by encouraging this new style of scientific research.[10] Experiments with phosphorus were representative of this kind of research (figure 13).

One complicating factor in the experiments was that phosphorescent substances were difficult to produce and hence very expensive. Samples were circulated in minute quantities. Their rarity made phosphorescent materials a suitable currency, one that could also be used for social advancement. In 1676 Baldwin provided the Royal Society with a relatively large sample and shortly afterwards, as a *quid pro quo*, was elected a Fellow. Part of his sample was presented to Charles II, the Royal Society's patron. Phosphorus was a 'currency in the economy of prestige', writes Golinski, a 'noble substance' in various senses.[11]

In using his phosphorus metaphor, Hooke was appealing to an audience of researchers who had already shared his experience – they had all either attended the demonstrations and experiments or read about them in the Society's journal, the *Philosophical Transactions*. The reference to the Bologna luminescent stones enabled everyone to picture the special properties Hooke was attributing to brain matter. There was no clear explanation for phosphorescence, but neither was there for the visual memory: how our brains absorb, store and reproduce light impressions was a mystery similar to the effect produced by the Bologna stone or Baldwin's phosphorus. What better metaphor could there be for the operation of the visual memory than the substance that still retained an aura of mystical alchemy and refused to surrender its secrets to even the most modern scientific instruments – a substance which did not reflect light, but was itself luminescent, a substance that had been presented to monarchs and was one of chemistry's most glorious products. By his choice of this particular metaphor Hooke linked the sense of awe at the miracle of human memory with the miraculous powers residing in phosphorus.

The microcosm of memory

The phosphorus metaphor for the visual memory, which has just been expanded upon, was taken from a text which is interspersed with analogies, metaphors and comparisons. This in itself was controversial enough, since in the intellectual circles in which Hooke moved, metaphors were treated with

13.   Allegorical print by Corbould. The goddess of science, globe in hand, turns
to the young chemist who is igniting a piece of phosphorus with a burning
glass and giving a superior smile. The old man brooding over his retort represents a farewell to the bygone age of alchemy. A comparison of this print
with Wright's painting (in figure 12) reveals phosphorescence as a popular
symbol for both the old and new styles of chemistry.

suspicion or downright hostility. The founding fathers of the Royal Society set
high standards for the 'manner of discourse', the kind of language used to
describe experiments and formulate theory. In 1667 Thomas Sprat wrote in
his *History of the Royal Society* that members were expected to keep to succinct
and simple language, purged of the 'trick of Metaphors'.[12] Following in the
footsteps of Bacon, Sprat railed against imagery in science. A year before

another member, Samuel Parker, had gone much further.[13] Parker advocated a general ban on the use of figurative language in scientific discourse. He cited the same reasons as Sprat, albeit in more flowery terms. He expressed a particular horror of metaphors, whose 'wanton & luxuriant fancies climbing up into the Bed of Reason, do not only defile it by unchast and illegitimate Embraces, but instead of real conceptions and notices of Things impregnate the mind with nothing but Ayerie and Subventaneous Phantasmes'.[14] Clearly, the logic of the author's imagery has its own inevitability. Sprat and Parker were expressing a common view: nature, it was felt, could only be reflected truthfully in literal language.

Hooke's treatise could not possibly pass as the kind of simple, literal use of language prescribed in the Royal Society, as Hooke was undoubtedly aware. Scattered throughout his text are various comments on his lavish use of imagery. In his lecture he presented not only a mechanistic theory of the operation of memory, but also a handful of reflections on the kind of language in which memory can be described. Hooke's theory of memory is worthy of our attention in the context of the history of science, the value of his comments on metaphorical discourse lies more on the philosophical plane.

All things considered it is quite odd that Robert Hooke should have written a treatise on human memory: he was an exceptionally versatile man, but most of his research was in the field of science and technology. Between 1664 and 1677 Hooke conducted weekly experiments and demonstrations for the Royal Society. He acted as an assistant to Christopher Wren in the rebuilding of London after the Great Fire of 1666, worked on scientific instruments for Boyle, built microscopes, telescopes, pendulum clocks and pocket watches, wrote treatises on earthquakes, comets, cryptography and magnetism. His principal scientific contribution was the book *Micrographia* (1665), describing his microscopic observations. Hooke's discoveries included the 'cell', so-called because its shape reminded him of the cells in a honeycomb.

Hooke lived in Gresham College, where he had been appointed professor of geometry. He had the reputation of being a difficult man to deal with. In a biographical sketch preceding *The Posthumous Works of Robert Hooke*, Richard Waller described his character as 'Melancholy, Mistrustful and Jealous'.[15] His diaries only confirm that impression.[16] A later biographer, Margaret 'Espinasse, analysed several conflicts in which Hooke was embroiled – with Newton, Henry Oldenburg (Secretary to the Royal Society and in Hooke's opinion a 'lying dogg'), the clockmaker William Clement – and reached the conclusion that Hooke had unjustly acquired a reputation as a malcontent.[17] Nevertheless the length of the list gives one pause for thought. It can be said in his defence that his position as a Fellow of the Royal Society was an extremely difficult one. Hooke worked under the patronage of Robert Boyle, Earl of Cork. Many of the other Honourable Fellows belonged to English nobility. Hooke, by contrast, was of humble origin. As a student at Oxford he was obliged to take on numerous assistantships. He was paid as 'Curator of Experiments', which made him, in a sense, a servant to many masters. Hooke was recognised, Shapin explained, as a person of 'ambiguous autonomy'.[18] Perhaps it is fair to say that there was an unfortunate mismatch between Hooke's low social prestige and his prominent position in the informal hierarchies of inventiveness, technical skill and intellectual brilliance. This mismatch, combined with an extreme sensitivity to insulting treatment, meant that there always seemed to be an element of grievance in Hooke's dealings with others.

Hooke's theory of memory followed an exposition on time and the consciousness of time.[19] Our knowledge of time, he argued, cannot be derived from our senses, since sense impressions are transient in nature. Perception of duration and frequency presupposes the operation of a memory. In Hooke's view, the estimated duration of a period is a derivative of the number of remembered events in that period. It was this hypothesis that led him to a discussion of memory.

Hooke conceived of memory as a material organ, explicable in purely mechanical terms. That our faculty to recollect has a corporeal nature is demonstrated by the fact that it can be influenced by physical factors like fever or excessive drinking. It may even be completely destroyed by an external force, like 'a Fall, or great Blow upon the Head'. In this case the soul, 'tho' it be an Incorporal Being', cannot make use of memory and is unable to effect its will. Hooke invited his audience to think of memory as a 'Repository' or 'Storehouse' of ideas. Our senses act as 'Collectors or Carriers', delivering impressions to the storehouse. Actual storage, however, requires the simultaneous activity of the soul, which gives the impressions a certain shape and motion before inserting them in the common repository. This action of the soul, Hooke explained, 'is commonly called *Attention*'. Once stored in the repository, impressions are preserved and retained for future use by the soul.

Hooke did not wish to be bothered with the question of the exact location of the soul. He simply assumed that there was 'a certain Place or Point somewhere in the Brain of a Man, where the Soul may have its principal and chief seat'. From this position the soul could direct its powers, receive impressions and form new ideas. Ideas, Hooke pointed out, are preserved in the order in which they are formed, like the links in a chain. The idea most recently shaped, the psychological present, is the beginning of the chain, the oldest idea is the last link. Each new idea shifts the chain one position further into the past. The order in memory is simply one of succession:

> So that there is as it were a continued Chain of Ideas coyled up in the Repository of the Brain, the first end of which is farthest removed from the Center or Seat of the Soul where the Ideas are formed; and the other End is always at the Center, being the last Idea formed, which is always the Moment present when considered: And therefore as there are a greater number of these Ideas between the present Sensation or Thought in the Center, and any other, the more is the Soul apprehensive of the Time interposed.

To become sensible of time, then, the soul has to make use of the organ of memory and the succession of ideas lined up in its repository: distances in time are marked by the length of the chain. In Hooke's theory, time came to be conceived of as a spatial quantity. Thus both time and memory were brought 'under the Consideration of Geometry and Mensuration'.

The brain is furnished with a variety of matter, adapted to the type of information supplied by the specific senses. Hooke referred to luminous substances for the material substratum of visual memory. Other sorts of matter were capable of receiving and retaining the impressions of sound, 'somewhat like those Bells or Vases which *Vitruvius* mentions to be placed in the antient Theaters, which did receive and return the Sound more vigorous and strong' or certain glasses 'answering the Tone by the same Tone of their own'.

Hooke saw the ideas stored in the brain as truly material entities, and in so doing, introduced a new type of question into theories of memory. For what is the *rate* at which these ideas are formed? What is the *number* of ideas in the memory? And what is their *location*? In traditional spiritual theories, memory was interpreted as a non-spatial entity and such questions hardly made sense. St Augustine took memory to be a *quasi*-space, 'an inner place – though it is wrong to speak of it as a place'.[20] The fact that every human being gathers innumerable quantities of memories in his lifetime will not lead to a lack of space, since memory has no physical limits: 'It is a vast, immeasurable sanctuary. Who can plumb its depths?'[21]

Hooke could not accept these 'solutions'. He energetically addressed the questions surrounding the quantification of memory processes. The rate at which the soul forms ideas and inserts them in memory may vary widely from person to person. For some there may be 'Four of them formed in a second Minute of Time, in others possibly not One in two Seconds of Time'. He then proceeds to estimate the number of ideas in the memory of a man of normal mental and physical constitution, being 'neither very quick, nor very dull'. If such a man were to live a hundred years, Hooke reckoned, he would have stored 'a thousand Millions of distinct Ideas'. His calculations deserve to be quoted at length:

> A hundred Years contain 36525 Days, and 36525 Days contain 876600 Hours, and 876600 Hours contain 3155760000 Seconds. Now one with another, when the Soul is intent and acting, there may be 3600 formed within the compass of an Hour, and so one in a Second of Time. So that if the Soul could through the whole Course of 100 Years be continually so intent, and so acting and forming these Ideas, and inserting them into his Repository or Organ of Memory, there might be 3155760000 Ideas. But by reason of Sleep interposed, one third Part of the Number will be taken off, the Soul then for the most part ceasing to form Ideas, or when it does, they are only imperfect and lost. So that there will remain but 2103840000, or to take a round Sum,

but 21 hundred Millions. Now if we examine this remaining two thirds of Time or Moments, and therein consider what part of the time remaining is lost in Infancy, Old Age, Sickness and Inadvertency, we may well reckon that two thirds of these remaining Moments are lost, and no Ideas at all formed in them; and so instead of 21 hundred, there will remain but the number of 7 hundred Millions. And if we again consider how small a part of these are industriously and carefully stored up, we may very well agree, that not above a seventh Part of these are stored up: and so one hundred Millions may be a sufficient Number to be supposed for all the Ideas that may have been treasured up in the Organ of Memory through the whole Course of a Man's Life, though of a hundred Years continuance; and consequently one Year with another may be supposed to add to this Store about one Million of Ideas.

On second thoughts, Hooke considered this spectacular outcome of one million ideas per year, which amounted to 2,738 ideas every day, to be probably far too high. He then switched to a different manner of calculation, informed by introspection rather than by calculus. If a man reflects on how many ideas he may have added to his store in the last month, he will probably find that the number will not exceed two or three hundred a day, perhaps as little as one hundred. So a man of fifty (Hooke himself was forty-seven at the time) may have deposited 1,826,200 distinct ideas in his storehouse, a little less than two million ideas. Hooke concluded that this would seem a realistic figure.

Hooke felt that even the initial figure of one hundred million ideas was not a physical impossibility. Very small quantities of matter may contain an infinite number of living creatures, each with its own shape and with sufficient room to move. As a pioneer in microscopic research, Hooke was familiar with small dimensions. A few years earlier he had observed 'animals' in rainwater that were no bigger than a thirtieth part of the breadth of a hair. This would mean that one cubic inch could contain 'eight millions of millions' of these minute creatures.[22] In the human brain, it would appear, there is no such thing as a lack of space.

Returning to his description of memory Hooke indicated that the stored ideas were 'little Images', with the 'Stamp, Seal or Mould' of the soul. Because the ideas are continually pushed further away by newly formed ideas they may change shape or be completely lost. In order to clarify the position and actions of the soul, Hooke introduced a second metaphor, more elaborate than the coiled chain of ideas: memory as a microcosm. 'The Soul', Hooke argued, 'forms to itself a Microcosm, or Picture of the Macrocosm, in which it radiates, and is sensible of every thing contain'd therein, in the same manner as the Sun in the Macrocosm'. By radiating in every direction, the soul knows what is present in memory.

The representation of the human mind as a microcosm of the universe was a popular one in the Hermetic tradition which had influenced Hooke so much in

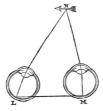

14. Engraving illustrating the Cartesian explanation of the perception of dis-
     tance. In estimating distance, the soul employs the fact that the closer that
     objects are to the observer, the more focused the eyes are. The distance to
     the arrow N is governed by the size of the angles L and M.

his youth, but Hooke gave a personal slant to the principle 'as above, so below'
by citing all kinds of optical and astronomical laws as analogies for the processes of memory. Forgetting, for example, may be due to the interruption of
the soul's rays by other images. Hooke likened this to an eclipse of the moon:
when the earth passes between the sun and the moon, the sun's rays cannot
reach the latter. Hence an image may be apparently lost and recovered immediately the obstacle is removed. Images that are closer receive more powerful
radiation from the soul, 'in a duplicate proportion to their Distance reciprocal,
much the same with that of Light', which is why memories become fainter with
time.[23] An apparent exception to this law is that some events make a particularly deep impression and are then remembered clearly, however long ago the
image was formed. Hooke's explanation is that powerful impressions are
remembered more often and subsequently constantly recreated, so that they
always remain close to the soul at the centre.

Hooke uses metaphors which are a precise reflection of contemporary views
on the nature of light and radiation, particularly in the passages on attention.
Those views had been inspired by Descartes's *Dioptrique*.[24] This treatise represented light as a pressure that is displaced instantaneously in a transparent
medium.[25] Descartes explained this theory by using an analogy of a blind man
who 'sees' with his stick: when the stick touches an object the blind man can
tell the shape of the object by the resistance that the stick produces. Light is the
pressure exerted on the optic nerves by objects via a transparent 'plenum'. In
his *Traité de l'homme*, published posthumously in 1664, Descartes put forward a
similar explanation for the perception of distance[26] (figures 14 and 15).

Many aspects of Hooke's *physics* were inspired by Cartesian views like that on
the plenum.[27] But in his description of *psychological* processes too, Hooke takes
his cue from Descartes's optical theory. In Hooke's microcosm the soul becomes
aware of the content of stored ideas by 'propagating from itself every way *in
Orbem*, a Radiation like the Sun, by which, as by a Stick, it becomes sensible of
all those Ideas that are yet unwasted within the Repository, feeling as it were
their Form, their Resistance, and their Reactions to its Radiations'.

15.   The blind man from the *Dioptrique* reappears in Descartes's drawing of his
       analogy of the perception of distance. The blind man can 'see' how far away
       the object is from the size of the angles f and g at the base of the triangle
       that he forms with two sticks.

Besides the perception of shape, 'as by a Stick', the estimate of the mental
images' distance from the soul, and the age of memories, also operates along
Cartesian lines: Hooke explains with great precision how the soul can deduce
from the angle that the reflected rays make with the surface of the sun the distance of an image. In short, in the microcosm of memory Descartes's optical
laws apply: Hooke has quite directly projected a prevailing physical theory into
his theory of memory.

Whereas Hooke's metaphors for attention were taken from what was considered as modern physics at the time, Hooke's metaphor for 'association by
similarity' derived from an older scientific tradition. If there is a certain
similarity of form and movement between two impressions, Hooke suggested,
it probably means that there will be a 'Sympathetick Agreement' between
them. In this case one impression will be capable of evoking the other, 'in the
same manner as a Musical String being moved, does make another String that
is unison or harmonious with it, move also, and so together make the Sound
the louder, or the Impression the stronger'.[28] In alchemy, 'sympathy' and
'antipathy' were designations of harmonious or conflicting relationships
between substances. The English physician William Gilbert used these two concepts in his *De Magnete* (1600) to describe the attraction and repulsion of magnetic objects. This use of psychological terms for natural forces fitted in with
the alchemical tradition, in which psychological idiom abounded. But by
Hooke's day, because of their frequent application to physical phenomena, sympathy and antipathy gradually acquired a physical meaning and their metaphorical character had been largely lost sight of. In describing association

between mental images as a 'Sympathetick Agreement' Hooke was making sympathy, once more, into a metaphor, since association was now being viewed as analogous to the attraction between *physical* objects. Some designations, we find, meander in the course of time between a literal and a figurative meaning. The somewhat hybrid nature of Hooke's metaphors shows clearly that his treatise exemplifies a period of transition between an alchemical and a mechanistic tradition.

Over three centuries later we can see that Hooke's theory of memory anticipates modern theory in a number of interesting ways. Examples include the relationship between the number of memories and estimate of duration, the clear distinction between storage and reproduction and the stress on the active role of attention in the formation of enduring memories. The metaphor of the 'Storehouse' can be recognised in standard theoretical terms like 'long-term store', 'storage duration' and 'storage capacity'. That stored material may disappear as a result of 'decay' or because other material makes it inaccessible ('interference'), are still the two main hypotheses on forgetting and both are mentioned by Hooke. In addition, Hooke provided an explanation for the fact that powerful impressions are vividly remembered irrespective of the time that has elapsed, which is identical to the current hypothesis of 'trace consolidation': whenever we remember the event concerned the trace is renewed and reinforced. Anyone tempted to make sarcastic observations on the laborious calculations regarding the number of stored ideas in the warehouse should look at the way in which the number of 'bits' in the human brain is currently calculated. The author of an article giving an overview of the field, Landauer, uses a method essentially identical to Hooke's.[29] He makes an accurate as possible estimate of the *rate* at which material is added to the memory and multiplies that by the length of life. On the basis of memory tasks after reading tests, Landauer arrives at an 'input rate to long-term memory' of 1.2 bits per second, where Hooke's estimate had been one mental image per second. For someone aged seventy that gives a total of 1.8 billion bits. Like Hooke, Landauer deducts one-third for sleep. Landauer's reflections on the 'loss rate' also show a striking parallel to those of Hooke. Landauer introduces a model where forgetting is attributed to an 'overwriting or masking of old information by new'.[30] This model assumes the availability of a fixed amount of storage capacity or 'writable bits'. Each newly learned bit, Landauer argues, 'occupies one of these loci, either filling a previously unused one or "overwriting" one previously occupied'.[31] Whereas Hooke evoked the image of a space in which the mental images already present are eclipsed by newly arrived images or are even completely lost, Landauer takes his inspiration from the terms used to describe the memory capacity of computers. Using different jargon, Hooke and Landauer specify identical hypotheses on the mechanisms of forgetting.

'Only by Similitude'

Given the audience he was addressing on that June day in 1682, Hooke's *Explication of Memory* contained a twofold provocation. Firstly, his theory of memory had an openly materialistic slant. A note in the minutes states that the paper 'seemed to tend to prove the soul mechanical'.[32] Although Hooke assured his audience at the meeting 'that no such thing was hinted, or in the least intended in it', he could not possibly maintain that his theory was a pious extension of the current spiritual theories of memory. Even almost twenty-five years after the lecture was delivered, Richard Waller, the editor of Hooke's post-humous writings, thought it advisable to mention in an afterword that the exposition might be considered 'too mechanical'. Just to be on the safe side, Waller added: 'I hold my self not in the least obliged to defend or maintain any of his Opinions or Discourses, but fairly present them to the Ingenious as he left them.'[33] As Secretary of the Royal Society Waller had his position to protect.

A second potential cause of dispute was the abundance of metaphors and analogies which Hooke permitted himself in his 'manner of discourse'. In a sense, his text preempted the discussion by giving arguments in advance for having departed from the sober, literal style prized by the Royal Society. Hooke justified himself on two grounds. The first was that processes in the human mind fundamentally elude literal description. The second was that graphic images enable the imagination to grasp the relationships between hypothetical processes. There is more to be said about both these arguments.

In the seventeenth century the philosophical status of the soul and memory was linked to the question of human immortality. As a result, reflections on the material substratum acquired religious significance. Hooke wrote his treatise against the background of Cartesian dualism and was careful to represent only the memory, not the soul as a material instrument. For Hooke the soul was a non-corporeal, non-spatial substance. Hooke's contemporaries denied the phys-icality of memory by placing memory *within* the soul. The neo-Platonist Henry More, for example, had stated some years before Hooke's lecture that it was self-evident that 'the power of Memory does not consist in such Marks or Figures in the Brain, nor in any Vibration or Motion there', and that 'Memory is wholly in the Soul herself, and that She is the sole Repository of all the Perceptions she has had.'[34] Hooke, possibly in response to More, located memory *outside* the soul.[35] This enabled him to describe memory processes in spatial and physical terms similar to those used in describing the material world.

This created a conceptual problem for Hooke. Because how does one 'locate' a non-spatial entity like the soul, in relation to a spatial and material memory? Hooke, as we have seen, did not pronounce on the exact position of the soul ('somewhere in the Brain of a Man'). Other indications of place are always linked to metaphors: at the distribution point of the warehouse, at the start of the chain of memories, in the centre of the microcosm. Towards the end of his paper, writing on the relationship between soul and memory, Hooke states, 'It is not, I conceive, possible to be truly understood or described, but only by Similitude.' The relationship between soul and memory can be described and explained only through comparison. Metaphors are quite simply indispensable.

But Hooke ingeniously made a virtue of this necessity. To fully appreciate the subtleties of his logical dexterity, a short digression on the mechanistic tradition is required, as it had emerged in the circles around Boyle and the Royal Society. Following Boyle, as strict as possible a distinction was made between facts and theories. *Factual* discourse comprised statements on 'matters of fact': observable phenomena which may or may not have been produced experimentally. *Theoretical* discourse comprised hypotheses on the explanation of the 'matters of fact'. The epistemological status of the terms in theoretical discourse was uncertain.[36] Generally they were described, without further definition, as 'notions'. For example, in his research with the vacuum pump Boyle had introduced the term 'spring of the air' to explain the elasticity of air, a property manifested by the observation that the pressure exerted by air increases as the volume containing the air decreases. This 'spring' was explained in turn by the theory that air consists of particles with a spring-like structure. The compression of these tiny springs was supposed to explain the resilience of the whole, just as a bale of wool can be compressed because of the elasticity of the constituent fibres. Boyle, quite deliberately, did not answer the question as to how the resilience of the particles was to be explained: in his view 'notions' should be linked as directly and graphically as possible with 'matters of fact'. A figurative explanation like the 'spring of the air' met those requirements, a hypothetical explanation of the causal mechanisms underlying the 'spring' did not. Using a clockwork metaphor borrowed from Descartes, Boyle pointed out that what we perceive of nature are the external movements of the hands, while the mechanisms producing those movements are hidden inside the case. Because a skilful clockmaker could produce two clocks which are completely identical from the outside, but whose movements do not share a single mechanism, those mechanisms can be described only by conjecture.

In his papers on physics, Hooke followed these ideas on research and theory as well as he could. In an article (probably dating from 1666), Hooke explicitly defines how hypothetical mechanisms can be linked to 'matters of fact'.[37] The good experimenter, writes Hooke, should have some provisional hypotheses prior to the experiment, and only if that is the case will the experimental outcome have real informative value. In order to acquire a sufficiently extensive repertoire of hypotheses, the experimenter would be well advised to compare nature with as many 'mechanical and intelligible ways of working' as he can think of.[38]

Returning to the treatise on memory, we are struck by the fact that here too Hooke is trying to follow the criteria for physical research. The idea that hypothetical explanations for memory processes are 'notions' which can be understood only through mechanical, graphic analogies recurs early in the introduction of the *Explication of Memory*, as does the recommendation that in formulating hypotheses one should use comparisons with familiar 'mechanical and intelligible ways of working'. Hooke states this in virtually identical terms:

> Now because nothing is so well understood or apprehended, as when it is represented under some sensible Form, I would, to make my Notion the more conceivable, make a mechanical and sensible Figure and Picture thereof, and from that shew how I conceive all the Actions and Operations of the Soul as Apprehending, Remembring and Reasoning are performed.

Metaphors, analogies and graphic images are not only necessary for the understanding of memory processes, as Hooke indicated, but they can also play the same role as in physical research: they have a heuristic value. Analogies like association-as-resonance, attention-as-radiation, forgetting-as-lunar eclipse or visual memory-as-phosphorescence, give the imagination a hold on what would otherwise remain vague 'notions'. Appealing to the need for graphic imagery Hooke included the same metaphors and analogies in his theoretical discourse which had met with such suspicion in the Royal Society.

This already constituted a dialectical triumph over his own principles. But Hooke went further still. He claimed to have brought memory within the scope of 'Geometry and Mensuration', in modern terms, to have subjected memory processes to mathematical treatment. On closer inspection one can see that here, too, Hooke has used a trick: he has smuggled in size and number along with the metaphors. Time and time again it is the figurative descriptions that make 'quantification' possible. By comparing the ordering of mental images with an ever-lengthening chain Hooke was able to take the distance between a given mental image and the beginning of the chain as a measure of duration. By placing memories in a quasi-solar system, Hooke was able to specify his 'inverse square law' on the relationship between the strength of a memory and its distance from the soul. Both quantifications only have meaning within a purely imaginary space. Hooke ordered mental processes by metaphorically presenting them as spatial. Metaphors were the tools he used to create space in a memory that otherwise would have remained closed to the imagination.

A physicist's memory

With the exception of Graham Richards, who included Hooke in his section on 'forgotten anticipations of psychology', historians of psychology have largely ignored Hooke's theory of memory.[39] Considering the topic of his lecture, this is a sorry paradox. Mechanically based psychology is generally considered to have started with Hartley or Lamettrie, authors whose theories date from the mid-eighteenth century. The *Explication of Memory* lets the history of mechanistic psychology start over half a century earlier. Hooke had no immediate followers. His theory, says Richards, 'rests in glorious isolation as a one-off piece of proto-psychological theorizing of a kind for which the intellectual climate was quite unripe'.[40] Yet, Hooke's work is an early example of a style of theorising which over the centuries has constantly associated itself with new technologies. His theory exemplifies a psychology in which state-of-the art techniques for storing and reproducing images provide metaphors for hypothetical processes in memory.

Hooke's theory is of interest to the history of science because it reflects its author's social and scientific environment. The metaphor of the microcosm was derived from his heliocentric cosmology. The 'law' governing the strength of a memory arose from his research into astronomy and optics. The calculation of the number of mental images in the memory was closely linked with his research into microscopy. The passages on the visual memory are infused with the glow of experiments with phosphorescence. In the explicit justification of imagery one hears the echo of the distrust of metaphors in Royal Society circles. The visualisations and 'quantifications' betray the almost regulation requirement of the Society that theories and hypotheses should be presented graphically and preferably in mathematical terms. Hooke's religious and metaphysical background (he was a devout Christian and believed the soul to be noncorporeal), is evident from his theory on the relationship between soul and memory.

Seventeenth-century still-life and portrait painters sometimes hung a gilded globe somewhere in a corner, which afforded a glimpse of the artist himself, half-hidden behind his easel. The *Explication of Memory* reflects the personal universe of a research with a scientific bent and a predilection for quantification and graphic examples. In his theory of memory Hooke designed a microcosm of what inspired and motivated him.

Notes

1   R. Boyle, 'A short Memorial of some Observations made upon an Artificial Substance, that shines without any precedent Illustration', in R. T. Gunther, *Early Science in Oxford*, vol. VIII, Oxford, 1931, pp. 273–7. Crafft was both a physician and an alchemist. In his 'memorial' Boyle spells Crafft's name as 'Kraft'.

2   Gunther, *Early Science*, p. 277.

3   E. Newton-Harvey, *A History of Luminescence: From the Earliest Times to 1900*, Philadelphia, 1957.

4   Quoted in J. V. Golinsky, 'A noble spectacle. Phosphorus and the public cultures of science in the early Royal Society', *Isis*, 80 (1989), 11–39 (20).

5   Leibniz was a friend of both Brand and Crafft. See also R. Finster & G. van den Heuvel, *Gottfried Wilhelm Leibniz*, Reinbek bei Hamburg, 1990, p. 14.

6   The lecture can be found in R. Waller, *The Posthumous Works of Robert Hooke*, London, 1705. Since the text is less than nine pages long, I have not given separate references for each quotation.

7   Bolonia was the Latin form of Bologna.

8   M. 'Espinasse, *Robert Hooke*, London, 1956, p. 161.

9   Golinsky, 'Noble spectacle', 26.

10 S. Shapin and S. Schaffer, *Leviathan and the Air-Pump. Hobbes, Boyle, and the Experimental Life*, Princeton, 1985.

11 Golinsky, 'Noble spectacle', 27.

12 Th. Sprat, *History of the Royal Society*, London, 1667, pp. 113ff.

13 S. Parker, *A Free and Impartial Censure of the Platonick Philosophie*, Oxford, 1666.

14 *Ibid.* p. 76.

15 Waller, *Posthumous Works*, p. xxvii.

16 Diaries are available for two periods of Hooke's life: H. W. Robinson & W. Adams (eds.), *The Diary of Robert Hooke, 1672–1680*, London, 1935; *Hooke's Diary for 1688–93*, in Gunther, *Early Science*, vol. x, pp. 69–265.

17 'Espinasse, *Robert Hooke*, p. 139.

18 S. Shapin, 'Who was Robert Hooke?', in M. Hunter & S. Schaffer (eds.), *Robert Hooke. New Studies*, Woodbridge, 1989, pp. 253–85 (256).

19 B. R. Singer, 'Robert Hooke on memory, association and time perception', *Notes and Records of the Royal Society*, 31 (1976), 115–31.

20 St Augustine, *Confessions*, trans. with an introduction by R. S. Spine-Coffin, Harmondsworth, 1961, p. 217.

21 *Ibid.*, p. 216.

22 Gunther, *Early Science*, p. 319. Hooke took the thickness of his own hair as a yardstick: $1/640$ of an inch.

23 In a letter to Newton of 6 January 1680 Hooke declared that the ratio, known as the inverse square law, also applied to gravity: 'My supposition is that the attraction always is in a duplicate proportion to the distance from the centre reciprocal.' Quoted in V. I. Arnol'd, *Huygens and Barrow, Newton and Hooke*, trans. from the Russian by E. J. F. Primrose, Basle, 1990, p. 22.

24 The *Dioptrique* is one of the constituent essays of the *Discours de la méthode*, Leiden, 1637.

25 R. S. Westfall, *The Construction of Modern Science, Mechanism and Mechanics*, Cambridge, 1977, pp. 52ff.

26 R. Descartes, *Traité de l'homme*, Paris, 1664.

27 M. Hesse, 'Hooke's vibration theory and the isochrony of springs', *Isis*, 57 (1966) 4, 433–41 (434).

28 On music as a 'controlling metaphor' in Hooke's theories, see J. C. Kassler, *Inner Music. Hobbes, Hooke and North on Internal Character*, London, 1995.

29 T. K. Landauer, 'How much do people remember? Some estimates of the quantity of learned information in long-term memory', *Cognitive Science*, 10 (1986), 477–93. Obviously Landauer's 'bits' are not identical with Hooke's 'ideas'; what the two notions have in common is that both function as units of calculation for quantifying information.

30 *Ibid.*, 485.

31 *Ibid.*

32 Singer, 'Hooke on memory', 117.

33 Waller, *Works*, p. 148.

34   H. More, *The Immortality of the Soul*, London, 1662, p. 16.

35   Singer, 'Hooke on memory', 127.

36   Shapin & Schaffer, *Leviathan*, p. 50.

37   M. Hesse, 'Hooke's philosophical algebra', *Isis*, 57 (1966) 1, 67–83.

38   Hesse, 'Hooke's algebra', 69.

39   G. Richards, *Mental Machinery. The Origins and Consequences of Psychological Ideas from 1600 to 1850*, London, 1992, pp. 66–9 (66).

40   *Ibid.*, p. 69.

4   A vast labyrinth

> Then one must clamber down on all fours, the dark hole is so *very* dark, and Lord only knows how long the ladder may be! But we soon see that this is not a single ladder running into the black eternity, for there are many of them of from fifteen and twenty rungs apiece, each standing upon a board capable of supporting a man, and from which a new hole leads in turn to a new ladder.
>
> Heinrich Heine, after his descent into the *Caroline*, a mine in the Harz Mountains.[1]

At a certain moment, writes Jean Clair in an essay on nineteenth-century psychology, the soul ceased to belong to God.[2] After this revolution the soul was no longer the exclusive domain of priests and clergymen, but literally everyone had something to say about it: artists and doctors, writers and charlatans, scholars and spiritualists, neurologists and craniometrists, psychiatrists and diviners. All these spokesmen created as many different souls. The silent secularisation of thinking about the human mind gave scope for widely differing interpretations, each with their own expressions, images and analogies.

This diversity can also be found in the iconography of memory. In the nineteenth century the memory appeared as a cell on the cranial maps of phrenologists, as a landscape or labyrinth in the work of Romantic writers, as a mineshaft in papers on the unconscious, as the depths of the ocean in poems, as a neurological process in the manuals of brain anatomists, as the photographic plate in a camera in theories on the visual memory. Looking back at the nineteenth century it seems as if memory underwent a transformation every ten or twenty years.

In text books, the beginning of the psychology of memory is usually given as 1885, the year that Hermann Ebbinghaus published his celebrated monograph *Über das Gedächtnis*.[3] In this, Ebbinghaus presented the results of a long series of experiments and so became the founder of the experimental study of memory. His work inspired later researchers to design ever more accurate experimental procedures, to construct apparatus for the standardised application of stimuli and to develop quantifying schemes for processing the results. This determined the nature of memory psychology in the twentieth century: a subject that was pursued in university laboratories, with a scientific slant which is found in research right up to the present day.

This experimental-quantitative orientation was a relatively recent development in the long history of the study of memory and the dominance that it gained after 1885 had the unfortunate effect that older contributions, by researchers who did not use the experiment as their tool of preference, disappeared from view in the history of the discipline. In the most favourable cases what preceded empirical research into memory is presented in the historical sections of textbooks as 'pre-scientific', more often it is dismissed as irrelevant. Those who go along with this and refuse to separate themselves from contemporary criteria for what counts as 'scientific' will be able to skip much of the nineteenth-century theorising about memory, and consequently pass by a subtly varied collection of interesting ideas.

One could equally point to 1839 and 1877 as the revolutionary years in thinking about remembering and forgetting. In those years the two most important artificial memories since writing were invented. From 1839 onwards photography developed through a hectic series of new procedures into an impressive technique for storing and reproducing optical information; in 1877 Edison with his phonograph presented an instrument which did for the ear what photography had done for the eye. In this way, in the space of scarcely forty years, technology provided our two distance senses with external memories, at first quite clumsy, with images and sounds which quickly faded, but after a short while so convincing that photography and phonography became efficient media for the recording and reproduction of information, artificial memories which seemed almost as boundless as those of human beings. Up until now our other senses have had to make do without artificial memories: what we feel, smell and taste can only be kept in the privacy of our memories.

Just as doctors introduced the camera obscura in their anatomical papers as an analogy for the eye, photography (in essence a procedure for preserving the images in a camera obscura), developed into a metaphor of memory. In the first articles on photography, the photographic plate was described as a 'mirror with a memory'. This metaphor was quickly to take a new turn, the brain was represented as the neuronal equivalent of a light sensitive plate, an organic medium that preserves a latent trace of light stimuli and reproduces them.[4] The same happened with the phonograph. The way in which this machine recorded sounds, preserved them in a soundless medium and made them audible again, inspired psychologists and neurologists to specify theories about the acoustic memory. In these theories the brain was compared to tin foil (later the wax cylinder), on which the phonograph drew a trace of sound stimuli.

Whereas the memory was represented as a mechanism for storing and repro-ducing information and was itself investigated with mechanical aids, nine-teenth-century views seemed to be an extension of the memory theories which Descartes and Hooke published in the seventeenth century, as though a mechanistic idea were unfolding historically, without interruption or stagna-tion. That impression is misleading. For wedged between these two mechanistic episodes lies Romanticism, a brief but violent movement, countering a science which modelled reality in accordance with the deterministic structure of a machine. Romantic authors saw mechanical metaphors for memory as an insult. Such a refined ability as remembering, the citadel of our mind, the seat of our thinking, feeling and knowledge, could only be denoted by organic meta-phors. Romantics were inspired in their imagery by nature, by growth and change; mechanical metaphors figure in their texts only by way of contrast.

The contrast between mechanistic and Romantic metaphors of memory is just one of the many contrasts in the psychology of the nineteenth century. The history of memory takes us past the paintings of Caspar David Friedrich and the dissecting tables of neuro-anatomists, past the popular consulting rooms of phrenologists and demonstrations of the phonograph, past the silvery shimmer of the first daguerreotypes and the clicking of *Gedächtnis-Apparate* in the psycho-logical laboratories, a tour, which is in short, just as confusing as the nine-teenth century itself, but certainly as lively.

The decline of the mechanistic approach

The Cartesian universe was a machine, an automaton in which the wheels drove each other cog by cog in accordance with the laws of pressure and thrust. Stars, planets and moons revolved round the heavens like gleaming cogwheels, in orbits which could be calculated and described by the same laws which deter-mined the movements in a clock. Descartes had declared that these mechan-istic principles applied to everything that lay outside the thinking intellect of man, not only to inanimate nature, such as mountains and objects, but also to organic nature. The clockwork metaphor was even useful for the development of a seed into a tree: 'so it is no less natural for a clock constructed with this or that set of wheels to tell the time than it is for a tree which grew from this or that seed to produce the appropriate fruit'.[5]

In the history of philosophy, Descartes's name is linked with the theory of the *bête machine*, the doctrine that animals are pure automatons.[6] The move-ments of animals were no more than the perceptible effects of machine-like processes. Memory too partook of this mechanisation of the animal soul. What looked from the outside like the operation of a memory, was in reality a ques-tion of mechanics. The objection of one of Descartes's correspondents, Henry Cavendish, Marquess of Newcastle, that swallows returning in spring to the place where they nested the previous year, have obviously remembered that place and hence have a memory, was dismissed by Descartes. The behaviour of swallows was completely determined by design and adaptation. One does not after all say of a clock that it 'remembers' when it has to strike. Birds are carefully adapted automatons: 'Doubtless when the swallows come in spring, they operate like clocks.'[7]

With the memory of animals reduced to machinery and human memory represented as an instrument determined by physical processes in the brain (remember Hooke's theory of memory), the mechanisation of the memory had advanced as far as was compatible with Christian views of the soul as a non-material, God-related substance. The final step, the human soul as a machine, was to be taken only in the century after Descartes and Hooke.

In 1747 the French doctor and freethinker Julien de Lamettrie had a pamphlet published by a Leiden printer entitled *L'Homme machine*.[8] It appeared anonymously. Not without reason: the unadorned materialism that was defended with a great deal of polemical flourishings branded the author as an 'atheist'. When Lamettrie's authorship was established, he was forced to leave the country and to exchange the Dutch Republic for a stay at the Court of Frederick the Great, who had seen fit to offer asylum to 'the victim of fools and theologians'. We owe what little we know about this doctor–philosopher to Frederick's eulogy, written after Lamettrie's death in 1751.

Lamettrie had studied the mechanistically orientated medicine of Boerhaave in Leiden and before that had come to the conclusion on the basis of personal experiences that the Cartesians, who had assumed two different substances in man ('. . . as if they had seen them, and positively counted them'), had counted one substance too many.[9] During a campaign in the service of the French army Lamettrie had contracted a disease which was accompanied by a high fever. The observation of his own perceptions strengthened him in his materialistic convictions. In the elegant Baroque prose of Frederick the Great:

> For a philosopher an illness is a school of physiology; he [Lamettrie] believed that he could clearly see that thought is but a consequence of the organisation of the machine, and that the disturbance of the springs has considerable influence on that part of us which the metaphysicians call soul. Filled with these ideas during his convalescence, he boldly bore the torch of experience into the night of metaphysics; he tried to explain by the aid of anatomy the thin texture of understanding, and he found only mechanism where others had presupposed an essence superior to matter.[10]

And for Lamettrie 'mechanism' meant, as it had done a century earlier for Descartes, clockwork. Man is a 'machine which winds its own springs. It is the living image of perpetual movement.'[11] This automaton differs only in complexity from the mechanical animals of Descartes: 'He is to the ape, and to the most intelligent animals, as the planetary pendulum of Huyghens is to a watch of

Julien Leroy.'[12] According to this theory the human memory was a piece of apparatus that worked purely mechanically, with springs and cogwheels adjusted to
make the appropriate movements at the right time.

Lamettrie's work was both the culmination and the conclusion of this
mechanistic episode. No one before him had dared to place the human mind
within the province of mechanics; after him the mechanical approach fell into
discredit and the interpretation of living organisms as a collection of cogwheels
was felt to be inappropriate. Towards the end of the eighteenth century the tide
turned. In philosophical treatises clockwork metaphors became increasingly
scarce and eventually disappeared. In the new philosophical approach mechanistic analogies seemed out of place, just as the wrought iron clockwork from
Descartes's time seemed clumsy and awkward compared to the elegant silver
pocket watches of the late eighteenth century. Perhaps the French scientific
researcher and writer Saint-Pierre was thinking of the Cartesian clockwork tree
when he wrote in 1784:

> Plants, it has been said, are mechanical bodies. Well, then, try to construct
> a body so slim, so tender, so fragile, as that of a leaf, which shall for whole
> years resist the winds, the rains, the keenest frost, the most ardent Sun. A
> spirit of life, independent of all Latitudes, governs plants, preserves them,
> re-produces them. They repair the injuries which they may have sustained,
> and skinover their wounds with a new rind.[13]

The contrast could not be sharper. In the Romantic period the 'life spirit', the
vital principle in organic nature, was opposed to the clockwork of the mechanistic approach.

Romanticism: the landscapes of memory

In the history of science, Romanticism has the subdued sound of a nocturne.
Following the Enlightenment and preceding the mechanistic renaissance in
the second half of the nineteenth century, Romanticism was an unexpected
intermezzo in the trust in technology and classical science. For about fifty
years, between 1790 and 1840 (in fact an episode with blurred borders), reality
seemed to lose its transparency and art, science and philosophy veered towards
the nocturnal side of nature, man and the soul. Romanticism had all the features of a counter-movement. Romanticism provided the negative (the metaphor is an anachronism) of the orientation which dominated science before
and after it – trance and dream as opposed to lucid thought, vision as opposed
to logic, harmony and unity as opposed to analysis, intuition as opposed to
reflection, and the unconscious as opposed to the waking consciousness. The
nocturnal scenes of Caspar David Friedrich were so many icons of this era, as
were the stories of E. T. A. Hoffmann in literature.

In science and philosophy the notion of reality as an indivisible and organic
whole was given form in German *Naturphilosophie*.[14] The mechanistic principle

of pressure and thrust gave way to the magnetic attraction between poles and magnets which were surrounded with so much more mystery. In *Ansichten von der Nachtseite der Naturwissenschaft*, published in 1808, the physician Schubert pointed to magnetism as the hidden force which permeated both the organic and the inorganic world and so linked man with the cosmos.[15] As an all-permeating polarity or charge, and finally as inspiration, magnetism gradually acquired a psychic meaning. Once in a magnetic trance a widening consciousness was supposed to be capable of miracles: reading with eyes closed, the 'seeing' of internal organs, the curing of nervous attacks. Absorbed into a cosmos which was no longer a machine, mechanistic analogies for the human soul seemed inappropriate. In 1795 Coleridge wrote of the soul as an organic Aeolian harp; individual human souls are 'organic hearts diversely fram'd', he wrote, 'that tremble into thought' when the wind of experience brushes them.[16] The soul is an element of nature, played upon by nature.

The man who more than any other has the right to act as a spokesman for Romantic ideas on memory, Carl Gustav Carus (1789–1869), was a passionate landscape painter. Together with his friend Caspar David Friedrich he is considered the principal representative of German Romantic landscape painting (figure 16). In 1819 both men spent several weeks painting on the Baltic island of Rügen. Their views on the relationship between landscape, painter and viewer were closely parallel and were expressed by Carus in nine essays in letter form.[17] Unlike Friedrich, painting was not a principal activity for Carus. He had studied physics, philosophy and medicine and after specialising in obstetrics became professor in that subject at the University of Dresden. In psychology Carus is known as the discoverer of the unconscious, before Freud.[18]

The books, paintings and letters of Carus are a microcosm of the ideas which were circulating among scholars and artists in the Romantic period. His work embodied the idea of organic unity; Carus's writings on landscape are also about the soul, just as conversely, his lectures on psychology took inspiration from landscape painting. Nothing was further removed from Romantic views on nature, organism or soul than the image of clockwork, which could be disassembled or replaced part by part at will. The Romantic metaphors and analogies referred to natural processes, to what grew and flowed without links or interruptions. Carus wrote in his first letter on landscape that even if science has dissected a plant fibre by fibre, cell by cell, that knowledge will still not be sufficient to make a single leaf.[19]

Carus wrote his psychology using the imagery of nature and landscape. The third landscape letter deals with the correspondence between the events in nature and what happens in the soul. In nature everything develops according to the four stages of growth, completion, decline and destruction, whether it be the cycle of a plant, the advent and dispersion of a thunderstorm or the changing of the seasons. Anyone who looks into his own soul, perceives in the course

16.   Carus shared Caspar David Friedrich's predilection for the themes of death, decay and desolation. His painting of a snow-covered cemetery near the ruined abbey of Obyn (*Cemetery at Obyn in Winter*) encapsulates these Romantic themes and recalls the 'shrouds of the winter night' that he wrote of in his letters on landscape. The painting hangs in the Arts Museum of Leipzig.

of his imaginings the same four stages: first the beginnings of growth, then the calm of the completed image, then the beginnings of fading and finally the disappearance of the idea. These stages of the processes in nature cause strings to resound in the human mind. Eye to eye with landscape, nature and the inner self become one. The bright morning light of a spring day encourages one, the clear blue firmament and the full summer foliage of a tree bring calm and inner clarity. The discolouration and stiffening in autumn make one melancholy and the 'shrouds of the winter night' may stir feelings of death in us.[20]

In Carus's eyes no-one painted the landscape of his soul in a more virtuoso way than Caspar David Friedrich. His melancholy became visible to the viewer in tombs and sunsets, his despair in the ruins of an abbey, his loneliness in the desolation of an Arctic plain.[21] In Carus's observation one can see an allusion to two psychic mechanisms which Freud was later to call identification and projection. Friedrich could only paint when he had brought the outside world and his inner self into harmony: 'I have to become one with what surrounds me, identify with clouds and rocks to be what I am . . .'[22] This identification was also felt by the viewer. He projected his passions and dreams freely into the landscape until the outer and the inner became reflections of each other. He let the landscape serve as a metaphor for his own soul: a wood, the edge sunny, two steps further on impenetrable darkness, rocks and ravines, boundless seas, mists, storm clouds, curtains of rain. Friedrich's *Der Mönch am Meer* inspired Von Kleist to write that people looked at it 'as though their eyelids had been cut off'.[23] No wonder: they saw their own introspection in paint. Their own soul was hanging on the wall, in a frame.

In the winter of 1829–30 Carus gave a series of lectures on psychology in Dresden.[24] The eighth lecture was devoted to memory. Sensory representations, Carus explained, are projected into our mind like rays of light onto a mirror. The memory stands like a living magnet behind this constantly shifting surface and preserves them.[25] Carus used the image of scudding clouds reflected in calm, clear water surrounded by rocks for the way passing experiences project themselves onto the memory.[26] The clear-minded will reflect the representations all the clearer: the clarity of, say, Lichtenberg gives a truer reflection than the murky water of 'a native of Tierra del Fuego or an idiot'.[27] The power of memory will also depend on the clarity with which the stimulus is reflected in our soul, just as reflections of white buildings and sailing ships are more distinct than dull colours and vague shapes.[28]

Consciousness is set above memory like the sun above the landscape. ('We cannot think of a better comparison.'[29]) The fiercer the sun, the greater the surface that can be overseen. By banishing darkness and shadow our consciousness can view the representations in memory and form them into new combinations. Just as with the mirror metaphor individual differences occur here too: the bright sun which burns in the souls of Gauss or Kepler makes mathematical representations visible which are infinitely more sophisticated than the dim recesses of the soul of a 'North-American savage' for whom everything above the number three dissolves into a vague 'many'.[30]

For Carus, the essence of the soul is thought; thinking is the breath, the pulse of our spiritual life, reflection, however, thinking about thinking is the most elevated activity. This operation of the mind, in which thought is both the subject and the tool, is like the dissecting of Brazilian light beetles by their own light.[31] But consciousness also has, as in the case of falling asleep, a steady darkening. In this semi-darkness, images are released from our memory which float through our soul 'like autumn leaves on a woodland stream'.[32] Both by day and by night the processes in our memory exhibit variation and mobility, one can scarcely speak of real laws of memory. For Carus the old Platonic notion that experience should be preserved in our soul like an imprint on a wax tablet, is absurd.[33] What goes on in 'this vast labyrinth' of our memory resists simple regulation and is most similar to the way in which a master weaver makes his bobbins flash quickly back and forth, linking thousands of threads together with movements that are far too swift to follow.[34]

By using the metaphor of a loom Carus is referring to a mechanism, just as Descartes had done previously. But there is an essential difference. Whereas the Cartesian analogy of a machine expressed the transparency of mechanical laws, the reliability and predictability of determinism, Carus's metaphor points to precisely the unfathomable quality of memory. It is impossible to understand how experience weaves representations into our memory, there are too many threads, they are moving too fast; our memory is an instrument whose operation is hidden from us.

One cannot say that Carus regretted this unfathomability; on the contrary, he was prepared to reserve a place in his psychology for the compartments of our mental life which were not accessible to introspection or reflection. The opening line of his *Psyche* has become a classic: 'The key to knowledge of the nature of conscious mental life lies in the realm of the unconscious.'[35] This unconsciousness, inaccessible but not for that reason vague, is a reservoir of vitality, a source of creativity, the origin of conscious mental life. There is no question of a sharp demarcation between the two spheres; their border is like that between day and night. Hypnotic phenomena, Carus felt, revealed psychic processes which were hidden from the individual himself and became visible only in the particular circumstances of a trance.

As well as 'twilight' the unconscious appeared in psychology and in literature as 'depth'. In the topography of the Romantic's soul 'inward' generally meant 'downward', down the shafts, to the 'subterranean gardens' of which the mining engineer and poet Novalis spoke, with their 'metal trees and crystal plants'.[36] Or it meant to the depths of the sea, as in Heine's *Die Nordsee*: 'I love this sea like my soul. Often I even feel as if the sea is really my soul itself; and just as in a sea hidden water plants grow which rise to the surface only at the moment when they bloom and when they finish blooming disappear again into the depths, so occasionally splendid images of flowers float up from the depths of my soul, which spread their perfume and shimmer and finally disappear again.'[37]

The Romantic penchant for what Carus called *die Nachtseite des Seelenlebens*, the notion that some rooms in the soul always remain sealed and that we shall never know what lies within, did not mean that *all* psychic processes were inaccessible to scientific research. Some doors were ajar, others wide open, and where direct access seemed impossible, one could still try to venture a hypothesis in an indirect way. In the Romantic period the underlying principle was: 'As it is outside, so it is inside'; the external was seen as a reflection of the internal.[38]

There is really no end to the creativity with which the external was conceived of as a sign or depiction of the internal. People read someone's character from handwriting, personality from facial features, fate from the lines on the hand, emotions from gestures, temperament from physical build. At the end of the eighteenth century the Swiss theologian Lavater had explained how the human face could be the expression of inner harmony, but also of sin, and even of criminal propensities: 'Whoever is familiar with the details of the human face in hospitals and prisons, will often scarcely be able to believe his eyes and shudder inwardly at the signs with which lewdness brands its slaves.'[39] Carus was an admirer of Lavater and expressed the resemblance between inside and outside through the symbolic meaning of the various parts of the human body, interpreting their shapes and proportions as an expression of character and temperament.[40] For Carus the structure of the skull in particular was a mark of great significance. In a cranioscopic atlas he collected skulls, death masks and plaster casts of celebrities such as Luther, Kant, Tiedge and Beethoven, together with the skulls of, for example, a poisoner, a patricide, an Egyptian pharaoh, an African Negro, a mentally defective girl and a Greenlander. In an intriguing alternation of measurement and interpretation Carus specified how patterns of personality and giftedness were reflected in external proportions. For example, he pointed to Kant's broad forehead, which matched the latter's great analytical powers, and the contrast with the central section of the skull, the seat of the emotional life, that 'was relatively weak in the creator of the Pure Criticism'[41] (figure 17). In Goethe's face Carus particularly praised the high forehead of over five French inches, and the delicate swellings around the eye sockets pointed to 'benevolent lucid judgement'.[42]

The link between internal and external was seen in the Romantic period in terms of a harmony which had a symbolic rather than a causal meaning. The differences in facial expressions or skull shapes might occasionally be connected to physiological differences which in turn were connected to differences in personality or giftedness, but there was no question of a direct causal relationship between the hidden psychic processes and the external. Therefore in the Romantic vision a landscape or a rock formation could also have a physiognomic expression. Against this background it is understandable that Carus wanted nothing to do with a rival tradition in the research into the brain and skull, phrenology. His cranioscopic atlas contains a number of irritated asides on the doctrine of Gall, who in contrast *did* assume that there was a direct causal link between the form of the skull, the properties of the brain and differences in personality and giftedness. Looking back at the development of neurology one can see a watershed between the cranial theories of Carus and Gall. Carus's belonged to the Romantic view of science orientated towards interpretation and symbolism, and after the middle of the nineteenth century was to share the fate of Romantic science at large. Gall's cranial theory became a stage in the development of an empirical and experimentally orientated neurology.

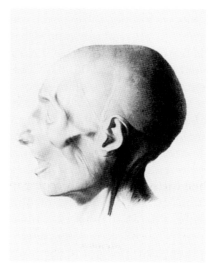

17.   In his *Neuer Atlas der Cranioskopie* (Leipzig, 1864) Carus collected visual
      material for his study of the connection between the structure of the skull
      and psychological qualities like intelligence, character, temperament, etc.
      The illustration shows the death mask of the philosopher Immanuel Kant,
      who died in 1804 at the age of eighty.

In the study of memory this meant a move from the writing table to the dissecting table.

Localisation: Gall, Flourens, Broca

Research into the localisation of psychic functions in the brain got underway
towards the end of the eighteenth century through the work of Franz Joseph
Gall (1758–1828), a Viennese doctor who excelled in cranial anatomy.[43] Gall was
the first to distinguish between the 'grey matter' on the surface of the cortex
and in the heart of the spinal cord and the 'white matter' which links these
areas together. He also discovered that the white fibres from the spinal cord
cross at the base of the brain, so that one half of the body is governed by the
opposite half of the brain. In addition, he developed new dissection techniques. His strength lay in comparative cranial anatomy. Based on research
into the brains of animals and human beings of different ages, Gall was able
to specify a link between brain and mind by tying it down to a link between
the size of the cortex and the higher mental functions. Speech, memory and a
capacity for thought turned out to be a direct function of the amount of intact
cortex.[44]

   If Gall had left it at these findings, writes Fancher, his work would have been
remembered with respect in the history of science.[45] Unfortunately he included
the non-controversial part of his results in a theory which Spurzheim dubbed

'phrenology' and later fell into discredit. According to this theory every psychic function had a corresponding 'organ' in the brain. The size of that brain organ was supposed to be proportionate to the development of the psychic function. Gall reports that it had struck him in his schooldays that boys who were good at learning things by heart had slightly protruding eyes ('so-called bulging eyes').[46] Gall attributed this to the swelling in the physical substratum of this kind of memory, at the front of the brain, immediately behind the eye sockets. Since most functions are located in the cortex just under the surface of the skull, the indentations, bumps and curves in the surface of the skull could be interpreted as a projection of the human mind. For example, if there is a pronounced talent for mathematics, then the swelling in the accompanying organ causes a protuberance. The trained hands of the phrenologist will sense this as a mathematical knob, a bony cupola for whatever is above the mediocre.

This notion, the skull as a landscape in which the irregularities refer to the tectonics of the underlying brain organs, led to one of the most ambitious projects in the science of the human mind. Gall's cranial theory, in the judgement of a Dutch follower, the doctor Jacobus Doornik, most resembled cartography: 'The skull proper has become the map, on which, just as in an atlas, the regions and localities are circumscribed in which man as in a tiny world, is described. Nowadays one travels around man's skull, as if on a globe, to seek and discover the places where our perceptions, desires, inclinations and mental abilities are housed.'[47] In this way Gall became a Columbus of the 'new world *in* us', whose discoveries were recorded in atlases and collected in skull cabinets. One of the most celebrated collections of skulls was Gall's own, a collection which thanks to generous donations from mad houses and institutions quickly increased in size, much to the alarm of his contemporaries, who saw in the enterprise a macabre *Kopfjägerei*. Had not Haydn's remains reached Prince Esterházy headless? In one of his letters Gall complained that everyone grabbed for his head when he entered the room.

Besides post-mortem research Gall conducted observations on the skulls of living people in an attempt to link the pattern of character qualities and specific gifts with the development of their 'brain organs'. For example, it was his practice to 'invite ordinary street urchins for cakes and brandy, with a promise of some money, who then gladly came to his house, and having been invited willingly told of each other's villainies, after which he investigated the greatest eaters, greatest liars, greatest jokers etc. as tests of his assumptions'.[48] Gall drew up a list of twenty-seven faculties, varying from sexual instincts, loyalty and vanity to feeling for language, musicality, religiosity and steadfastness. All these 'inward' properties appeared on the outside as anatomical signs, so that anyone 'who is able to decipher this sign language, has also discovered the axis around which man's mind and heart turn'.[49]

In March 1805 Gall, with his pupil and partner Spurzheim, had begun a 'cranioscopic journey', a lecture tour which would occupy almost three years and would take the two anatomists through half of Europe.[50] Gall himself had at that point not yet published anything about his brain and cranial theory – he did that only from 1808 onwards – but various books had already appeared, based on his lectures. Gall imagined memory as a series of separate faculties, each with their own position in the brain. They were however located close together, just above and behind the eye sockets. There were six forms of memory: memory for facts, places, numbers, words, names and for people.[51] Gall situated the memory for facts directly above the nose. A bump in that position pointed to a highly developed memory for facts. Did not the elephant, with its proverbial good memory, have a thick bump above its trunk? The memory for places, situated immediately on either side of the memory for facts, enabled its owner to orientate himself spatially and was important to field marshals and engineers, astronomers and landscape artists. Memory for numbers was on the edge of the eye sockets and pushed the eyes, when particularly well developed, somewhat towards each other, 'which gives a slightly cross-eyed look to the eyes. One notices this particularly with the *Jews*, who for many generations, have lived from calculation and trade.'[52] How great, the translator wondered, must this tool be in Leibniz, the inventor of differential calculus? He answered the question with an observation of his own: 'The fact that in making difficult calculations mentally one often goes cross-eyed is an observation which seldom fails. The portrait of Leibnitz, which I have in front of me, is indeed cross-eyed.'[53]

The partnership between Gall and Spurzheim ended in 1813 in a quarrel.[54] At that moment Spurzheim took a popularised version of cranial theory – plus ten or so faculties which he discovered himself – to the New World and in lucrative lectures gave an applied twist to them: in his hands phrenology developed into an instrument for choosing a marriage partner and a profession, and ultimately even into a personality test (figure 18). Phrenology had already become a caricature of psychological theory. Lacking recognition by orthodox science Gall and his pupils began addressing non-scientific audiences and gradually quite a few bits of hocus-pocus became mixed up with phrenological doctrine.[55] By the time of Gall's death, in 1828, his theory had no significant support in academic circles. His own skull was prepared by a pupil and was later included in the collection of the Musée de l'homme in Paris under catalogue number 19216.

In France, established science marshalled considerable opposition forces. By far the best known opponent of phrenology was Pierre Flourens (1794–1867). Like Gall, Flourens was a brilliant brain anatomist, with a special talent for comparative anatomy. The difference between the two researchers was a technique which Gall regarded as useless and which Flourens mastered to perfection: surgical extirpation. Flourens was extremely skilful at removing tiny sections of brain tissue, usually in the form of slices so thin that he could even use the technique with bird brains. By observing the behaviour of the animal after recovery, he tried to ascertain a general distribution of functions across the brain. This extirpation technique brought experiment into the repertoire

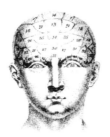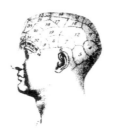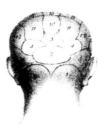

18.   Gall's theory of the brain and the skull was popularised by Spurzheim, who
        expanded the theory further and presented it to the public as 'phrenology'.
        Spurzheim devoted great care to the illustrations. These diagrams of cranial
        maps are from the frontispiece to his *Phrenology, or, the Doctrine of the Mind;
        and of the Relations between its Manifestations and the Body* (London, 1825).

of brain research, albeit that, for the time being, incisions were only made into
animal brains.

One of Flourens's findings concerned the behaviour of a dog which had had
increasingly deep slices of its cerebellum removed. As a result of this surgery
the dog gradually lost the ability to move in an orderly way: when it wanted to
move forwards, it fell backwards, if it wanted to go left, it turned right. The processing of sensory stimuli remained intact, and only the coordination of the
motor system disappeared. In another experiment a pigeon lost the whole of its
cortex. Consequently the bird no longer reacted to visual or auditory stimuli
and no longer made voluntary movements. From these and similar experiments Flourens concluded that while functions were distributed in a general
way across different brain structures, *within* those structures no separate faculties could be pinpointed.[56] He argued that the higher mental functions such as
speech, thought and memory were distributed evenly over the brain. This
conclusion fitted in elegantly with Flourens's philosophical conviction that the
human mind is a harmonious and indivisible whole, with its seat in an integrated brain. He dedicated his dismissal of phrenology to Descartes. It brought
him membership of the Institut de France, which Gall had been refused in 1808.

In the mass of observations and findings accumulated in Gall's œuvre one case
can be found which could not be reconciled with Flourens's conclusions and
which was eventually to lead to a partial rehabilitation of localisation theories.
Gall described the case of a soldier who had suffered brain damage as a result of
a sword thrust just below the left eye. Since the accident he had lost the ability
to name objects or people. Gall then provided the first description of partial
aphasia as a result of a lesion in the left frontal lobe. Aphasia had already been
known about for a considerable time and had also been previously linked to brain
damage, but not until now linked to an injury in a specific place. After Flourens
such a link was not considered plausible in French neurology. The notion of a
separate language centre was kept alive by Bouillaud, a doctor, physicist and a

pupil of Gall's, and the former's son-in-law, the neurologist Aubertin. It was by following the latter's directions that the Paris neurologist Pierre-Paul Broca (1824–80) was able to identify the site later to be named after him.[57]

As with Columbus, when Broca made the discovery of his life, he was quite unclear about what exactly he had found. The brain which he presented to his medical colleagues at a meeting of the Société d'Anthropologie in 1861, had a hole the size of a pigeon's egg in the left frontal lobe. The edges had become pulpy: obviously the brain tissue from the centre of the injury had become infected and had oozed away. Broca had removed the otherwise intact brain the day before from the skull of a certain Leborgne, a shoemaker, of whom the history of neurology has preserved only the nickname, Monsieur Tan, after the stopgap 'tan' with which he replied to all questions.

At the time of his death Tan had lacked the ability to speak for twenty-one years, and it was only reasonable to assume that this disfunction was connected to the lesion in the left frontal lobe. The exact nature of the link was less clear. Tan could produce noises and sounds, so that his inability to speak had nothing to do with the muscles and nerves of his speech apparatus. Tan could also understand what was said to him, so that he still retained what Broca called 'the memory for words'. But what then had oozed out of his brain? Broca maintained that in Tan 'the memory for the movements necessary to pronounce words' had been affected. Autopsies of other aphasic patients confirmed the conclusion that the speech centre is located on the underside of the third convolution of the left frontal lobe, not far from the place of the sword wound of Gall's unhappy soldier. There must have been a babble of agreement from a cabinet in the Musée de l'homme.

Broca discovered the neurological site of (expressive) aphasia in 1861. In the next two decades there followed a whole series of findings in the area of function localisation. Those results were partly due to new techniques.[58] The discovery of sensory and motor projection areas by the German physiologists Fritsch and Hitzig was based on electrical stimulation of the cortex. Other researchers succeeded in following the course of nerve groups through the brain and hence of mapping the most important connections. Extirpation experiments in apes led to the discovery of the capacity for sight in the rear lobe. Not long afterwards an auditive centre was also identified. The hypothesis that the projection areas were linked together by association areas was confirmed by extirpation and post-mortem examinations. Wernicke's more theoretically driven research into the relationship between the motor system of speech and the representation of the meaning of words provided new insights into the form of aphasia which was later to be named after him. After all these developments, the brain of 1875 was no longer the brain of 1800 nor even that of 1850. Whereas Gall had localised a far too specific and largely arbitrary list of faculties and Flourens had distributed the functions rather too generally over the various brain structures, the neurologist of 1875 had at his disposal a fairly accurate map of the brain. In neurological atlases the white areas of *terra incognita* began to shrink and became enclaves in known territory.

'Mental physiology'

What was the significance of these developments on theories regarding memory? The various pathologies – expressive and receptive aphasia, apraxia, agraphia – made it seem plausible that the memory consisted of constituent functions, each with its own neurological location. The motor memory for speech was obviously located in a different place to the memory for the meaning of words or the memory for objects. But as for *how* these constituent memories were linked with processes in the brain or what those processes in the brain precisely consisted of, brain scientists in the second half of the nine-teenth century were none the wiser than in Descartes's and Hooke's time. The prevailing ideas on the physical substratum of memory were very general in nature. The French philosopher–psychologist Fouillée grouped the hypotheses for the forming of memory traces into three categories.[59] According to the first hypothesis, experience caused a pattern of continuing *movement* in the brain in the form of vibration. The second hypothesis attributed the formation of memory traces to permanent changes in the *structure* of the brain cells. The third hypothesis assumed that in the brain a *disposition* could arise for the repetition of the identical pattern of excitation.

The most fully developed ideas on the neurological substratum of memory are found within a group of theoreticians who historically have been assembled under the title 'mental physiologists'. This orientation emerged in the 1860s and flourished in the same two decades which had been so fruitful for localisa-tion research. The best-known representatives were the Britons William Carpenter (who coined the term 'mental physiology') and Henry Maudsley.[60] Both were doctors. Carpenter, Maudsley and like-minded researchers were opti-mistic about the scope for materialistic explanations of psychic functions.

In 'mental physiology' one publication had an exceptionally great influence. In 1870 the physiologist Ewald Hering gave a lecture on memory to the Austrian Akademie von Wissenschaften.[61] Hering defended two propositions. The first was that 'memory' is a general characteristic of organic matter; the second that all inherited or acquired characteristics are contained in the organism and are transmitted to posterity as 'memory'. This last proposition was to share the fate of Lamarck's heredity theory and fall into discredit, but the first proposition developed into a much discussed hypothesis in theories of memory. Hering maintained that organic matter is predisposed to preserve and reproduce stimuli. A muscle which is trained increases in size and this makes repetition of the movement increasingly easy. Obviously facilitation processes take place at cellular level which simplify the reproduction of a particular condition and which in that way 'remember' that condition in the form of a disposition. According to Hering this is a universal characteristic of organic matter. The human memory is a special case of this feature. In the same way that movements work their way into the motor nervous system, so mental functions can wear their way into the brain. The retention and reproduction of perceptions, thoughts and images are a function of the organic matter of which our brains are constructed.

This hypothesis managed to attract quite a few advocates from the ranks of 'mental physiology'. The views of authors like Maudsley and Carpenter in England and Ribot in France on the neurological substratum of memory processes virtually coincided with Hering's theory of the 'organic' memory. The standard explanation of memory was as follows. The processing of experience in the brain takes place through neural activity. This activity is electrical in nature: stimuli are guided from nerve cell to nerve cell through a moving excitation. By being subjected to the stimulus the nerve cell undergoes a modification making it more sensitive to activation. Pathways of these nerve cells form circuits and it is these circuits which are the physiological basis of retention. A reactivation of the identical neural pathway evokes the original experience. If reproduction is the result of an external stimulus outside the brain, one speaks of recognition; a stimulus from the brain itself leads to remembering. Memory is nothing but the conscious side of this purely physiological disposition of brain cells.[62] Mental physiologists were unanimous on the physiological explanation for retention: a memory is the reactivation of a trace laid down by earlier experience.

This theory suggested an explanation for association. William James, himself a physiologist, maintained that the brain corresponded to 'the great communicating switch-board at a central telephone station', an instrument that establishes communications between the processes in varying parts of the brain.[63] In accordance with this mechanistic metaphor James had sketched in an older publication how the laws of association of similarity and contiguity could be derived from processes in networks of nerve cells.[64] When two neural processes have occurred simultaneously or immediately following each other, there is a tendency that the repetition of one process will also activate the other. Bearing in mind such factors as electrical currents in nerve tissue and the summation of excitations, James specified a physical law of association: the chance that a neural impulse will follow a certain path is determined by the number of times that the impulse has previously followed that path and of the intensity of the activation. Because of the purely physical course of stimuli and reactions, there is no *operator* in the 'switch-board' of our brain: all connections are made automatically, without the intervention of a selecting agent.

Fouillée has a corresponding physical explanation for association by contiguity in which he compares neural pathways with railway tracks which at certain parts of the track come closer, merge with each other and redivide. The fact that two representations become linked in our memory is because the neural pathways which form the substratum of these images join at a place 'analogous to that where a signalman determines the course of trains'.[65] With reference to this passage Ladd asked the offhand, but profound question: 'Is there, then, something to be said of a mental "switchman" determining the course of *these* trains of ideas?'[66]

Explanations like these presuppose a very close connection between brain and memory, but outside the field of mental physiology the notion that memory processes coincide with brain processes was far from common. Various researchers denied that the human memory can be directly linked to processes in the brain; others opposed the claim that this hypothesis could offer an adequate explanation for reproduction. Even the apparently so solid theory of physiological retention was not uncontroversial. An awkward empirical problem, for example, was the exact nature of the change in the nerve elements. How long did the change remain intact? Weren't brain cells far too plastic for such static changes in their structure? A more philosophical objection focused on arbitrary remembering. How could the apparently free decision to remember this or that be linked with the determined course of electric currents through neural circuits? And why was the repetition of the original pattern of excitation experienced as a memory instead of a perception or a thought, like the first time? Where did the awareness come from that the excitation was a repetition of a previously identical excitation? Was that consciousness itself based on an excitation, elsewhere in the brain? Both from an empirical and a philosophical point of view, the physiological explanation of retention seemed to raise quite a few problems. In order to present this as a plausible theory the authors in the 'mental physiology' tradition had to use all the empirical and conceptual means at their disposal. And one of those means was the metaphor.

Phonograph and memory

As early as the sixteenth century, there was a great deal of fantasising about the possibility of retaining sound and later replaying it. In *Pantagruel* (1533) Rabelais described how the sounds of a winter campaign were frozen in the ice and in the spring, as the thaw set in, again became audible.[67] A century later Sorel in a report of an imaginary journey to the South Seas, mentioned people who communicated across long distances by speaking a message into a sponge and despatching the sponge. The addressee could hear the sponge by holding it to his ear and squeezing it[68] (figure 19). In reality, the means for giving sound permanence were very restricted. Though there were procedures for amplifying sound, such as the constructions of Vitruvius to which Hooke referred, or the sounding bowls with which waves of sound could be concentrated, these devices were based on resonance and echo and *lengthened* the acoustic stimulus instead of preserving it.

A first step in the direction of the phonograph was taken in 1857 by the Frenchman Leon Scott de Martinville. He designed an apparatus – according to

19.   A nineteenth-century engraving from *Le Courrier véritable* of 1632: when squeezed the sponge releases the words it has absorbed earlier.

tradition, after reading a book of physiology – whose construction was inspired by the anatomy of the human ear. This 'phonautograph', or automatic sound writer consisted of a horn as an ear and a membrane as an eardrum (figure 20). Attached to the centre of the membrane was a hog's-hair bristle, which drew a trace over the regularly turning soot-covered glass cylinder. In this way the vibrations were converted into a pattern of wavy movements and sound was

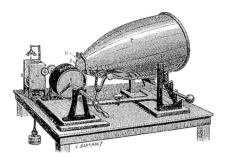

20.   The 'phonautograph' of Leon Scott de Martinville. Sounds captured by the
horn P are recorded in the soot-coated cylinder E via the membrane M and
the hog's-hair bristle s.

transformed into a lasting visual trace. Conversely the trace could not be recon-
verted into sound: the machine recorded but did not reproduce. In 1857 Scott
was granted a patent for his phonautograph. After that developments stag-
nated.

On 18 April 1877 the Parisian poet–painter–inventor Charles Cros delivered
a sealed envelope to the Académie des Sciences containing, according to the
caption, 'a description of a process for recording and reproducing phenomena
perceived by the ear'.[69] When, at the end of 1877, Cros heard of Edison's invention, he ordered the Académie to open the envelope and to publish its contents
as quickly as possible in its proceedings.[70] It is clear from the description that
Cros had anticipated the principles of the process patented by Edison. He proposed letting an extremely fine needle draw a trace on a membrane over a soot-
covered cylinder – as in the case of the phonautograph – and subsequently to
convert the sideways movements of the trembling needle into a relief, engraved
into a disk of durable material. The trace was in this way turned ninety degrees
and formed a groove. By having the disk rotate again under the needle, the
vibrations became audible again through the membrane.

After having deposited his idea with the Académie, Cros tried to find
someone who could build such a piece of equipment for him. He had no success
and by the end of 1877 the unfortunate Cros found himself overtaken by
developments in America, where Edison had been able to convert the same idea
into a machine, protected by solid patents. Compared with Cros's procedure
Edison's had been simplified in one respect, and in all probability that one
point meant a difference between the theoretical specification of a mechanism
and an operational machine: where in the case of Cros the trace drawn had to
be subsequently converted into a relief, Edison had the needle itself engrave a
relief. Figures 21 and 22, taken from an article from *Nature* of 1878, specified the
operation of the machine.

Edison had had his prototype built by his assistant John Kruesi. During the
first experiment which has since become legendary, Edison shouted a few lines

21.   The front view of Thomas Edison's phonograph. A horizontal threaded axle
runs through the holders A and B and when the handle D is turned moves
slowly sideways. The flywheel E ensures uniform motion. On the cylinder C
a groove is cut in time with the thread on the axle. The cylinder is covered
with tin plate. An arm with the mouthpiece F rests against the cylinder. A
cross-section of this mouthpiece is shown from the side.

of the children's song 'Mary had a little lamb' into the mouthpiece and a
moment later these sounds were reproduced audibly (Kruesi: *Gott im Himmel, it
has spoken!*). The apparatus became known as the 'Talking-Machine' and indeed
in the beginning was only suitable for storing spoken language. Edison
arranged the first demonstrations himself. In the *Scientific American* of 22
December 1877 we are told how Edison came into the editing room and put on
the table a 'simple little contrivance'.[71] After a turn of a handle 'the machine
inquired as to our health, asked how we liked the phonograph, informed us that
it was well, and bid us a cordial goodnight'.[72] In the spring of 1878 Edison
instructed his representatives to give demonstrations of this amazing invention
all over the world, spreading the news outside scientific and technological
circles. The demonstration for the Académie des Sciences on 11 March 1878 has
become famous because of an incident that illustrates the extent to which the
notion of storing sound conflicted with the prevailing intuitions (figure 23).
Shortly after Edison's representative had addressed the gathering with
'Monsieur Phonograph présente ses hommages à l'Académie des Sciences' and
had this sentence repeated by the phonograph, the physicist and doctor
Bouillaud (the previously mentioned pupil of Gall) jumped up, denounced the
representative as a 'fraud' and shouted that the noises had been produced by
ventriloquy. Later demonstrations were not able to dissuade him from this
opinion. In the *Revue Scientifique* there was a report a month later that Bouillaud
could not be convinced even by replication experiments under laboratory
conditions that the spoken words were actually being repeated by the phonograph: in two cases he had seen minimal lip movements from the speaker when
the words were repeated. Personal experiments had taught him meanwhile
that one could make sounds via the nostrils without moving the mouth per-
ceptibly and these observations proved that the phonographic question was far
from having been decided. The report mentioned that Bouillaud insisted on
replications under the strictest possible precautions – 'jusqu-là, M. Bouillaud ne
croira pas au phonographe'.[73]

22.   The side view of the mouthpiece from Edison's phonograph. Membrane A is made to vibrate by the sounds made in the mouthpiece. These vibrations are engraved on the tin plate via the needle P. The machine is now ready to record sound: one puts one's mouth close to the opening of the disc 'and *the metal plate is talked to* while the cylinder is revolved with a uniform motion'. The sound vibrations are then converted into a pattern of depressions and bumps in the tin plate and thus they are permanently preserved. In order to reproduce the sound the head is removed, the cylinder is wound back and the needle replaced in the groove. As the tin plate revolves again under the needle, the needle transmits the sounds to the membrane: 'The consequence of this is, that the iron plate gives out the vibrations which previously fell upon it, and *talks back to you what you have said to it.*'

Just as in the case of phonography, making recordings permanent was a big problem. Just as the first photographs faded when they were exposed to light, the phonographic track soon lost its sharpness when the recording was played. In reproduction the needle wore away the groove and after a couple of plays the recording had been erased. Only with the introduction of wax (1887), soft enough to record the traces, firm enough to retain them, did the phonograph develop into a convincing memory for sound. In 1889 the phonograph was an enormous attraction at the World Exhibition in Paris (figure 24).

However simple the phonographs were mechanically, the possibility of storing sound made a deep impression. *Nature* spoke of 'the acoustic marvel of the century'.[74] The *Scientific American* wrote: 'No matter how familiar a person may be with modern machinery and its wonderful performances, or how clear in his mind the principle underlying this strange device may be, it is impossible to listen to the mechanical speech without his experiencing the idea that his senses are deceiving him.'[75] The apparatus opened enchanting perspectives. Sound became transportable in space and time. Music, traditionally the most

23. Engraving of a demonstration of Edison's phonograph at the Académie des Sciences, 11 March 1878.

transient of the arts, became reproducible almost overnight. The voices of famous singers, wrote the anonymous journalist in *Scientific American*, would now no longer have to die with them. In trials witnesses could be confronted with the repetition of their own testimony under cross-examination. The testator would be able to read his own will out, so that there need no longer be any doubt of his mental condition. It was already possible to project stereoscopic photographs of people onto a screen for the public. 'Add the talking phonograph to counterfeit the voices, and it will be difficult to carry the illusion of real presence much further.'[76] The phonograph preserved what until then had been unrepeatable, transient, tied to the moment. As in the case of photography Edison's invention was seen as an instrument which perhaps did not bring immortality any closer, but was at least able to alleviate the consequences of transience.

The brain as a conscious phonograph

Whereas the phonograph was associated with preservation and reproduction of sound, with an acoustic memory, it was only a matter of time before this same invention was to serve as an analogy in theories on the auditive memory. It occurred soon after the first demonstrations and articles in the popular press. In his *Phonetical Memory* which appeared in 1880, Appleby discussed the similarities between the phonograph and the auditive memory.[77] In that same year Delbœuf praised the phonograph as 'a remarkable example of fixation', and defined the memory as 'an album containing phonographic sheets', ready to reproduce what had been recorded in the past.[78]

24.   Engraving of the public listening to Edison's phonograph via rubber tubes at the World Exhibition of Science and Technology, Paris, 1889.

The most fully developed analysis of the relationship between the phonograph and the memory was published in 1880 by the French psychologist and philosopher Jean-Marie Guyau.[79] Guyau introduced the phonograph as a metaphor of memory with a number of general observations. Analogic reasoning plays an important part in science. Discoveries often originate from metaphors. In psychology, a science still in its infancy, metaphors are an absolute necessity in order for us to understand mental functions: before we can *know* anything we have to be able to *imagine* it. The human brain, Guyau believed, had been compared up until now with relatively crude artifacts. Spencer imagined the brain as a mechanical piano which could play an infinite number of tunes; Taine compared memory with a printing works which keeps clichés of what has been printed. Such metaphors described the brain at rest, but fail to do justice to the dynamic aspects of a memory which contains not ready-made replicas but potential images. Moreover such metaphors only explain preservation and not reproduction. Both these objections were overcome by the metaphor of the phonograph. When one speaks in front of the phonograph sound waves are converted into a trace. An analogous process takes place in the brain: sound impressions engrave 'invisible grooves' in the brain cells which function as bedding for nerve currents. Later stimulation will again follow the course of the bedding and hence reproduce the perception which led to the creation of the bedding. Exactly the same phenomenon takes place in the phonograph when the needle runs through a groove which has already been made: in this case the same sound waves are created as in recording. 'If the phonograph membrane had a consciousness of its own', writes Guyau, 'it would say, when we made it reproduce a tune, that it remembered this tune; and it would perhaps perceive as a marvellous ability what seems to us to be simply the output of a machine'.[80] Moreover, this imaginary phonograph would be able to distinguish new impressions from stored memories: in an existing groove the needle experiences less resistance than in cutting a new track. What one calls the ease of the familiar, of memory, corresponds to the ease with which the needle slides through the familiar groove. The daydream, the effortless succession of images, is the intro-spective experience which belongs to the frictionless course which the currents of neurons follow in our brain.

This difference between a newly engraved track and an existing groove, argues Guyau, bears a striking resemblance to the phonograph and the memory: neither instrument is capable of reproducing what has been recorded in all its richness of sound. The human voice, remembered or recorded, retains something incomplete and abstract. If the phonograph could listen to itself it would immediately hear the difference between the real and the reproduced voice. Another similarity is that the frequency of the vibrations can radically alter the nature of stored material; by making the handle rotate faster one can make tones sharper or higher. Does this not resemble the operation of atten-tion, which after all results in vague notions gradually becoming sharper? And might this not be connected to the frequency of the brain cells?

But there is also a difference. In the case of the phonograph there is no transi-tion from movement to consciousness: the metal trace in the phonographic disc 'is essentially deaf to itself'.[81] Precisely that transition is the mystery which is unceasingly accomplished in the brain. The metaphor of the phonograph leaves the mystery of body and soul intact, writes Guyau, but perhaps this mystery is less astonishing than it seems. After all, someone who listens to the phonograph is also taking sound vibrations into his consciousness: obviously movement *can* transform itself into consciousness. Moreover, these movements come to the listener from outside; it will be simpler for the brain to convert its own vibrations into perceptions. 'From this point of view', argues Guyau, 'it would seem neither too inexact nor too outlandish to describe the brain as a perfect phonograph, a conscious phonograph.'[82]

As one sees, the pattern repeats itself. Once more we have an advanced tech-nique which is absorbed without much fuss into psychological theorising; again it is a technique with impressive public effects; this time too, the tech-nique is to serve as a proof of existence. If a machine can convert acoustic stimuli into latent, reproducible tracks, so can our brains. Whereas in 1682 Robert Hooke still had to resort to the echoes in the classical theatres, to glasses and strings which vibrated with a mysterious 'sympathy', Guyau and Delbœuf were able in 1880 to refer to a differentiated and theoretically completely trans-parent technique for preserving and reproducing sound. Michon has pointed out that the use of metaphors for functionally orientated authors like Guyau was simply a question of necessity: 'In their desire to describe and explain the complex functional relations of the mind, they have usually no other option than to describe a physical architecture, *any* physical architecture, that seems to be able to carry at least part of the weight of the functionalistic description.' For this purpose functionalists turned to the 'the most intricate information processing structure that happens to be available. For Guyau this was appar-ently the phonograph.'[83]

With his reflection on memory as a phonograph Guyau hoped not only to analyse the processes of memory, but also to specify their relations to the brain. The vibrations of the needle corresponded to the vibrations in the brain cells, the grooves with association paths, the dents in the tin foil with latent neural pathways. This close correspondence fitted in with the tradition of 'mental physiology'. This tradition was soon to come to an end. When Guyau's article appeared in 1880, a young private teacher in philosophy, Hermann Ebbinghaus, had just completed an intricate series of memory experiments in which the link between memory and the brain no longer played any part. Within a few years these experiments were to give a completely new orientation to research into memory.

Hermann Ebbinghaus: the mathematisation of memory

The convention of dating the beginning of memory psychology in 1885, with the appearance of Ebbinghaus's *Über das Gedächtnis*, is open to dispute. There is no reason at all why the psychology of memory should coincide with *experimental* research into memory; moreover experiments were conducted before Ebbinghaus. For example, in 1740 Segner designed an ingenious experiment to measure the duration of after images.[84] He attached a glowing coal to a wheel – today called 'Segner's Wheel' – and caused it to revolve in the dark. The coal drew a luminous track whose length increased with the speed of rotation. Segner increased the speed until the circle closed and subsequently, he calculated from the circumference and the number of revolutions the storage duration of what today is called the 'iconic memory'. Before Ebbinghaus the German physiologist Weber conducted empirical research into memory processes. In 1834 he presented experimental studies into the sensitivity of nerves to touch. He tapped the skin twice with a sharp tip and then recorded how accurately experimental subjects could estimate the distance between two touches after varying intervals between the two contacts.[85] But even if Ebbinghaus did not mark the beginning of the experimental study of memory (a status which he never claimed for himself), he does have the honour of being the first to design and conduct an experimental *programme*.

Hermann Ebbinghaus (1850–1909) first studied history, but was later drawn to philosophy.[86] He gained his doctorate in 1873, writing a dissertation on the concept 'unconscious'.[87] In 1869, the year in which Carus died, the philosopher Eduard Von Hartmann published his *Philosophie des Unbewussten*, a compendium of the treatises on unconscious processes in organic nature and in the human mind in the preceding half century.[88] Von Hartmann argued that every process that is accessible to consciousness presupposes a multiplicity of processes which are *not* accessible and hence must be located in the unconscious. A simple and apparently transparent process like recognition was in reality the result of a 'vast apparatus' of hidden mental operations.[89] Consciousness, argued Von Hartmann, is aware of the results, not the processes themselves.[90]

Ebbinghaus was extremely critical of the work of Von Hartmann, which was greatly influenced by the literary–philosophical tradition of Carus. He himself considered psychology as a natural science. The assertion that virtually all mental processes take place hidden from view did not seem a particularly fruitful starting point for quantitative research.

Between 1875 and 1878 Ebbinghaus spent time in France and England. In those years he made a discovery which gave him the idea that memory could be made accessible for scientific research. In a second-hand bookshop in London he found Fechner's *Elemente der Psychophysik* (1860) which gave a list of experiments on the relationship between stimulus and sensation. Fechner had succeeded in expressing the link between the strength of physical stimuli and the intensity of sensations in quantitative laws. Ebbinghaus hoped to achieve the same with memory processes.

If psychology aspires to become a science, Ebbinghaus considered, then it will have to find in the human mind a place where 'the powerful levers of exact scientific research, experiment and measurement' can be applied.[91] In the study of memory two factors needed to be taken into account: the *time* which elapses between the presentation and reproduction, and the number of *repetitions* required to learn something by heart. Experience teaches us that a poem which has once been learned by heart, but has been partly forgotten, can be less effort to learn a second time around. This 'saving', however, tends to decrease in proportion to the length of the interval between the first and the second time that one learns the poem. In order to quantify this relationship learning a poem is not the appropriate method: the experimental subject will be distracted by his associations and therefore retain one thing more easily than another. Real precision, access to the pure laws of memory, can be achieved only with homogeneous material. To this end Ebbinghaus wrote over 2,300 syllables on cards, always a vowel between two consonants, such as 'bif' and 'lep'.[92] By putting these syllables randomly into sequences of eight, twelve or more, Ebbinghaus assured himself of stimuli which were as uniform as possible, in the hope of being able to detect in this way the naked mechanisms of memory; by eliminating associations he could in the words of Bem, 'always begin with a cleaned section of memory'.[93]

The experiments took several years and were conducted by one experimental director, Ebbinghaus, and one experimental subject, Ebbinghaus. They were arranged in a fixed pattern. Ebbinghaus shuffled cards, took out a predetermined number and wrote the series of syllables in a notebook. He then read the series to himself in an even tempo and repeated it until he could reproduce the series perfectly. After a predetermined interval – which could vary from twenty minutes to six or even thirty-one days – he learned the list again and calculated how few repetitions he needed compared to the first time around. This 'saving' method gave a measure for retention. Combining the results of hundreds of experiments, Ebbinghaus constructed his famous 'forgetting curve'. He transformed the general assertion that one forgets more, the longer the interval between learning and relearning into a curve which showed varying percentages of decrease at different points on the time axis. In the first twenty minutes the curve drops very rapidly, decreases slightly after an hour and then after a day switches to a gradual, almost flat decline. With similar experiments Ebbinghaus investigated such phenomena as the learning speed as a function of the number of nonsense syllables in the series, retention as a function of the number of repetitions and the difference between spread learning and 'cramming'. Using six couplets from Byron's *Don Juan*, he also investigated how much easier it is to learn material which is rich in rhyme and rhythm.[94] Ebbinghaus gave a mathematical expression to each of these factors in the form of curves or formulae.

The first report on the experiments, written in 1880, was left unpublished by Ebbinghaus.[95] Meanwhile he had become a private teacher at the University of Berlin, and in 1883 he repeated all his experiments. Finally, in 1885 his memorable monograph appeared. Ebbinghaus prefaced the report of the results with an extensive methodological study in which he specified the statistical and experimental principles which future memory psychologists were to accept as canons for their research. Reviews praised the heroic nature of his efforts, but thought the results themselves unremarkable. The 'laws' which Ebbinghaus had stated, in the judgement of the reviewer in *Mind*, 'seemed scarcely calculated to set the Spree on fire'.[96] General feeling was that its merit lay mostly in a demonstration that even a 'higher' mental process like memory could be investigated empirically. This new development was seen by some psychologists as a revolution of historical dimensions. In the view of Wundt's pupil Titchener, the nonsense syllable was 'the most considerable advance in this chapter of psychology, since the time of Aristotle'.[97]

Ebbinghaus's psychophysics of memory had succeeded in expressing the relationships between retention and forgetting in terms of measurement and number and had hence opened up a new field of research. Ebbinghaus left the exploitation of this field to others. In the psychological laboratory at Göttingen, Müller and his assistants undertook a long series of experiments, concentrating on the formation of associations, the effect of the order of the material to be learned and the improvement of learning by spreading repetitions. Müller, or more accurately his wife, was also the discoverer of retroactive inhibition, the disturbing effect of material learned later on, on top of material learned previously: Mrs Müller complained that her memory of the first list became vaguer after she had had to learn the second list.[98] In other laboratories, like the one at the Sorbonne, researchers replaced the nonsense syllable with meaningful material such as whole sentences, and people focused on the practical consequences for education.[99] Memory research quickly established contact with the psychology of individual differences – differences in personality, talents, intelligence, gender, age – which resulted in a large number of comparative

25. Woodcut of Ernst Zimmermann's rotation apparatus in his 1903 catalogue. This rotation apparatus for the study of memory was designed by G. E. Müller and A. Pilzecker. It was a clockwork mechanism, which turned a cylinder to which lists of stimulus words were attached. The speed could be regulated by rotating vanes and a counter recorded the number of rotations. The test subject had to learn the pairs of words that appeared in the window. Subsequently, by closing the left- or right-hand side of the window, the association between the words could be tested.

studies. Almost immediately after Ebbinghaus's pioneering work, the study of memory underwent a rapid thematic and geographic expansion.

There was also expansion at the level of methods and techniques. Whereas *Über das Gedächtnis* was the work of one man and his memory, his followers severed the personal union of researcher and research project. The first generation of memory psychologists separated the role of experimental subject from experimental director.[100] Experimental conditions were mechanised. Ebbinghaus himself had conducted his experiments with no other aids than a notebook and a pocket watch, but after him an impressive experimental technology developed. Around the turn of the century engravings appeared in the catalogues of psychological instrument-making companies depicting all kinds of *Gedächtnis-Apparate* and *Mnemometers* (figure 25). Prominent memory psychologists like Müller, Pilzecker, Wirth, Ach and Ranschburg gave their names to apparatus which presented stimuli in a standardised way, often in combination with metronomes, chronoscopes and other pieces of high-tech from the beginning of experimental psychology. The material to be learned was recorded on discs, cylinders or paper rolls and from then on the stimuli turned, clicked and slid past the eyes of the experimental subjects at speeds which had been determined down to a tenth of a second. Their reactions were recorded, again down to a tenth of a second, and entered in a refined statistical machinery which arranged the raw material into curves and tables. All this paraphernalia helped to give memory psychology the look of a natural science: an experimental, quantifying discipline, practised with instruments which made precision measurement possible. Memory provided, as Ebbinghaus had hoped, a pur-chase for the 'powerful levers of exact scientific research'. In the first ten or fifteen years after *Über das Gedächtnis* memory research acquired the features which it has preserved right down to the present day.

One might assume that the far-reaching mathematisation to which Ebbinghaus had subjected memory would lead to a reduction or even replace-ment of metaphors in the description of memory processes. Leafing through *Über das Gedächtnis* it looks as if curves, tables and formulae have ousted imagery. Ebbinghaus did his best to reinforce that impression. In the intro-ductory section he wrote that psychologists are wont to use all kinds of meta-phors, such as 'engraved images' and 'well-beaten paths', which had in common the fact that they were inadequate. He himself tried to refrain from meta-phorical descriptions as far as possible and to limit himself to what he called, with ingenuous self-confidence, 'das thatsächliche Verhalten' (the actual state of affairs).[101] He succeeded in doing this in the methodological and experi-mental parts of his monograph, but in the theoretical passages Ebbinghaus slid almost automatically into the familiar metaphors for memory. As soon as *explanations* had to be articulated, imagery turned out to be unavoidable. For example, Ebbinghaus saw associations as 'threads' which were strung between the elements of a series, varying in 'strength' with the distance between them.[102] Ebbinghaus also used the metaphor of memory as a record of traces. He maintained that a series of images 'dig in ever deeper' by repeated learning, and that forgetting was the result of the 'fading' or the 'falling apart' of traces.[103] The implicit metaphor in his work is in reality that of Plato's wax tablet and his experiments, Marshall and Fryer wrote, gave a quantitative formulation of a traditional 'stamping-in' model.[104]

Anyone who tries to form a picture of the activity in a memory laboratory around the turn of the century, of the equipment for presenting stimulus words, the strict experimental protocols, the careful registration of the reac-tions, the reporting in articles with sometimes more tables than text, and then thinks back to the literary treatises on memory which appeared in the heyday of Romanticism, must be struck by the contrast. The memory, which at the beginning of the nineteenth century could be described as a landscape full of woods and streams, ravines and plateaux, skies and gleaming lakes, had nothing in common with the memory which towards the end of the same century is subjected to research with 'mnemometers' and other *Gedächtnis-Apparate*. The publications of Carus and Ebbinghaus seemed to come from different worlds. This contrasting relationship also exists between Ebbinghaus and other nineteenth-century authors on memory. Broca's efforts to find the neurological locus for speech resulted in a distinction between 'memory for words' and 'memory for the motor mechanisms of speech'. Distinctions like these played no part in the mathematisation of memory which Ebbinghaus advocated. The same applied to Guyau's attempt to present the phonograph as a graphic analogy for the way in which the memory for sound could be linked with processes in the brain. From Ebbinghaus's perspective this was irrelevant. What mattered in experimental research into memory were measurements and numbers, not the links between memories and neurons. Viewed in this way, it seems as if the work of Ebbinghaus stands at the end of the nineteenth century like a funnel, narrowing the diversity of Romantic literary and neurological traditions into the uniformity of formal memory laws. This representation of matters, however, is misleading. Each of these traditions had its own continuation: in art, philosophy, psychiatry, sometimes even in psychology. But equally incorrect is the argument found in the 'preface history' of many contemporary textbooks, that the study of memory began with the reduction to the learning and relearning of experimentally and mathematically accessible material. Ebbinghaus's work was first and foremost the conclusion of an era.

Notes

1   Quoted from A. Werner (ed.), *The Sword and the Flame. Selections from Heinrich Heine's Prose*, New York, London, 1960, pp. 249–50. Heine's walking tour of the Harz mountains took place in September 1824.

2   J. Clair, 'Beilhieb im Kopf', J. Clair, C. Pichler and W. Pircher (eds.), *Wunderblock. Eine Geschichte der modernen Seele*, Vienna, 1989.

3   H. Ebbinghaus, *Über das Gedächtnis*, Leipzig, 1885.

4   The camera obscura, photography and film have each been linked to memory. This parallel persists throughout the nineteenth century and is the subject of the next chapter.

5   R. Descartes, *Principles of Philosophy*, trans. V. R. Miller and R. P. Miller, Dordrecht, 1983, p. 288.

6   On the *bête machine*, see L. Cohen Rosenfield, *From Beast-Machine to Man-Machine*, New York, 1940. On the *bête machine* as an episode in the debate on the mechanisation of psychological processes, see D. Draaisma, *Het verborgen raderwerk. Over tijd, machines en bewustzijn*, Baarn, 1990.

7   From a letter to the Marquess of Newcastle (23 November 1646). In R. Descartes, *The Philosophical Writings of Descartes (Vol. III: The Correspondence)*, trans. J. Cottingham, R. Stoothoff, D. Murdoch, A. Kenny, Cambridge, 1991, p. 304.

8   J. O. de Lamettrie, *L'Homme machine*, Leiden, 1747.

9   J. O. de Lamettrie, *Man a Machine*, G. C. Bussey (ed.), La Salle, 1912, p. 86. The mechanistic approach is first and foremost a methodological position and does not imply materialism (neither Descartes nor Boerhaave were materialists); however, the converse *is* true.

10   *Ibid.*, p. 6. The eulogy was read to the Berlin Academy of Sciences.

11   *Ibid.*, p. 93.

12   *Ibid.*, p. 140.

13   H. B. de Saint-Pierre, *Etudes de la nature*, Paris, 1784. Quoted from *Studies of Nature*, 5 vols., trans. M. Hunter, London, 1796, I, p. 296.

14   S. Poggi and M. Bossi (eds.), *Romanticism in Science. Science in Europe, 1790–1840*, Dordrecht, 1994.

15   G. H. Schubert, *Ansichten von der Nachtseite der Naturwissenschaft*, Dresden, 1808.

16   Quoted in M. H. Abrams, *The Mirror and the Lamp. Romantic Theory and the Critical Tradition*, Oxford, 1953, p. 61.

17   C. G. Carus, *Neun Briefe über Landschaftsmalerei*, 1830, Villingen edn, 1990.

18   H. F. Ellenberger, *The Discovery of the Unconscious*, New York, 1970, pp. 207–8; G. H. E. Russelman, *Van James Watt tot Sigmund Freud. De opkomst van het stuwmodel van de zelfexpressie*, Deventer, 1983, pp. 61–5.

19   Carus, *Briefe*, p. 15.

20   *Ibid.*, pp. 27–8.

21   C. Sommerhage, *Deutsche Romantik. Literatur und Malerei, 1796–1830*, Cologne, 1988, p. 84.

22   Quoted in E. von Schlebrügge, 'Zur Topographie der romantischen Seele', in J. Clair et al. (eds.), *Wunderblock*, Vienna, 1989, p. 119.

23   *Ibid.*

24   C. G. Carus, *Vorlesungen über Psychologie*, Darmstadt, 1958.

25   If Carus had given this lecture ten years later, he would most probably have replaced the rather forced analogy of a magnet which preserves images with a photographic metaphor.

26   Carus, *Vorlesungen*, p. 155.

27   *Ibid.*, p. 155. The aphorist G. C. Lichtenberg (1742–99) was considered one of the keenest minds of his age.

28   *Ibid.*, p. 163.

29   *Ibid.*, p. 158.

30   *Ibid.*, p. 159.

31   *Ibid.*, p. 160.

32   *Ibid.*, p. 160.

33   *Ibid.*, p. 161.

34   *Ibid.*, p. 162.

35   C. G. Carus, *Psyche, zur Entwicklungsgeschichte der Psychologie*, Pforzheim, 1846, p. 1.

36   Von Schlebrügge, 'Topographie', p. 115.

37   Heine, *Die Harzreise und andere Reisebilder*, Berlin, 1915, p. 92.

38   See also D. Draaisma, 'Een iconografie van de ziel', *Vrij Nederland*, Boekenbijlage, 23 September 1989, 6–7.

39   J. C. Lavater, *Physiognomik. Zur Beförderung der Menschenkenntnis und Menschenliebe*, Vienna, 1829, vol. I, p. 144.

40   C. G. Carus, *Symbolik des menschlichen Gestalt*, Dresden, 1852.

41   C. G. Carus, *Neuer Atlas der Cranioskopie*, Leipzig, 1864, table VII.

42   Carus, *Atlas*, table XI.

43   A selection of Gall's writings with a biographical introduction was edited by E. Lesky: *Franz Joseph Gall; 1758–1828, Naturforscher und Anthropologe*, Bern, 1979.

44   Gall published his most important papers jointly with his pupil and partner Johann Caspar Spurzheim: *Anatomie et physiologie du système nerveux en général, et du cerveaux en particulier*, Paris, 1810–19.

45   R. E. Fancher, *Pioneers of Psychology*, New York, 1979, p. 45.

46   Quoted in Lesky, *Gall*, p. 74.

47   J. E. Doornik, *Voorlezingen over F. J. Gall's herssen-schedelleer*, in *Felix Meritis en Doctrina et Amicitia, winter 1805–1806*, Amsterdam, 1806, p. 4.

48   M. Stuart, *Herinneringen uit de lessen van Frans Joseph Gall, Med. Doctor te Weenen, over de Hersenen, als onderscheiden en bepaalde werktuigen van de geest*, Amsterdam, 1806, p. 44.

49   Doornik, *Voorlezingen*, p. 3.

50   On Gall's visit to the Netherlands in 1806 and the reception of his theory there, see M. Conradi, 'Franz Joseph Gall in Nederland', *De Psycholoog*, 7 (1995), 320–3.

51   J. C. F. Leune, *De leer van Gall over de herssenen en de schedel*, Amsterdam, 1804, pp. 121–9.

52   *Ibid.*, p. 128.

53   *Ibid.*

54   W. Krauss, 'Franz Galls Schädellehre', in J. Clair et al. (eds.), *Wunderblock*, p. 203.

55   Cantor and Shapin have conducted an interesting debate on the reception of phrenology in academic scholarship and the status of phrenology as a counter-culture. G. N. Cantor, 'The Edinburgh phrenology debate: 1803–1828', *Annals of Science*, 119 (1975), 195–218; S. Shapin, 'Phrenological knowledge and the social structure of early nineteenth-century Edinburgh', *Annals of Science*, 32, (1975), 219–43.

56   P. Flourens, *Examen de la phrénologie*, Paris, 1824.

57   F. Schiller, *Paul Broca. Founder of French Anthropology, Explorer of the Brain*, Berkeley, 1979.

58   M. A. B. Brazier, *A History of Neurophysiology in the Nineteenth Century*, New York, 1988.

59   A. Fouillée, 'La survivance et la sélection des idées dans la mémoire', *Revues des deux mondes*, 69 (1885), 357–89.

60   W. B. Carpenter, *Mental Physiology*, London, 1874; H. Maudsley, *The Physiology of Mind*, London, 1868.

61   E. Hering, *Über das Gedächtnis als eine allgemeine Funktion der organisierten Materie*, Vienna, 1870.

62   See, for example, Maudsley, *Physiology*, 1876, p. 513.

63   W. James, *Principles of Psychology*, New York, 1890.

64   W. James, 'On the association of ideas', *Popular Science Monthly*, March 1880.

65   Fouillée, 'Survivance', 380.

66   G. T. Ladd, *Physiological Psychology*, London, 1887, 1891 edn, p. 424. This

'mental switchman' would in that case have a similar position to that of the 'master weaver' about whom Carus spoke.

67   F. Rabelais, *Pantagruel*, Paris, 1533, 1548 edn, ch. LVI, book IV.

68   C. Sorel, *Le Courrier véritable*, Paris, 1632.

69   D. Marty, *The Illustrated History of Phonographs*, New York, 1981, p. 13.

70   Cros wrote his letter on 3 December; his application was granted the same day.

71   Anon., 'The Talking Phonograph', *Scientific American*, 22 December 1877, 384–5.

72   *Ibid.*, 384.

73   *Revue Scientifique*, 30 September 1878, 358. Bouillaud himself wrote about the phonograph in the article 'Remarques sur le phonographe et le téléphone', *Comptes rendus des séances de l'Académie des Sciences*, 87 (July–December 1878), 473–7.

74   A. M. Mayer, 'Edison's Talking Machine', *Nature* (11 April 1878), 469–71.

75   Anon., 'Phonograph', 385.

76   *Ibid.*

77   J. Appleby, *Phonetical Memory*, London, 1880.

78   J. Delboeuf, 'Le sommeil et les rêves: leurs rapports avec la théorie de la mémoire', *Revue philosophique*, 9 (1880), 129–69; 413–37 (160).

79   J.-M. Guyau, 'La mémoire et le phonographe', *Revue philosophique*, 9 (1880), 319–22. This article was included as chapter 4 in Guyau's posthumously published book *La Genèse de l'idée de temps*, Paris, 1890. A new edition and an English translation were published by J. A. Michon, V. Pouthas and J. L. Jackson (eds.), *Guyau and the Idea of Time*, Amsterdam, Oxford, New York, 1988.

80   Quoted from *Guyau and the Idea of Time*, pp. 118–19.

81   *Ibid.*, p. 322.

82   *Ibid.*

83   J. A. Michon, 'Guyau's idea of time: a cognitive view', Michon et al. (eds.), *Guyau*, p. 174.

84   J. A. Segner, *De raritate luminis*, 1–12, Göttingen, 1740.

85   H. Gundlach, 'Über das Gedächtnis und der Weg dorthin', in W. Traxel and H. Gundlach (eds.), *Ebbinghaus-Studien I*, Passau, 1986, pp. 23–40.

86   D. Shakow, 'Hermann Ebbinghaus', *American Journal of Psychology*, 42 (1930) 4, 505–18; contains a bibliography of Ebbinghaus.

87   H. Ebbinghaus, *Über die Hartmannsche Philosophie des Unbewussten*, Düsseldorf, 1873.

88   E. von Hartmann, *Philosophie des Unbewussten*, Berlin, 1869, 1870 edn.

89   Von Hartmann, *Philosophie*, p. 252.

90   *Ibid.*, p. 253.

91   Ebbinghaus, *Gedächtnis*, v.

92   These syllables are mostly called 'nonsense syllables'. This is due to an unfortunate translation of 'sinnlose Silbenreihe': it is not that the syllables were lacking meaning, but their sequences. Many of the syllables are perfectly normal German words.

93   S. Bem, *Het bewustzijn te lijf*, Amsterdam, Meppel, 1985, p. 263.

94   Ebbinghaus, *Gedächtnis*, pp. 110–22; the time required to learn eighty sylla-
      bles of Byron was only one-tenth of that required to learn eighty nonsense
      syllables.

95   H. Ebbinghaus, *Urmanuskript 'Über das Gedächtnis'*, Passau, 1983.

96   J. Jacobs, *Mind*, 10 (1885), 454–9 (458). The Spree flows through Berlin, where
      Ebbinghaus was living in 1885.

97   E. B. Titchener, *Textbook of Psychology*, New York, 1910, pp. 380–1.

98   G. E. Müller and A. Pilzecker, 'Experimentelle Beiträge zur Lehre vom
      Gedächtnis', *Zeitschrift für Psychologie*, Ergänzungsband, 1 (1900), 1–300.

99   A. Binet and V. Henri, 'La mémoire des phrases', *l'Année psychologique*, 1,
      (1894), 24–59.

100   H. Gundlach, 'Experimentelle Gedächtnisforschung', in J. Clair et al. (eds.),
      Wunderblock, pp. 351–5.

101   Ebbinghaus, *Gedächtnis*, p. 7.

102   *Ibid.*, pp. 128–9.

103   *Ibid.*, p. 71.

104   J. C. Marshall and D. M. Fryer, 'Speak memory! An introduction to some his-
      toric studies of remembering and forgetting', in M. M. Gruneberg and P. E.
      Morris (eds.), *Aspects of Memory*, London, 1978, pp. 1–25.

5   A mirror with a memory

Oh Mister Daguerre! Sure you're not aware
Of half the impressions you're making[1]

The human eye is a watery globe, held together by membranes, set in a bony, semi-circular socket. Conjunctiva, iris and cornea at the front of the lens, sclera, retina and choroid on the opposite side, stretched around three chambers full of liquid, each with transparent walls, together achieve an optic miracle: in a complicated process of refraction and reduction they introduce light in and give it a form which makes it processable by the brain. Once it has hit the retina, which in turn consists of ten microscopically fine layers of cells and is in fact an ultra-thin layer of brain tissue, photochemical processes transform the optical stimulus into a pattern of firing nerve cells and the 'picture' becomes a neuronal code. Seeing begins with optics and ends with electrical impulses. Darwin classified the eye among the 'organs with extreme perfection and complication'; and the possibility that the eye should have been created in a process of blind evolution, was almost beyond his imagination.[2]

From an early period the eye was surrounded with optical devices and aids. In the Middle Ages glasses were ground to make magnifying glasses and spectacles. Through the lenses in microscopes and telescopes the eye penetrated new spatial domains. Prisms refracted the daylight into all the colours of the rainbow. Through tinted glass one could see the world in any colour one chose. Flat mirrors doubled the visual image, convex and concave mirrors deformed it, reflective cylinders restored the fantastic forms of an anamorphosis to a recognisable shape. By about 1800 there was a range of possibilities for manipulating visual experience, for enlarging, reducing, lengthening or shortening, colouring or doubling perception at will.

Aids like the lens were and still remain unavailable for the other senses. Only with the ear can the stimulus be strengthened, in the case of what we taste, smell or feel we have to make do with the naked sense. There are no spectacles for smelling better, there is no mirror to double the taste, no coloured glass for changing what we feel, no prism that scatters everyday smells into a spectrum of perfumed scents. Touch, smell and taste are always naked.

The eye's primacy among the senses is reflected in the imagery for higher mental activities. In the Classical period the intellect was the natural light, the *lumen naturale*; when you have a luminous idea you see the light. In many languages 'vision' has the secondary meaning of understanding. We speak of the light of reason and a lucid intellect. The seer is a wise man, even if – an archetype in literature – he is blind. Introspection too, literally, 'looking inward', is a quasi-visual process, as is reflective thought. The eye is the only sense that has an inner pendant in the 'mind's eye'.

Ryle designated metaphors like these with the term 'para-optics': they reconstruct the image of consciousness as a ghostly theatre in which quasi-sensory images are projected.[3] Theories on visual memory have always partaken of this para-optics. Hypotheses on the relationship between the images which appear on the retina and the preservation of visual memories were inspired by optical processes known through physics, such as the phosphorescent substances of Hooke, or optical apparatuses. Writing about visual memory in 1747, Lamettrie compared the brain to a 'medullary screen upon which the objects painted in the eye are projected as by a magic lantern'.[4] A century later the invention of photography provided a revolutionary new technique for preserving images. From the mid-nineteenth century onwards, when developments in photochemistry and improvements in the construction of cameras produced sharp photographs, photographic metaphors of all kinds appeared in papers on the visual memory, gradually changing the human brain into a light-sensitive plate, the memory into an album full of silent snapshots, consciousness into a gallery, its walls covered with long rows of daguerreotypes and talbotypes, ambrotypes and kalotypes. Until the invention of cinematography, in 1895, photography was the dominant metaphor in the para-optics of the mind.

But let us begin at the beginning.

The camera obscura

The camera obscura in its simplified form is a darkened chamber with a hole in one of the walls. In bright light the rays entering through the opening will project an image of the outside world on the opposite wall. This projection is upside down, left and right are reversed. The enormous reduction of format and strength of light made camera obscuras suitable aids for astronomical observations (figure 26). The earliest drawing of a camera obscura can be found in the work of Gemma Frisius, who observed the solar eclipse of 24 January 1544 with this instrument. In about 1560 the camera obscura was made in a form which hardly changed until the eighteenth century: a lens and a diaphragm were placed in the aperture to gather the rays and to control the amount of light. These two refinements made it possible to reduce camera

Maculæ et Faculæ ex uariis obferuandj modis ftabiliuntur.

26.   Engraving of a camera obscura in use as an instrument for astronomical observation.

obscuras to a portable size. The smallest specimens, in which the image was projected onto ground glass via a mirror, were very similar to the first photographic cameras.

At the beginning of the seventeenth century there occurred the change in direction which the historian Maier has designated so aptly as 'the mechanisation of the world picture'.[5] In anatomical books mechanical techniques like pumps and pulleys were introduced as analogies for musculature, joints and organs. In this tradition the camera obscura developed into an analogy for the eye (figure 27). Kepler already knew that at the back of the eye, on the retina, there appears an inverted image of what the eye 'sees' at the front. In his *Dioptrique* Descartes developed the comparison between the camera obscura and the eye. The hole in the wall corresponded to the pupil, the glass lens to the vitreous humour and the white linen screen onto which the image was projected, to the retina. One could check this for oneself, wrote Descartes, by taking the eye of a recently deceased person or a large mammal like an ox and removing the back membranes. If one then holds the eye in a piece of paper, stands in a darkened room and allows light to fall only through the eye, one will finally – 'possibly not without admiration and pleasure' – see a beautiful perspective image on the retina. By squeezing the eye gently one can lengthen or shorten the image at will. In the drawing which Descartes included of this procedure the observer is depicted in a camera obscura (darkly shaded), absorbed in the image on the retina (figure 28).

Because of the optical pathways which cross each other in the eye, both left and right and top and bottom are reversed (figure 29), but this inversion was no problem for Descartes. In his theory of perception, light stimuli were patterns of movement and it was as movement that the 'image' was processed by the

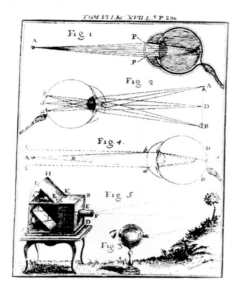

27.   Engraving of the camera obscura as an analogy for the optical processes in
      the human eye.

optic nerves. In the *Traité de l'homme* Descartes included a drawing of binocular
vision in which the standing arrow ABC projects an inverted image in both eyes
(figure 30). These images cause vibrations in the nerves leading to the pineal
gland, the seat of the soul. The nerves of the corresponding places in both eyes
each end in a single site in the pineal gland and are, moreover, linked crossways
with that gland, so that the images arrive both merged and the right way up.
In this way, the soul receives an integrated and upright projection of the arrow
ABC, reduced to abc. This miniaturisation of visual experience, with the retention of correct spatial orientation, was an ingenious neuro-psychological
answer to the problem of the inverted image in a camera obscura.[6]

In the century after Descartes, technology found a way of dealing with this
problem. With the aid of mirrors and prisms the image in the camera obscura
was turned upright and some camera obscuras even successfully projected an
image onto a flat table top (figure 31). In this way one could keep a watchful eye
on the outside world with a glass and prism. Situated at the bend in a river or
positioned in an outside wall on a market square this instrument reported
silently but faithfully on what was happening outside the darkened room.
Some camera obscuras were positioned in special domes and developed, with a
revolving 'eye' sticking outwards like a periscope, into a tourist attraction. The
camera obscura was – with the magic lantern – the optical marvel of the eighteenth century, an illusionistic wonder. Travel accounts and journals from that
time testify to the fact that the camera obscura had an enchanting effect when
first encountered. In 1747 John Cuff, a London dealer in optical instruments,

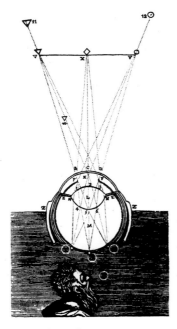

28. Engraving of Descartes's representation of the eye as a camera obscura.

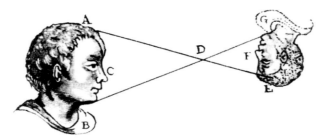

29. Engraving illustrating the principle that the inversion of the image and the reversal of left and right leave the geometrical proportions intact.

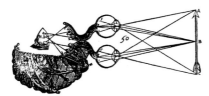

30. Engraving explaining the Cartesian theory of binocular vision. The optical pathways cross in the eye. Because the nerves also cross after the eye – and hence the image is inverted again – an upright projection abc of the arrow ABC appears on the pineal gland.

31.   An eighteenth-century engraving showing how the image of a camera
      obscura could be projected onto a flat surface with the aid of a mirror and
      a prism. Note that the lens is set into an outside wall.

prefaced an advertisement for his firm with an ode to the camera obscura
which opened: 'Say, rare Machine, who taught thee to design? / And mimic
Nature with such Skill divine?'[7]

As well as being used as an instrument for entertainment the camera
obscura served to demonstrate the laws of optics. Scientific societies often had
a camera obscura installed in the room where their instruments were kept. The
Batavian Society for Experimental Philosophy in Rotterdam, for instance, had
an impressive collection of high-tech devices, including a huge burning glass
with which metal could be melted and a telescope with which one could tell
the time on the Cathedral of Utrecht, but most visitors regarded the camera
obscura as the pinnacle of the collection. In order to demonstrate its operation
the amanuensis closed the blinds and placed a sheet of white paper some distance behind a round glass in the wall. A visitor wrote in 1839 that one saw the
bridge with all the ships and houses 'in their natural colour, drawn on that
white paper only by the rays of daylight'.[8]

Most camera obscuras had a practical use. Painters and draughtsmen used
camera obscuras to record the contours of landscapes and views of towns.

According to the Venetian patron Count Algarotti, the camera obscura was as indispensable to the artist for a pure presentation of nature, as a microscope was to the scientific researcher or a telescope to the astronomer.[9] Some camera obscuras were no more than simple collapsible boxes, but others had the shape of a comfortable tent in which the artist could trace the image on matt glass at his leisure. This process resulted in works with a 'photographic accuracy' and the typical perspective inherent in the use of lenses.

Most of all, the colourful, mobile miniatures in a camera obscura resembled film. It was precisely with regard to movement that the images in a camera obscura were more faithful than any kind of painting. The seventeenth-century author Leurechon wrote: 'Above all there is the pleasure of seeing the movement of birds, men or other animals and the quivering of plants waving in the wind; for although all that is reversed, nevertheless, this beautiful painting, beyond being foreshortened, represents ingeniously well that which no painter has ever been able to represent in his painting, to realize movement continued from place to place.'[10] But for all the movement, it lacked durability. The little films which, standing in the dark, one saw projected in that pool of light were fleeting and fragile. If one let in so much as a chink of light the image was erased; when dusk fell the image dissolved into the darkness. Nothing of the movement could be preserved; a still picture could only be recorded by laborious tracing. The camera obscura had no memory.

The obstacle with which optical science was confronted here was, in effect, a technical variant of the same problem with which researchers of human perception were confronted. Descartes had been able to follow the image that entered the eye up to its projection onto the retina; how this image was taken in further and, most importantly of all, how it was finally taken into the memory as a memory image, still remained a mystery. That the human mind gave durability to the changing images on the retina was an established fact, but it was not possible to discover what mechanisms were responsible for it.

That the camera obscura was not capable of preserving the delicate film was, however, scarcely experienced as a fault. It was only the invention of photography that made the camera obscura, retrospectively, a flawed apparatus. Before 1839 the transience of the image appeared to be an inevitable consequence of natural laws. In the whole of the literature of eighteenth-century science fiction there is only one author who fantasised over a process for saving images. In *Giphantie* the French writer Tiphaigne de la Roche gave a prophetic description of a miraculous substance with which images could be preserved. Cloths were soaked in a substance and then exposed to the light of the objects which were to be painted. The writer declaimed that,

> the first effect of the canvas is that of a mirrour; there are seen upon it all
> the bodies far and near whose image the light can transmit. But what the
> glass cannot do, the canvas, by means of the viscous matter, retains the

images. The mirrour shows the objects exactly; but keeps none; our canvases show them with the same exactness, and retain them all. This impression of the images is made the first instant they are received on the canvas, which is immediately carried away in some dark place; an hour after, the subtle matter dries, and you have a picture so much the more valuable, as it cannot be imitated by art nor damaged by time. We take, in their purest source, in the luminous bodies, the colours which painters extract from different materials, and which time never fails to alter.[11]

Giphantie appeared in 1760. It was not until eighty years later that this dream of a mirror preserving images was to be fulfilled.

Photography: the chemical memory

Photography is a product of a marriage between optics and chemistry. The camera obscura offered everything that could be achieved with purely optical means: colour, movement and image; recording the image required chemical processes with light-sensitive materials. As early as the seventeenth century, alchemists experimented with phosphorescent materials. The experiments and demonstrations which Robert Hooke described for the Royal Society were part of an intensive international research programme which focused on the production of substances which could retain light.

In 1727, in his attempt to make a 'luminous stone', the German doctor Schulze experimented with silver nitrate, a material which was in use as a disinfectant for treating wounds. Schulze made a mixture of chalk and silver nitrate but achieved the opposite of what he was hoping for: the mixture darkened when exposed to light and hence preserved precisely what was dark.[12] Like his compatriot Crafft and his spectacular experiments with phosphorous, Schulze had an amazing experiment up his sleeve; he filled a transparent bottle with a mixture of chalk and saltpetre acid containing silver, cut a letter out, stuck that to the bottle and let everything stand for a while in the light. The mixture slowly darkened, but behind the letter it remained light. In this way an illuminated letter would appear in the liquid, only to disappear if the bottle were to be shaken again. The experiment could of course also be reversed so that a dark form appeared in the chalky white mixture. With this Schulze demonstrated the first negative–positive process.[13]

Experiments with silver nitrate were also conducted in England. In 1802 Thomas Wedgwood (son of the pottery manufacturer) and Humphrey Davy, a professor of chemistry, described how one could copy glass drawings onto paper moistened with silver nitrate.[14] The lines and contours left an impression of usable resolution on the paper. These 'shadowgraphs' could, moreover, be kept, at least providing the image was not exposed to light. In the dark or seen by candlelight the image remained intact, but in full daylight the prepared paper turned out to have a short memory; after just a few minutes the image dissolved in the darkening paper. The process, in other words, did make an exposure, but was unable to fix it. This latter, decisive, step in the invention of photography was to be taken in France.

In their account of 1802 Wedgwood and Davy reported that they had tried to record the images of a camera obscura but that they had been unable to do so because of the low strength of light. The images were too weak to leave even the slightest trace on the paper. In France Joseph Niépce, of noble extraction but greatly impoverished by the Revolution, experimented with a substance which was not only more light-sensitive and hence absorbed an impression more quickly, but was also easier to fix. This substance, 'bitumen of Judea', came from the Dead Sea and had the property of hardening in sunlight. Niépce coated a glass plate with a very thin layer of bitumen, laid a transparent drawing on top of it and exposed the plate to light. The unilluminated parts remained soft and could be washed out with a mixture of turpentine and lavender oil. What remained was a copy of the drawing on glass, in hard and preservable bitumen. Considering that the image had been drawn by the sun Niépce called his process 'héliographie'.

From 1822 onwards Niépce, who felt encouraged by the excellent results with his 'héliographie', attempted to record the images of a camera obscura using the same process. The trials were unsuccessful. The low intensity of light and the blurred lens forced Niépce to use extremely long exposure times. He did not succeed in getting enough contrast into his exposures. Nevertheless one of those failed trials produced a record which entered history as 'the first photograph': in his workroom on the family estate of Le Gras in Saint-Loup-de-Varennes Niépce put his camera in the window alcove and so recorded the view of the courtyard (figure 32).

Niépce may have given the camera obscura a rudimentary memory, but there was still no question of a usable and convincing photographic process. This was perfected by Louis Daguerre. Daguerre was a scenery painter with a predilection for illusionistic effects.[15] He had set up a lightshow theatre in Paris, the Diorama, in which hung screens measuring fourteen by twenty-two metres and which were painted on two sides. These huge *trompe-l'œils* could be made visible alternately by the manipulation of the lighting so that a sunny alpine landscape changed before the eyes of the astonished public into an enchanting nocturnal scene. Daguerre made use of camera obscuras in his work and heard from his optician about Niépce's trials. The two men entered into a legally sealed agreement and exchanged their data. After Niépce's death in 1833 Daguerre continued the research and began a period of feverish experiment.

In the period between 1833 and 1837 Daguerre was confronted with the same problem that had tormented Wedgwood and Davy in 1802: he succeeded in making exposures, but did not have the means of fixing the image. Daguerre's exposures, on silvered copper plates, dissolved when exposed to light into the

32. This exposure of Joseph Niépce's dates from 1826 or 1827 and is regarded as the 'first photograph'. The exposure time was a full eight hours. In this way an 'impossible' image was created: the opposite walls have *both* caught the sunlight. The afternoon sun erased the morning shadows.

faded colour of silver iodide. The improvements that Daguerre made to Niépce's process were connected with the three basic processes of photography: the sensitising of the plate, developing and fixing. For the first process Daguerre used iodine vapour which was deposited on the plate. Later he discovered, by chance, that mercury vapour could make the exposure visible again – an under-exposed plate had been put into a cupboard with an open dish of mercury and had developed all on its own. And in 1837, finally, he discovered that a solution of kitchen salt fixed the exposure. With this the process was so perfected that Daguerre could start profiting from his invention, under the name 'daguerreo-type'.[16]

In the final months of 1838 the rumour of Daguerre's process spread through Paris. On 6 January 1839 the first newspaper article about the new discovery appeared in the *Gazette de France*. The author was a certain Gaucheraud. His report of what he was shown on a visit to Daguerre is bathed in a glow of enthu-siasm and astonishment:

M. Daguerre shows you the piece of bare copper, he puts it in his apparatus before your eyes, and at the end of three minutes – if the summer sun is shining, a few more if autumn or winter weakens the strength of the sun's rays – he takes out the metal and shows it to you covered with an enchanting drawing of the object towards which the apparatus was pointed. It is only a matter of a short washing operation, I believe, and there is a view which has been conquered in so few minutes, everlastingly fixed, so that the strongest sunlight can do nothing to destroy it.[17]

In terms derived from things familiar to the reader he explained that Daguerre had found a method of preserving the images which paint themselves in a camera obscura, in a permanent impression which could, like a painting or engraving, be taken away from the objects. Unlike the camera obscura, movement could unfortunately not be reproduced (figure 33). In a shot of a boulevard, Gaucheraud told his readers, a waiting coach horse had moved its head, with the result that the animal appeared headless on the copper plate. The still life, the city view, this was the true glory of Daguerre's invention, and it would not be long before travellers could take their shots of monuments, cities and landscapes from all over the world back to France with them. And then it would become apparent, Gaucheraud predicted to his readers, 'how far from the truth of the Daguerreotype are your pencils and brushes'.[18]

Through the agency of the astronomer Arago, a member of the Chamber of Deputies, the French government offered Daguerre an annual pension in exchange for the publication of his process. This took place on 19 August 1839 during a celebratory session of the Académie des Sciences. After the unveiling of the process there were public demonstrations. Daguerre was able to ensure supplementary income by selling complete kits for making daguerreotypes – camera, chemicals, plates, developing box – and marketing manuals. In 1840 the first professional daguerreotypists set up their studios in major cities. Within a few years daguerreotypists were active on all continents.

Illustrative of this unprecedented rapid progress is the advent of daguerreotypes to the New World. Its crossing of the Atlantic has been traced almost from day to day by the historian of photography Taft.[19] The introduction of daguerreotypes into America owed much to the efforts of a man whose name is now mainly associated with telegraphy, Samuel F. B. Morse.

Morse was a portrait painter and also a professor in the arts of design at the University of New York. In the spring of 1839 he was staying in Paris in order to request a French patent for his electromagnetic telegraph. He heard about the new photographic processes and made Daguerre an offer of demonstrating his own telegraph in exchange for becoming acquainted with the daguerreotype. Daguerre accepted the offer, and invited Morse into his Diorama. Morse was astonished by the quality of Daguerre's pictures. In his own efforts to preserve the image of the camera obscura he had only obtained varying shades of

33. Daguerreotype of the Paris boulevard du Temple (1838). Like Niépce's expo-
     sure with the two walls both in the sun, this daguerreotype contains an
     almost surreal detail. Daguerre pointed his camera at a busy Paris boulevard
     along which carriages were driving up and down and people were strolling.
     But in the exposure the boulevard is eerily empty: everything in motion was
     moving too quickly to leave any traces on the light-sentive copper plate. Only
     the man who paused for a few minutes to have his shoes shined was cap-
     tured (see opposite). Those who moved remained unseen.
         Arguments arose later about the question of whether photographs could
     'lie'. The first works of Niépce and Daguerre show that such a question is
     rather naive: photographs have 'lied' from the very beginning.

shadow, and now Daguerre presented him with silvery plates of an almost
unimaginable sharpness. In a letter of March 1839 to the New York *Observer*,
Morse described one of the plates, probably the view of the boulevard du Temple
(figure 33):

> You cannot imagine how exquisite is the fine detail portrayed. No painting
> or engraving could ever hope to touch it. For example, when looking over a
> street one might notice a distant advertisement hoarding and be aware of
> the existence of lines or letters, without being able to read these tiny signs
> with the naked eye. With the help of a handlens, pointed at this detail, each
> letter became perfectly and clearly visible, and it was the same thing for the
> tiny cracks on the walls of buildings or the pavements of the streets.[20]

33 (*cont.*)

Daguerre had also printed a microscopic shot of a spider in an enlarged form, which revealed a 'minuteness of organisation' the existence of which no-one had suspected. Morse predicted that the scientific researcher would have to explore a totally new kingdom, as far removed from the microscope as the microscope was from the naked eye.

Daguerre kept the details of his process secret from Morse. Morse returned to New York and – like the rest of the world – had to wait for the official announcement on 19 August. Within a few days, English newspapers published the technical description of the daguerreotype and in one of the first trans-Atlantic crossings under steam, on board the packet steamer *British Queen*, the news travelled from Portsmouth to New York. Immediately after its arrival on 20 September 1839 the description was published by the papers. Morse had his instrument-maker Prosch (who had also assisted him in building his telegraph) build a Daguerre camera. At the end of September he presented the first success-ful daguerreotypes.

Morse's experiments were eagerly followed by one of his colleagues, the pro-fessor of chemistry and physiology, John William Draper. Draper was a pioneer in research into the properties of light, and long before Daguerre's discovery had conducted experiments with the effect of light on iodine. In 1840 he himself discovered a phenomenon which was later to be called after an inde-pendent co-discoverer 'Moser images'. If one leaves an object on cold, polished metal, breathes on it, allows the liquid to evaporate and removes the object, nothing more can be seen on the metal. But if one breathes on the metal again, then the contours of the object immediately reappear, as though it were still lying there. Thanks to his background as a chemist, Draper was able to improve on Daguerre's process. Even with simple equipment – a spectacle glass in the short end of a cigar box – he achieved encouraging results. In the summer of 1840 he made a portrait which is considered to be the oldest preserved daguerreotype portrait.[21]

Morse and Draper decided to become partners and in 1840 moved into a glass studio which they had had built on the roof of their university. In the spring of 1840 Draper made one of the first daguerreotypes of the moon and developed a process of enlarging shots so that travelling cameras could be given a more convenient format. Morse concentrated more on the commercial aspects of daguerreotypes. As yet there were no revenues from his telegraph and from 1840 onwards he obtained an income by portrait photography and lessons to aspiring daguerreotypists. Morse spent hundreds of mid-nineteenth-century dollars every year on sensitised plates which he ordered from Paris. Mainly thanks to Morse and Draper, developments in America were at least as rapid as in the Old World. The first reviews of daguerreotype exhibitions appeared within a year of the arrival of the *British Queen*. Ten years later, in 1850, there were some two thousand professional daguerreotypists active in America.[22] For the price of a few dollars, anyone could have their portrait taken.

It is striking how the invention of photography was in the air. In the same 1830s when Daguerre was feverishly experimenting, the Englishman William Fox Talbot succeeded in making contact pictures of plants in his garden. These 'shadowgraphs' or 'shadows' were sharply focused but not stable. Like Daguerre, Talbot had difficulty in fixing. The 'shadows' which he sent to his sister-in-law faded before her eyes as soon as she opened the envelope. Talbot presented his 'talbotype' in 1839 within the same forum of the Royal Society which had received Hooke's paper on phosphorous and memory in the seventeenth century.[23]

Daguerreotypes were unusually sharp and seemed to glow in an ethereal, silvery light, but they also had disadvantages. They reflected light in an annoying way and because of the absence of a negative, the pictures could not be reproduced. This latter objection did not apply to the 'kalotype', developed in 1841. This process produced a negative from which in turn an exposure could be made thus giving a positive.[24]

After the publications of Daguerre and Talbot, there followed an explosion of new discoveries. Lenses and diaphragms were improved, the sensitising of light-sensitive substances underwent refinements, the methods of exposure for interior shots improved dramatically, processes were invented for enlarging photographs, and for printing from etched daguerreotype plates. In 1847 Claude Niépce de Saint-Victor, a distant cousin of Joseph Niépce, succeeded in

34.   The principle of ambrotypes, illustrated with the aid of John William Draper's portrait. On the left, the negative against a white background, on the right, the same negative on black velvet.

attaching the negative to glass instead of paper. After the invention of photography, Wheatstone was able to use photographs for his 'stereoscope', two photographs taken from a slightly different angle; projected alongside each other they gave the illusion of depth.[25] Within twenty years a stream of patents had been issued on the basic procedures of Daguerre and Talbot.

In 1851, the year of Daguerre's death, the English sculptor Frederick Archer introduced a process which marked the end of daguerreotypes. Archer used collodium, obtained by the processing of raw cotton and named after the Greek word for sticking. Collodion plates were extremely light-sensitive and produced considerably sharper photographs than the processes of Daguerre or Talbot. By giving a slightly exposed collodion negative a background of black velvet one could present the negative as a positive. These 'ambrotypes' were cheap alternatives to daguerreotypes and ousted the latter from the market. Portrait photography became known henceforth as simply 'ambrotypie' (figure 34). The introduction of collodion concluded the hectic early years of photography.

Photography entered society via the circuits of painting. Many photographers of the first generation had a background in painting, like Daguerre himself; Talbot and Morse were amateur painters, and before the invention of photography they had worked with camera obscuras. Photographers felt more like artists than craftsmen. They adopted the vocabulary and customs of painters. Photographers worked in studios with north-facing windows, made their customers pose, pursued classical genres like the still life, the nude or the historical tableau and exhibited in salons.[26] So great was the similarity between photography and painting that, at least in the eyes of the public, the photographers pointed out in their advertisements that posing for a group portrait took no longer than an individual portrait.[27] Caricaturists like Daumier were fond of portraying the photographer as an *artiste manqué*.

At the same time the inventors and the first photographers emphasised that their processes differed essentially both from painting and from the images in a camera obscura. What made photography such an astonishing invention was the combination of three qualities: the unequalled precision of the depiction, the automatic nature of the process and the durability of what previously had been ephemeral.

As early as the newspaper report of Gaucheraud (6 January 1839), the minute exactness of the representation was mentioned. Just like Morse a few months later, Gaucheraud was given a magnifying glass by Daguerre to observe that the details of the photograph were beyond the scope of the naked eye. The same quality also astonished Arago, who praised the 'mathematical' precision of the pictures at the ceremonial announcement. This precision was more than a neutral noting of what one later began to call the 'resolution' of photos. Precision referred to the true-to-life character of the depiction. Photographs had a measure of realism which was no longer taken as a relative concept, as it was in other genres in the visual arts, but as something absolute. An engraving or etching could be more or less true to life, a photograph was quite simply a depiction of reality itself, a visualisation of the truth. Gaucheraud's remark that photographs of travellers would eventually prove 'how far your pencils and paintbrushes are from the truth of daguerreotypes' summarises this turn of events succinctly.

Interpreting photography as the embodiment of the truth was not only concerned with sharpness and precision. Both Daguerre and Talbot argued in their first publications that their process enabled nature to reproduce *itself*. It made the intervention of the artist superfluous. Talbot defined his invention in the subtitle of his report as 'the process by which natural objects may be made to delineate themselves without the aid of the artist's pencil'.[28] Photography had an automatic character which was lacking in traditional visual arts. In a painting there was not a single detail that had not first been in the eye and mind of the painter; a photogaph gave a direct representation. It was more of a record than a depiction.

Where later the machine-like character of photography was cited as an argument for the inferiority of photography as a visual art, in the middle of the nineteenth century the semi-automatic recording of the outside world was seen as a decisive achievement of the new technology. In the report on his experiments for the Royal Society, Talbot describes how he had stretched photographic paper against the back wall of a camera obscura and hence obtained beautiful miniatures, as if painted by some Lilliputian artist.[29] In the summer of 1835 he had made a whole series of photographs of his country house. This house, Talbot added, 'I believe to be the first that was ever yet known *to have drawn its own picture*'(author's italics).[30]

But even more amazing than the unprecedented sharpness and the semi-

automatic character, was the third quality: the ability of photography to bring
the fleeting moment to a halt and record it. In the first descriptions of contemporaries the astonishment was expressed in terms such as 'wizardry' and 'black
magic'. The photographer appeared like a magician able to preserve what had
always been transient by using occult processes in a dark room. The fact that
Daguerre used mercury vapour in the process – mercury, the element of rapid
flight – seemed to increase the mystery even further.

The astonishment of the recording of the play of light and shadow was
expressed poetically by Talbot in his account of 'the art of fixing a shadow'.
Carried away by the awesome achievements of technology, he wrote:

> The most transitory of things, a shadow, the proverbial emblem of all that
> is fleeting and momentary, may be fettered by the spells of 'our natural
> magic', and may be fixed for ever in a position which it seemed only destined
> for a single instant to occupy . . . Such is the fact, that we may receive on
> paper the fleeting shadow, arrest it there and in the space of a single minute
> fix it there so firmly as to be no more capable of change, even if thrown back
> into the sunbeam from which it derived its origin.[31]

Even a century and a half later one can empathise with Talbot's astonishment:
shifting across sundials – then so much more common than today – shadows
were markers for elapses of time, for what precisely did not allow itself to be
held still.

Almost two decades after the introduction of photography, the American
Oliver Wendell Holmes, a doctor and amateur photographer, recalled the astonishment at the preservation of visual images. Daguerreotypes, he wrote,
managed to capture the image in a mirror, an invention more amazing than
chloroform anaesthesia or direct communication over hundreds of miles via
the telegraph. Had not the mirror image always been a metaphor for illusion,
for change? Photography captured what was transient, gave permanence to
what was fleeting; photography was the invention of a 'mirror with a
memory'.[32]

The memory as a photographic plate

In the autumn of 1839, Nicolaas Beets's *Camera Obscura* appeared – a classic
collection of Dutch prose sketches of everyday life. The writer prefaced the text
with a motto, which came from an 'anonymous' source, in which the camera
obscura was presented as a metaphor of the soul:

> The shadows and phantoms of Reflection, Memory and Imagination fall into
> the soul as into a Camera Obscura, and some so striking and delightful that
> one feels inclined to copy them, and by retouching them somewhat, colour-
> ing them in and grouping them, to make small paintings out of them . . .[33]

The motto continued with the warning that one must not expect true-to-life
portraits from these sketches, 'for not only is a nose of Memory imposed a
hundred times on a face of Imagination, but the expression of the face is

so unspecific, that the same features sometimes resemble fifty different people'.

The metaphor playfully articulates a caveat of what in our time is usually given as the common phrase that 'any similarity with actual persons, etc . . .', but it also had a wider importance. The camera obscura is being associated here with the changeability and manipulability of images in the memory. Whatever falls onto the screen of our soul through the opening of the senses, is out of focus, vague, they are outlines and contours which allow themselves to be recoloured and ordered by memory.

It is a strange coincidence that this motto should have appeared in the autumn when photography was introduced. From 1839 onwards it was no longer the camera obscura but the photographic camera which became the most advanced optical instrument and through this development, a new analogy for the processing of visual experience became available. The camera obscura was an optical apparatus which offered a physical model for the visual processes in the eye. As a metaphor for memory the camera obscura could illustrate change and variation (as in the work of Beets), but not the permanent recording of images. The chemical processes of photography on the other hand were suited *par excellence* as an analogy of what happened with visual stimuli *after* projection on the retina, their processing by the brain and absorption into memory. In psychological theory, Wendell Holmes's metaphor of photography as a 'mirror with a memory' was resolutely turned around a hundred and eighty degrees. After 1839 the human memory became a photographic plate, prepared for the recording and reproduction of visual experience.

It is natural to assume that one can find photographic metaphors mainly in the work of researchers who had first-hand familiarity with photographic processes. That assumption is correct. Francis Galton's theory of memory (to be discussed later) is a good example, but the previously mentioned Draper, a pioneer of American photography, also used photographic metaphors in his publications on memory. Besides being a chemist, Draper was a prominent physiologist. In 1856 he published a study of human physiology which quickly gained textbook status.[34]

Draper wrote that the human nervous system has the ability to retain 'relics or traces of impressions'.[35] Nerve cells which gather and integrate the stimuli from a large number of other neurones, the so-called ganglion cells, can store and compare these 'impressions'. This delayed process introduces the beginnings of a memory. Nothing is ever erased from this memory: every stimulus leaves a trace, however faint the impression. Photography was a striking metaphor for this fundamental indelibility: 'I believe that a shadow never falls upon a wall without leaving thereupon its permanent trace – a trace which might be made visible by resorting to proper processes. All kinds of photographic drawing are in their degree examples of the kind.'[36] Draper saw 'Moser images' as a convincing analogy for memory traces and concluded that in ganglion cells something similar happens: 'But if on such inorganic surfaces impressions may in this way be preserved, how much more likely it is that the same thing occurs in the purposely constituted ganglion!'[37]

These memory traces are located in our brains. They bear no similarity to the form of what is observed; in other words, they are stored in the form of a code. Draper also had a technical metaphor to hand for this code. Referring to the work of his fellow-professor and studio sharer Morse, Draper wrote that the external form of what was observed and the neuronal trace are related like 'the letters of a message delivered in a telegraphic office and the signals which the telegraph gives to the distant station'.[38]

In later work Draper gave a specification of the analogy between the brain and photography. The fact that all sensory impressions leave a permanent trace corresponds to

> the duration, the emergence, the extinction, on photographic preparations. Thus I have seen landscapes and architectural views taken in Mexico, developed, as artists say, months subsequently in New York – the images coming out, after the long voyage, in all their proper forms and all their proper contrast of light and shade. The photograph had forgotten nothing.[39]

The fact that the photograph 'had forgotten nothing' is typical of the gist of many photographic metaphors. As analogies for visual representations photographs particularly stress the *immutability* of what is stored as a memory: they suggest a memory that forgets nothing, that contains a perfect, permanent record of our visual experience. Accordingly Draper saw the mind as a 'silent gallery', with 'silhouettes of whatever we have done' on the walls. During the day we notice nothing of this colossal picture archive. Our attention is taken up with what presents itself to our senses. But when we are asleep or in delirium of a fever, when there is intense fear and undoubtedly also 'during the solemn moments of dying', these images regain their vitality, our mind turns inward and 'looks over the ambrotypes she has collected – ambrotypes, for they are truly unfading impressions – and, combining them together, as they chance to occur, constructs from them the panorama of a dream'.[40] The metaphor is elegant and conclusive: ambrotypes, you will remember, only revealed their image against the background of black velvet.[41]

Authors from various language areas have, independently of each other, used photographic metaphors to support the theory of physiological retention. Nervous elements, wrote the French neurologist Luys, attached to the Paris Salpêtrière, have the ability to retain a condition of vibration after the sensory stimuli which caused this condition have disappeared. Luys spoke of 'organic phosphorescence'. Thanks to modern physics it was known that the vibrations of the ether in the form of light waves might be retained in phosphorescent materials. He referred to the research on which his fellow-townsman Niépce de Saint-Victor had reported to the Académie des Sciences in 1857, in which it had been shown that light vibrations can be stored on paper as 'vibrations silencieuses' and kept there until certain chemical processes reveal the original representation again. A photographic plate which is exposed to sunlight contains a 'latent image' of that sun and after developing, 'a *memory* of the absent sun' (author's italics).[42] For that matter, the daily practice of photographic reproduction with collodium was in Luys's view sufficient proof that some inorganic materials had the ability to preserve traces of light vibrations. Well, one finds this same quality in the organic matter of a nervous system: here too sensory impressions are stored in the form of vibrations and later reproduced.

The German doctor Kussmaul also used photographic metaphors in expounding his theory. The traces left by sensory impressions, he wrote, can be compared with 'the invisible images, which the sun makes on a prepared silver surface'.[43] The Belgian psycho-physiologist Delbœuf compared the brain to a photographic plate and saw in memory processes the organic parallels of technical processes such as 'sensitising' and 'fixing'.[44] The English doctor Carpenter believed that photography shows how it is possible that memories sometimes seem to have disappeared for good, but under certain circumstances nevertheless reappear: 'Just as the invisible impression left upon the sensitive paper of the Photographer, is developed into a picture by the application of particular chemical re-agents.'[45] The same metaphor was used by the Yale professor Ladd, who like Luys pointed to the development processes of Niépce de Saint-Victor and the use of collodium plates.[46]

Another process that was linked with the operation of the human brain was colour photography. In 1861 the physicist James Clerk Maxwell presented a process for projecting a coloured image from three monochromatic images to the Royal Institution in London.[47] Maxwell had wound coloured ribbons round a bow and photographed this three times against a background of black velvet, through a red, green and blue filter respectively. The negatives and positives were printed on glass and subsequently projected over each other with three magic lanterns, each through its own filter. The three positives combined, reproduced the bow in its original colours. Following the colour theory of Thomas Young, published around 1800, that there are three kinds of optic nerve cells, sensitive to the three primary colours, Maxwell assumed that his three photographs corresponded to the parts of the coloured ribbon 'as they would be seen by each of Young's three sets of nerves separately'.[48] The human brain, he reasoned, separates the colour spectrum into three parts and joins them together again, a hypothesis which respects the principle of economy, because now each nuance of colour no longer required a separate type of nerve cell. The coloured magic-lantern projections of Maxwell offered a neat physical analogy for a neurological hypothesis which could not be tested directly.

But there were also deep differences of opinion on the scope of technical metaphors, even within the tradition of 'mental physiology'. In 1880 the doctor Théodule Ribot, the first director of the Psychological Laboratory at the Collège de France, argued against physical analogies for memory. Ribot wrote that in common usage 'the word *memory* has a triple meaning: the conservation of certain conditions, their reproduction, and their localisation in the past'. Taking the first two away eliminates the memory; if the third is taken away, 'memory ceases to exist in an objective, but not in a subjective, sense'.[49] Photographic metaphors have the disadvantage that they explain preservation but not reproduction:

> Analogies to memory have been sought in the order of inorganic phenomena, particularly in the property possessed by light of being stored up in a sheet of paper in a state of imperceptible vibration for a greater or lesser time, ready to appear upon the application of a proper developing medium . . . In our opinion, these and similar facts have too vague an analogy with memory to be of value as practical illustrations. Conservation, the first condition of recollection, is found, but that alone; for in these instances reproduction is so passive, so dependent upon the intervention of a foreign agent, that there is no resemblance to the natural reproduction of the memory. Hence, in studying our subject, it must never be forgotten that we have to do with vital laws, not with physical laws, and that the bases of memory must be looked for in the properties of organic matter, and nowhere else.[50]

Criticism was also made of photographic metaphors from 'outside' mental physiology. The German author Huber raised the matter in a monograph on memory, taking the metaphors of Draper and Kussmaul as a convenient nail on which to hang his objections to the physiological theory of retention.[51] According to Huber, matter is capable of preserving impressions. But a characteristic of the memory is precisely the reproduction of those impressions. This objection reminds one of that of Ribot, but Huber has something else in mind. The problem with photographic metaphors is that they presuppose a *consciousness*. The material residues of earlier psychic processes can only be reproduced in our consciousness 'if this consciousness is present as the mirror in which those traces are reflected'.[52] The reason is simple: 'The impressions cannot see themselves.' And even if physiology were capable of explaining how it is possible that impressions can be reproduced in consciousness, then one would still have to clarify how this representation is interpreted as *belonging to the past*. Photographic metaphors cannot do justice to the distinction between imaginings pure and simple and remembered imaginings. That immediately indicates a danger of metaphors: they may obscure the real problems. A metaphor like that of Kussmaul, believes Huber, not only fails to contribute anything to the explanation of memory, but indeed misrepresents it.[53] Where Huber himself had talked two pages before of the consciousness-as-a-mirror he impresses upon his readers that they must not confuse 'comparisons' with 'real insights'.

Draper, Ladd, Kussmaul and other authors in the tradition of 'mental physiology' took their metaphors for retention from advanced scientific procedures. Writing for fellow-specialists they could be sure of the persuasiveness of the point-by-point comparison between photographic manipulation of light and hypothetical neuronal processes. The sensitising of the receiving medium, the latent character of the trace, the conversion of an optic image into a neuronal code, reproduction as a process of development that could take place directly or after a long period, all these components of the analogy could be fitted into the physiological theory of retention and hence provided a coherent, graphic representation of processes which mostly took place unseen. At the same time, photography was a technique with impressive public effects. In books aimed at a larger readership such as Draper's *History of the Conflict between Religion and Science*, photographic metaphors facilitated the popularisation of new theories on visual memory. With their metaphors the 'mental physiologists' were addressing at once a scientific and a wider audience.

Anyone who took a few steps backwards to compare the photographic metaphors with the references to phosphorescence, which Hooke had included in his treatise on memory, would note the similarities. In both instances the analogies are derived from techniques which were advanced for their time. Manipulations with light by phosphorescent materials were spectacular and enchanting; in the mid-nineteenth century, photography was also a magical phenomenon. However different in nature and background, the public appeal of phosphorescence and photography was identical. A second similarity is their use as of a proof of existence. Hooke pointed to phosphorescence in order to show that matter is capable of retaining light impressions and therefore lent plausibility to the fact that there is a purely material explanation for the way in which the human brain stores and reproduces visual memories. References to photography had an identical function. The storing and reproduction of visual representations on a photographic plate provided the proof that optical stimuli leave unrecognisable latent traces in a suitable medium. If an impression can be preserved on inorganic surfaces, Draper argued, then it could certainly be so in ganglion cells which were especially suited for the purpose. This reasoning is a repetition of Hooke's observation on the relationship between artificial phosphorescence and the 'Chymistry of Nature' in the brain.

Besides these similarities there are also obvious differences. Whereas phosphorescent substances could only serve to show that matter has the capacity for retaining light impressions, in the nineteenth century one is able, thanks to optical and chemical theories, to show how light stimuli can be stored as well as reproduced. In the seventeenth century, phosphorescence was almost as mysterious as the visual memory itself. In the nineteenth century, photography is a well-understood technique. Moreover, photography is technically much more refined: a phosphorescent substance stores only undifferentiated light, a photographic plate preserves the distribution of light, colour, focus and depth.

In the third quarter of the nineteenth century more was known about the neurological substratum of the memory than in Hooke's day. Physiologists were familiar with the electrical nature of neural transmission and had an inkling of the processes of facilitation. Since the nerve elements of memory were assumed to be in a condition of vibration (Luys's hypothesis) the gap between the analogy, the vibrations on a photographic plate, and the actual neurological processes, narrowed. Indeed for Luys it was a question of identical processes in a different medium. Thanks to an increasing technical sophistication the proofs of existence became ever more precise and persuasive.

There are passages from the work of Ribot and Huber which illustrate that this increased precision had a downside as well. The more explicit and exact the presumed similarities between the terms of the comparison are, the clearer the *differences* become. If the hypothesis is that sensory stimuli cause physical changes in the brain like light stimuli do on a photographic plate, then this raises the question about what neuronal process corresponds with the development phase in photography. It is precisely the graphic representation of photography that makes it possible to indicate the gaps in the theory. The same applies to the philosophical objections to physiological theories of memory. By adopting the metaphor, Huber is able to give a graphic impression of the problem of the homunculus: impressions cannot see themselves, photographs cannot view themselves. Traces require a consciousness that interprets them.

The pictorial statistics of memory

Not all photographic metaphors derived from the domain of 'mental physiology'; nor were they always connected with physiological retention. Photography also provided metaphors for specific memory processes, such as the ability to form general impressions from a series of specific visual impressions.

In 1877 the English gentleman–scientist Francis Galton was approached by the Inspector of Prisons with the request to set up an inquiry into the possible connections between certain types of crime and facial characteristics.[54] In criminological physiology it had already been supposed that such a connection must exist. Galton was given the use of a large number of delinquents' photos, together with information regarding what they had been convicted for. He distinguished three groups of offences: (1) murder and manslaughter, (2) fraud and forgery and (3) sexual crimes. Next he made provisional selections of the portraits in the hope of achieving 'natural classes of faces'. This method turned out to be inadequate for a good quantitative analysis. Searching for a suitable procedure for calculating averages in relationships, Galton remembered an effect that occurs when two magic lanterns are used for making one image merge into another. The common element in both images becomes clearly visible as the pictures merge, and what belongs to only one of the images becomes blurred. Galton made use of this effect in a photographic variant. He photographed a series of portraits on the *same* photographic plate and divided the normal exposure time into as many parts as there were portraits. In this way the photographs represented a 'pictorial average'. The common features of the

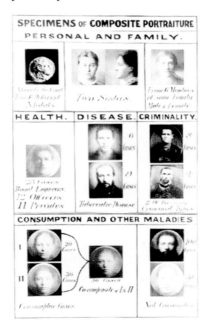

35.   Examples of 'compound photography'. Frontispiece to Galton's *Inquiries into Human Faculty and its Development* (London, 1883).

representations were stored, what was exceptional remained, literally, under-exposed and disappeared. If, for example, only one of the persons photographed had a moustache, then in the composite portrait it was scarcely visible; if they all had a moustache then an 'average' moustache appeared in the portrait. Besides the average the compound photograph gave a second statistical measure: 'variability'. The sharpness of the outlines, observed Galton, depended on the degree to which the components differed from the average: the more the faces resembled each other the sharper the compound portrait. Galton himself talked of 'pictorial statistics'.

The method of the compound photography was published in 1879 and caused a flurry of applications.[55] Scores of products of this impressive technique appeared not only in illustrated magazines but also in scientific journals: composite portraits of TB sufferers, men and women, the same person over the years, members of one family, twenty doctors of philosophy, etc. Galton selected a series of examples as the frontispiece to one of his books.[56] (See figure 35.)

The method did not work in the case of the mentally ill; according to Galton their features were too irregular for a composite portrait. One of the more spectacular uses was the production of composite portraits of historical figures such as Alexander the Great and Cleopatra. Five different portraits of the latter on coins and medallions were used to make a compound portrait. Her reputation

36.   Francis Galton's composite portraits of criminals.

for unequalled beauty was not confirmed. Galton wrote that to the ordinary English taste, probably his own, her features were 'simply hideous'.

Galton's attempts to give a face to the statistics of crime appeared to be successful initially. The suspicion arose that there were indeed systematic differences between the facial features of different kinds of criminals. For example, Galton obtained a different average face from a group of murderers than from a group of thieves, and these faces, he reported, were 'certainly not a common English face' (figure 36).

But he opposed the idea that there was such a thing as typical murderers' or frauds' faces. For that, the differences within a category were too great: 'The individual faces are villainous enough, but they are villainous in different ways, when they are combined, the individualities disappear and the common humanity of a low type is all that is left.'[57] No characteristic facial features corresponded with the 'ideal' type of a criminal – if one can express it in that way. Thus Galton opposed a prejudice of his time. He maintained, however, that the average face of criminals compared unfavourably with the expression of determination, intelligence and honesty that characterised the common face of officers and men of the Royal Engineers.

Compound photography found an application in the criminology of Lombroso and his pupils and in anthropological research into racial differences.[58] Merged portraits also found a place in philosophical studies on the nature of beauty. Galton himself used his newly discovered technique in theorising about memory. A classic problem in British empiricism and in the psychology which was grafted onto it, concerned the question of how general impressions or abstract notions arise. We can form a visual memory of a specific dog by looking at that dog and imprinting its image on our minds, but how do we arrive at the general notion 'dog'? Nothing in reality corresponds to that notion: 'general dogs' do not exist. Galton tried to find a solution to this problem. In his lecture to the Royal Institution he presented the technique of the compound portrait as a metaphor for the neuronal substratum of memory processes.[59] 'The physiological basis of memory is simple enough in its broad outlines', wrote Galton.

> When any group of brain elements has been excited by a sense impression, it becomes, so to speak, tender, and liable to be easily thrown again into a similar state of excitement. If a new cause of excitement differs from the original one, memory is the result. Whenever a single cause throws different groups of brain elements simultaneously into excitement, the result must be a blended memory.

The physical substratum of memory therefore rests on the fact that whenever a group of brain cells receives a pattern of sensory stimuli, the brain cells become more receptive to comparable patterns. If the same pattern activates two different groups of cells a 'blended memory' is created. The memory's extraction of the common elements from the separate impressions, is due to the fact that the brain has the same functional structure as the photographic plate in compound photography. Just as in a compound portrait common characteristics become clearer in the visual memory. In this way, more or less prototypical images occur of, say, 'dog'. Unique characteristics of separate dogs are as it were retouched by the memory. That compound traces underlie our visual memory images, is also confirmed at the psychological level, argues Galton, for it is precisely memories that are similar to each other that often get mixed up. A photo of a mountain plus a lake evokes in us a vague consciousness of previously seen identical images. Obviously the brain combines memories into forms which have the characteristic qualities of classes. Because we can study the qualities of photographic images at leisure we are, according to Galton, capable of drawing conclusions which throw light on mental processes too fleeting to be investigated directly.

In his *Inquiries*, Galton gave additional support to his metaphor. A possible objection to his representation of things was that generalisations are not so much determined by the number of components but by the extent to which those components make an impression. Galton's answer was that exactly the same thing happened in the case of compound photography, because if one of the portraits had sharp contours, it determined a disproportionate part of the final portrait: 'The cases seem to me exactly analogous. I get over my photographic difficulty by throwing the sharp portrait a little out of focus.'

This last turn of phrase already suggests that the metaphor of the compound photograph was not very productive as an experimental heuristic tool. Galton gave a graphic representation of a phenomenon that was already known in psychology, and his metaphor did not imply any predictions about hitherto unknown processes. Only *after* it has been made clear to him that generalisations are often determined by cases which make a greater impression than others, does Galton realise that something comparable happens in his photographic process. The metaphor would have heuristic value only if a quality of the technique had led to the discovery of a new psychological phenomenon. This is not the case. A more enduring achievement of Galton's research appears possible at the theoretical level. The hypothesis that various memories have a common neuronal substratum and that the brain therefore contains a large number of 'compound traces' was rediscovered in the memory psychology of the 1970s. The notion of 'compound traces' experienced a revival, particularly in the hologram metaphor for memory, and again in the context of photographic techniques.

Photographic memory: mathematical prodigies and blindfolded chess players

Whereas Galton presented a specific photographic technique as an analogy for an equally specific memory process, the French psychologist Alfred Binet was guided in his research by the more general question of whether visual representations in memory correspond to photographically exact representations. The type of visual memory which is commonly called 'a photographic memory' was connected with photography at an early period. In 1868 Maudsley described the case of a man who was capable of repeating a text he had just read, backwards. This is the kind of visual memory, writes Maudsley, 'in which the person seems to read a photographic copy of former impressions with his mind's eye'.[60] The metaphor of the 'photographic memory' is considerably older than the specialist term 'eidetic memory', which was only introduced in 1922.[61] Binet's research, carried out jointly with L. Henneguy, concerned the thought processes of mathematical prodigies and chess players. In 1894 Binet and Henneguy reported on their findings in *Psychologie des grands calculateurs et joueurs d'échecs*.[62]

In 1892 a twenty-four-year-old calculating prodigy appeared at the Sorbonne, one Jacques Inaudi. Inaudi was of humble origin and had spent his childhood as a shepherd. At about the age of six he developed a true passion for figures. By the age of seven he was multiplying five-figure numbers in his head. After having displayed his abilities for a while at markets and fairs he was taken under the wing of an impresario, who took him on a tour of great theatres. At the age of thirteen, Inaudi was examined by Broca. The latter noted that the boy had a comparatively large head and that his skull showed various irregularities. Eleven years later, in 1892, Charcot also took a series of measurements, but besides a slight asymmetry of the face, the head had few remarkable external qualities. It was the task of Binet, director of the Psychological Laboratory at the Sorbonne, to investigate the mysterious interior.

Inaudi was first questioned about his background and his present life. The interview provided a rather heterogeneous description of the young mathematical prodigy. Binet reported that Inaudi had been born into a poor family, that his brothers had tried in vain to master the art of mental arithmetic, that he was slightly built, was ambidextrous, that his hearing and sight were normal, that he had a placid, rather indolent character, spent his days mainly playing cards and billiards, ate a lot, slept for long periods, only remembered dreams when numbers occurred in them, had childish handwriting and so on. Binet was also able to report that Inaudi's sexual needs were well developed. The main striking feature was his general ignorance and exceptional forgetfulness in practical matters: 'His mind has extensive areas which are uncultivated.' Perhaps that was a necessary precondition for his astonishing mathematical ability, assumed Binet, because the 'mental calculations, or the huge mass of figures that have to be mobilised, need a great deal of room; that requires large empty spaces'.[63]

Inaudi's mathematical ability was indeed astonishing. He could subtract twenty-one-figure numbers from each other very quickly, calculate the square root of a nine-figure number and work out within a wink of an eye how many seconds there are in two years, forty-eight days and twelve hours. His memory must have had an enormous capacity; as a mental calculator he retained not only the numbers of the question and answer, but also those of the intermediary results. At the end of the presentation, Inaudi was able to faultlessly reproduce all questions and solutions – well over two hundred figures in all.

Binet first investigated whether Inaudi's other memory functions were just as well developed. Generally the memory for separate letters is the same as that for separate figures; after one presentation most people can reproduce approximately seven elements, the memory span. Inaudi turned out to be able to retain only five separate letters. However, his memory span for numbers had a spectacular size – forty-two figures. Imagine someone reading out a telephone number with forty-two digits – Inaudi could retain that. With repetition he could retain over one hundred figures. There was also a primacy and a recency effect: reproduction of the middle of the series, roughly between the fortieth and seventieth figure, caused Inaudi more effort than the beginning and the end. Inaudi worked purely by ear. The person conducting the experiment read the questions aloud slowly and Inaudi would repeat them, murmuring quietly to himself. When Binet made him hum gently while he was calculating, the solution took twice as long. Inaudi could not solve questions which were simply visual, i.e. work presented to him on a blackboard or a piece of paper.

Pericles Diamandi, a Greek, was another genius who reported to Binet's laboratory. Experiments showed that Diamandi had a completely different type of memory from that of Inaudi. Where Inaudi 'heard' figures as he calculated, Diamandi 'saw' them. He appeared to have a photographic memory. In several

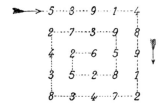

37.   A grid of twenty-five numbers, used by Binet in his investigation of the memories of mathematical prodigies.

shrewd experiments Binet investigated the question of whether this metaphor indeed applied to Diamandi's memory.

In the first place, reasoned Binet, someone who can really retain information in a photographic way should also be able to remember the actual colours of the figures without any extra effort. He asked Diamandi to learn a five-by-five grid of twenty-five black figures. Average learning time: three minutes. Next Diamandi learned a grid of twenty-five crosses in six different colours. That took on average eight minutes. Finally he learned a grid of twenty-five coloured figures. Learning time: eight minutes. This showed that the memory for colour was independent from the memory for figures: when Diamandi looked at a mental photograph, it was definitely not a colour one.[64] This finding corresponded with Diamandi's own explanation – he learned the figures separately and then the colours.

The metaphor of the photographic memory suggested a further experiment. If Diamandi really were to see a mental photograph, then he should be able to do so just as easily from left to right (the normal reading direction) as from right to left. In reality, Diamandi reproduced information from left to right three times faster than from right to left.

The metaphor of the photographic memory apparently clarified little about the thought and memory processes of mathematical prodigies, but a new experiment showed that the metaphor could be considered accurate for the difference between auditory and visual memories. Binet made both Inaudi and Diamandi learn a grid of twenty-five figures. Inaudi was read the figures line by line, Diamandi was shown the grid on paper. Diamandi learned the grid in three minutes. Inaudi was much quicker: forty-five seconds. Reproducing line-by-line both prodigies attained approximately the same speed. But when Inaudi and Diamandi had to reproduce the figures in the form of a spiral (figure 37), Diamandi was much quicker: he completed the task in thirty-six seconds as opposed to Inaudi's eighty seconds.

Binet had an elegant explanation for this pattern of times for learning and reproduction. In the case of auditory presentation the figures are arranged only in time. It is as though they are standing one behind the other in a straight line, a one-dimensional ordering. In Diamandi's visual presentation the figures are arranged two-dimensionally. That is why the learning of the numbers took

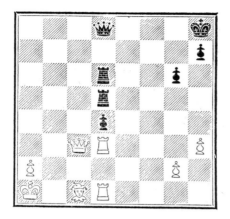 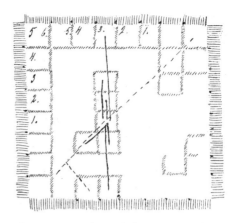

38.   A chess position (left) and a mental representation of the same position (right), drawn by the blind chess player Sittenfeld.

slightly longer with him. But in order to be able to reproduce information in a spiral, the figures have to be arranged two-dimensionally. For this, Inaudi had to convert his lines into a square first of all and that was why reproduction took him slightly longer. Binet's conclusion was that a visually orientated kind of memory may not have much in common with a photographic memory, but that the processes in the visual memory are indeed more like reading a photo than the processing in auditive-oriented memory.

Binet reached similar conclusions when he conducted research into the thinking and remembering of blind chess players. Blind chess players, who can play about ten games at once in their head and subsequently are able to reproduce them faultlessly, turned out like Diamandi not to have a depiction of the reality in a kind of 'inner mirror' as Binet first supposed. A survey showed that the mental image that most blind players 'see' was a radical abstraction of reality. In that process of abstraction the expertise of the chess player was crucially important. A position was not retained as a collection of separate pieces, but as a meaningful pattern, like a chord is for a musician. Chess players have no difficulty in remembering a game because the development has a *meaning* for them. It would be just as difficult for a non-chess player to retain a game as for an illiterate person to remember a sentence as a list of symbols. The fact that the memory image is an abstraction is also clear from the fact that blind chess players only 'see' that part of the board that is significant for the game. Colour, and the exact shapes of the pieces play no part in that abstraction. A drawing by the chess player Sittenfeld is characteristic of the kinds of images that many blind chess players reported: he remembered a chess position as a kind of 'force field', a pattern of potential moves (figure 38). This memory image was based on a well-developed spatial–visual memory and was the result of strict and expert selection. The mental image and reality were related, wrote Binet, like a portrait and photograph.

The final lines of Binet's research into the thinking and remembering of mathematical prodigies and chess players read:

> Though we search and examine in the most minute details, we cannot comprehend with precision the complexity of intellectual activity. The blindfold game contains everything: power of concentration, scholarship, visual memory, not to mention strategic talent, patience, courage, and many other faculties. If one could see what goes on in a chess player's head, one would find a stirring world of sensations, images, movements, passions and an ever changing panorama of states of consciousness. By comparison with these our most attentive descriptions are but grossly simplified schemata.[65]

The speed of calculation, memory span, the reproduction of colours and figures, the memory for chess patterns, all these phenomena can be isolated for the benefit of experiment and theory, but in the human consciousness they are inextricably bound up together.

Stationary trace, frozen image

According to Binet, our most refined descriptions are in reality no more than 'grossly simplified schemata'. And this was true *a fortiori* for the technical metaphors for psychical processes. A few years before his research into mathematical prodigies Binet was already criticising Galton's metaphor of the 'compound photograph'.[66] Binet found the idea that the human memory functioned like a photographic plate on which separate impressions merge purely mechanically into a general representation unconvincing. If the human eye took the place of the lens in Galton's apparatus and if it were to be presented with a series of visual images, this would certainly not create the equivalent of a compound photo in the brain. Whether something makes an impression on us depends on attention, emotion, interest and preconceived ideas. None of these factors plays a role in compound photography. Binet concluded that Galton's optical machinery was inadequate as a metaphor for the forming of general ideas.

It is not without irony that Binet focused his criticism on a variant of the photography metaphor which tried to do justice to the changes which impressions may undergo in the memory. Where the majority of photographic metaphors printed a static picture in a memory, the gradual merging of visual images into an 'average' picture, however mechanically Galton imagined that process, was at least a *movement*. Looking back on the development of photography from the camera obscura and the traces which it left in the psychology of memory, this is probably the sharpest contrast: that the moving images against the back wall of the camera obscura were associated with change and distortion, while photography became a metaphor for the recording of a stationary and constant image. With a photographic camera, images were fixed, in both senses of the word.

The developments in optical technology and the chemistry of light-sensitive substances in the mid-nineteenth century enabled neurologists and psychologists to follow the visual image from the retina to the visual memory, deeper into the brain; at the same time they had to accept that the memory image lost its changeability. A metaphor like that of Hildebrand, the narrator of the *Camera Obscura*, on the retouching and colouring of shadows and phantoms which fall into the mind applies solely to the camera obscura; as a metaphor of memory, photography defined our recollections as exact and permanent copies of reality. The photographic metaphor, however, also possessed some extremely attractive qualities. Unlike drawings or paintings, photos were the result of semi-automatic processes: once prepared the camera allowed the landscape, the nude, the still life to record themselves, without further intervention. Between the lens and the plate, entry and trace, the optical stimulus found its own way. Where in the camera obscura every image erased the previous one, in the photographic camera a trace was preserved, in a coded form unlike a visual copy. Only the development of the plate transformed the trace back into an optical image. Stored on the plate, the image remained a latent trace, 'submerged, ineffective, unnoticed', like the traces of the *eikons* of which Aristotle spoke. It is no surprise that neurologists and psychologists found this an irresistible analogy, suited *par excellence* to transform the brain into an instrument which preserves not replicas but the latent impression of experience. It was accepted as an unavoidable corollary that these images now came to a standstill and the changeability of experience froze into a motionless neuronal trace.

It was not until the turn of the century that the images of memory were to move again. One can guess what technique was able to achieve this feat.

In order to record the movement of marching soldiers, Henri Bergson explained, an effective way of proceeding would be

> to take a series of snapshots of the passing regiment and throw these instantaneous views on the screen, so that they replace each other very rapidly. This is what the cinematograph does. With photographs, each of which represents the regiment in a fixed attitude, it reconstitutes the mobility of the regiment marching. It is true that if we had to do with photographs alone, however much we might look at them, we should never see them animated; with immobility set beside immobility, even endlessly, we could never make movement. In order that the pictures may be animated, there must be movement somewhere. The movement does indeed exist here; it is in the apparatus. It is because the film of the cinematograph unrolls, bringing in turn the different photographs of the scene to continue each other, that each actor of the scene recovers his mobility; he strings all his successive attitudes on the invisible movement of the film . . . Such is the contrivance of the cinematograph. And such is also that of our knowledge.[67]

The discovery of the Lumière brothers finally provided the metaphor for a memory which not only preserved images but also allowed them to move. In the end, isn't human memory just like cinematography, a combination of movement and stasis, a magic marriage of camera obscura and photography?

Notes

1   First lines of an anonymous song that circulated in London in August 1839;
    quoted in H. and A. Gernsheim, *L.J.M. Daguerre*, New York, 1968, p. 105.

2   A few months after the publication of *Origin of Species*, Darwin wrote to his
    friend Asa Gray: 'the thought of the eye made me cold all over'. C. Darwin,
    The Autobiography of Charles Darwin and Selected Letters, F. Darwin (ed.), New
    York, 1892, p. 244.

3   G. Ryle, *The Concept of Mind*, London (1949) 1978, p. 153.

4   J. O. de Lamettrie, *Man a Machine*, G. C. Bussey (ed.), La Salle, 1912, p. 107.

5   A. Maier, *Die Mechanisierung des Weltbilds im 17. Jahrhundert*, Leipzig, 1938.

6   On the relationship between Descartes's theory of perception and the
    camera obscura, see W. van Hoorn, *As Images Unwind*, Amsterdam, 1972. Only
    the nautilus, a deep-sea fish, actually has a camera obscura for an eye: a
    retina behind a simple opening in the skin.

7   Anonymous, *Verses Occasion'd by the Sight of a Chamera Obscura*, London, 1747.
    The ode is discussed by H. Schwarz, 'An eighteenth-century English poem on
    the camera obscura', in V. D. Coke (ed.), *One Hundred Years of Photographic
    History*, Albuquerque, 1975, pp. 128–38.

8   M. J. van Lieburg and H. A. M. Snelders, *De bevordering en vervolmaking van de
    proefondervindelijke wijsbegeerte*, Amsterdam, 1989, p. 21.

9   Algarotti's essay on painting is discussed in A. Scharf, *Art and Photography*,
    London, 1968, pp. 22–3.

10 Quoted in A. K. Wheelock, *Jan Vermeer*, New York, 1981, p. 38.

11 An English translation of *Giphantie* appeared in 1761 as *Giphantia: or A View
    of What Has Passed, What is Now Passing, and During the Present Century, What will
    Pass, in the World*, London, 1761. The passage on the magic canvas is included,
    with a great many other primary sources from the history of photography,
    in B. Newhall (ed.), *Photography: Essays and Images*, New York, 1980. For some
    other older, but also vaguer adumbrations of photography, see J. A.
    Groshans, 'Photography foreshadowed', *Nature*, 10 January, 1878, 202.

12 Accordingly, his account was given the rather perplexed title:
    'Dunkelsheitsträger anstatt Lichtträger entdeckt; oder merkwürdiger
    Versuch über die Wirkung der Sonnenstrahlen'.

13 U. Tillmanns, *Geschichte der Photographie*, Stuttgart, 1981, p. 20.

14 T. Wedgwood and H. Davy, 'An account of a method of copying paintings
    upon glass and of making profiles, by the agency of light upon nitrate of
    silver', *Journal of the Royal Institute*, 1 (1802), 170–4; reprinted in B. Newhall
    (ed.), *Photography*.

15 Gernsheim, *Daguerre*.

16 Tillmanns, *Geschichte*, p. 31.

17 Included in Newhall, *Photography*, pp. 17–18.

18 Quoted in *ibid.*, p. 18.

19 R. Taft, *Photography and the American Scene. A Social History, 1839–1889*, New
    York, 1942.

20 Quoted in M. Frizot (ed.), *A New History of Photography*, Cologne, 1998, p. 28.

21 Taft, *Photography*, p. 29.

22 G. Freund, *Photography and Society*, London, 1980, p. 33.

23   The report was presented on 31 January 1839 and appeared later that year in book form: W. H. F. Talbot, *Some Account of the Art of Photogenic Drawing*, London, 1839. The text is included in Newhall, *Photography*, pp. 23–31. The astronomer Herschel renamed Talbot's procedure 'photography'. Calling daguerreotypes photographs is strictly speaking an anachronism.

24   Tillmanns, *Geschichte*, p. 36.

25   Before photography the images for a stereoscope had to be drawn or painted, with a laboriously calculated difference in perspective. Like the camera obscura previously, the stereoscope was presented as a physical analogy in perception theories. Stereoscopes were standard equipment in physiological and psychological laboratories.

26   On the history of the relationship between art and photography, see Scharf, *Art*.

27   The confusion was further increased by the fact that group portraits were nevertheless more expensive.

28   Talbot, *Account*.

29   Talbot, *Account*; quoted from Newhall, *Photography*, p. 28.

30   Newhall, *ibid.*; his house was very suited to the task, Talbot believed, because of 'its ancient and remarkable architecture'.

31   *Ibid.*, p. 25.

32   O. W. Holmes, 'The stereoscope and the stereographe', *The Atlantic Monthly*, June (1859) 3, 738–48. Also in Newhall, *Photography*, pp. 53–61.

33   Hildebrand [N. Beets], *Camera Obscura*, Haarlem, 1839.

34   J. W. Draper, *Human Physiology*, London, 1856. The 1868 edition used here was already the seventh.

35   *Ibid.*, p. 269.

36   *Ibid.*, p. 288.

37   *Ibid.*

38   J. W. Draper, *History of the Conflict between Religion and Science*, London, 1878, pp. 133–4.

39   *Ibid.*, p. 135.

40   *Ibid.*, p. 136.

41   J. Luys, *Le Cerveau et ses fonctions*, Paris, 1878.

42   Luys, *Cerveau*, p. 106.

43   A. Kussmaul, *Die Störungen der Sprache*, Leipzig, 1881, p. 35.

44   J. Delbœuf, 'Le sommeil et les rêves: leurs rapports avec la théorie de la mémoire', *Revue philosophique*, 9 (1880), 129–69; 413–37.

45   W. B. Carpenter, *Mental Physiology*, London (1874) 1879, p. 436.

46   G. T. Ladd, *Physiological Psychology*, London (1887) 1891, p. 422.

47   R. M. Evans, 'Maxwell's color photograph', *Scientific American*, November 1961, 118–28.

48   *Ibid.*, p. 118.

49   Th. Ribot, 'La mémoire comme fait biologique', *Revue philosophique*, 9 (1880), 516–47. Quoted from Th. Ribot, *Diseases of Memory*, London, 1882, p. 10.

50   Quoted from Ribot, *Diseases*, pp. 11–12.

51   J. Huber, *Das Gedächtnis*, Munich, 1878.

52   *Ibid.*, p. 28.

53   *Ibid.*, p. 30.

54   F. Galton, *Memories of my Life*, London, 1908.

55   F. Galton, 'On generic images', *Proceedings of the Royal Institution*, 9 (25 April 1879), 161–70. This lecture is included as an appendix in F. Galton, *Inquiries into Human Faculty and its Development*, London, 1883. The quotations are taken from this appendix.

56   Galton, *Inquiries*, frontispiece.

57   *Ibid.*, p. 15.

58   A. Sekula, 'The body and the archive', *October*, 39 (1986), 3–64.

59   Galton, 'Generic images'.

60   H. Maudsley, *The Physiology of Mind*, London (1868), 1876, p. 518.

61   By Erich Jaensch, 'Über die subjectiven Anschauungsbilder', *Bericht über den Kongress für experimentelle Psychologie*, 7 (1922).

62   A. Binet and L. Henneguy, *Psychologie des grands calculateurs et joueurs d'échecs*, Paris, 1894.

63   These are almost exactly the same terms used to express the relationship between the calculating and memory capacity of computers.

64   One can, however, conclude from the same data that these two memory operations are not *strictly* independent, because in that case the learning of coloured figures should take eleven minutes: three for the figures and eight for the colours.

65   Binet and Henneguy, *Psychologie*, p. 339. Before publishing his monograph on mathematical prodigies and blindfolded chess players, Binet had written a separate article on his study of chess players, 'Les grandes mémoires. Résumé d'une enquête sur les joueurs d'échecs', *Revue des Deux Mondes*, 117 (1893) 63, 826–59. An English translation by M. L. Simmel and S. B. Barron appeared as 'Mnemonic virtuosity: a study of chess players', *Genetic Psychology Monographs*, 74 (1966), 127–62. The quotation is taken from this translation.

66   A. Binet, *La psychologie du raisonnement*, Paris, 1886, pp. 107ff. A French-language article appeared as early as 1878 on this new technique: F. Galton. 'Les images génériques', *Revue scientifique*, 17 (1878), 2nd series, 221–5.

67   H. Bergson, *L'Evolution créatrice*, Paris, 1907; quoted from H. Bergson, *Creative Evolution*, New York, 1911, pp. 305–6. In a note Bergson mentioned that he had previously used this metaphor in a series of lectures on the notion of time at the Collège de France. He gave these lectures between 1902 and 1903. Cinematography was invented in 1895.

6   Digital memory

No new technology since the invention of photography and the phonograph captured the human imagination as much as the computer did. The first computers became operational during the Second World War. From the beginning their performance inspired mathematicians, philosophers and psychologists to reflect on the relationship between human thought and the behaviour of machines. From the 1950s onwards the computer was the dominant metaphor in cognitive science, the area of research that focuses on the processing of knowledge. This hegemony lasted until the mid-1980s.

It has been observed, however, that from the perspective of style and methodology, post-war psychology bears a resemblance to psychology as it was practised in the last decades of the nineteenth century more than the psychology that set the tone in the first half of the twentieth century.[1] That observation is confirmed by the use made of metaphors in those different periods. Whereas the psychologists of the nineteenth century, as we have seen, incorporated the most important new discoveries in the field of artificial memories and communication in their theories on memory, but this was not the case in the decades before the Second World War. The style of psychological theory in the inter-war years seems to diverge from what preceded it and what followed it.

The smaller frequency of metaphors in psychological theories and publications can be seen in the calculations carried out by Gentner and Grudin.[2] They used the *Psychological Review* as their source. For each first issue of the volumes 1894, 1905, 1915, and from 1925 up until 1985 they noted the number of metaphors used for psychological processes. Of the three periods into which they had organised their material (1894–1905, 1925–45, 1955–85) the middle one showed a significant decline. They attribute this to the influence of behaviourism, observing that the ban on references to non-observable mental processes at the same time removed the necessity for metaphors. For the connection between stimulus and response, the metaphor of the telephone exchange would suffice, and was indeed used by behaviourists with some frequency;

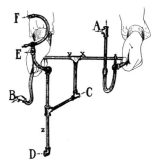

39.   Drawing of a tri-dimensional maze made of copper piping, used for research
      into the learning of motor-skills. The test subject had to manoeuvre a steel
      ball from A to a predesignated opening.

other technical inventions from this period would not have been compatible in
any meaningful way with stimulus-response psychology.

But one should not conclude from this analysis that the proportion of
behaviourist metaphors was negligible. The frequency and heterogeneity may
have been less, but the metaphors which *were* used, including those for learning and memory, acquired a central position in theories of human behaviour.
It was precisely in neo-behaviourism – which like classical behaviourism
focused on external behaviour, but in the explanation of that behaviour
allowed references to non-observable processes – that metaphors were used
which anticipated ideas usually attributed to the advent of the computer. The
metaphors of the behaviourists do not form a contrast with those of cognitive
psychology, as often portrayed in chronicles of the cognitive revolution, rather
they are the precursors of them.

The mechanism of behaviour

In the 1920s and 1930s neo-behaviourists like Tolman and Hull used metaphors
liberally.[3] Both researchers were strongly influenced by spatial representations.
In the case of Hull this took the form of electro-mechanical systems; Tolman
ordered his ideas in the form of maps and diagrams: 'I feel comfortable only
when I have translated my explanatory arguments into diagrams.'[4] Tolman was
mainly inspired by the twin metaphors of the maze and map. The maze was a
popular instrument in research into learning (mainly with rats), but also had
more complex variants which were used in experiments with human subjects
(figure 39). The map was a representation in the memory of the spatial knowledge acquired during learning. These maps could be 'broad and comprehensive'
or 'narrow and strip-like'. The 'central office' of the nervous system, explained
Tolman, 'is far more like a map control room than it is like an old-fashioned
telephone exchange'[5] – in a telephone exchange the incoming signals are not

processed and compared, as happens in a control room, but simply linked via 'one-to-one switches to the outgoing responses'.

For Tolman and his assistants the metaphors of the maze and map acted as a research programme: every problem was transformed into the diagram of a maze and subsequently its implications were examined.[6] The metaphor of the map, originally designed to order theories of learning and memory, was broadened to include the process of scientific research itself, which consequently became a kind of cartography: 'All science presents, it seems to us, but a map and picture of reality',[7] it is one of the ways in which we try to orientate ourselves in 'that great God-given maze which is our human world'.[8]

Tolman's contemporary Clark Hull had trained as an engineer. In his student years he constructed a 'logic machine' which through a turn of the handle produced all the valid conclusions of a syllogism.[9] In the 1920s he designed an automaton which calculated correlation coefficients (and is now preserved in the Smithsonian Institute). At that time he wrote in his intellectual journal – the 'Idea Books' of 1927/8 – the note that 'all kinds of action, including the highest forms of intelligent and reflective action and thought, can be handled from the purely materialistic and mechanistic standpoint'.[10] His machines carried out 'mental work', they were, according to Hull, 'psychic machines'. At one time Hull conceived the (never-realised) plan of housing his creations in a special museum for 'psychic machines' at Yale.

In 1926, Hull stated as the core of his 'robot approach' the view that thought-processes could in principle be imitated by a machine. The design of such a machine would force us to make a precise analysis of thought: 'To think through the essentials of such a mechanism would probably be the best way of analysing out the essential requirements of thinking, responding to abstract relations among things, and so on.'[11] This early articulation of the logic of simulation research was followed by the construction of mechanical and electro-chemical analogies for conditioning processes.[12] In the 1930s these analogies were refined by Hull and his assistants. One of the articles concluded with the observation that if it were to prove possible to duplicate more complex responses, 'the way would seem to be open to the design of mechanisms manifesting a wide range of adaptive behaviour considered by many psychologists as involving mind. It is possible that at a not very remote date the concept of a "psychic machine" may become by no means a paradox.'[13] It is clear that Hull found ammunition for robust optimism in his own analogies. Figure 40 shows the wiring diagram of a 'psychic machine' which was designed to imitate the learning and forgetting of natural organisms.

Hull and his co-authors saw the construction of such models as a contribution to the programme which was intended to liberate psychology from 'mysticism'.[14] They specified the latter as the explanation for actions in terms of 'soul, spirit, ego, mind, consciousness, or *Einsicht*'. Mechanical models would gradually force the mystics to retreat into the more marginal areas of psychology. In

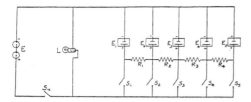

40.   An electro-chemical model for the conditioned reflex. The battery at E is connected to the bulb L. The compartments E1–E5 are storage cells, divided from
each other by rheostats R1–R4. The button at su represents the unconditioned stimulus: when the circuit is complete, the bulb lights up (the
unconditioned response). In order to encourage conditioning, the test director presses one of the buttons s1–s4 as well as su, for example s2. Besides L
lighting up, the storage battery E2 is also partly charged. By pressing these
two buttons again, suggesting the simultaneous presentation of two
stimuli, E2 is charged further, so that eventually s2 can make L light up by
itself and therefore the stimulus has become conditioned. The increasing
strength of s2 is revealed in the increasing brightness of L, the 'learning
curve'.

Batteries can also be charged when the strength of the adjacent battery
overcomes the resistance, which corresponds to 'overconditioning'. The
combined effect of two separate stimuli, 'summation', is revealed by the
greater brightness of L when two buttons are pressed at once. Even
'spontaneous recovery', the phenomenon where an extinguished conditioned reaction may reappear after a while, has an analogy in the system:
when the storage batteries seem to have become flat, a period of rest is
sufficient to obtain a reaction again. Finally 'forgetting' corresponds with
the gradual running down of batteries, even when they are not used.

the struggle against mentalistic idiom much was expected of technical
improvements in the 'psychic machines'. A definitive judgement could be made
only when as much ingenuity had been expended on the mechanical models as
on the steam machine, the electromotor or the printing press. A development
in that direction was quite conceivable, they believed, since 'in the demands for
higher and higher degrees of automaticity in machines constantly being made
by modern industry, the ultra-automaticity of the type of mechanism here considered, may have an important place'.[15] These were to prove prophetic words.

In a previous publication Hull had expressed the underlying logic of his
electro-chemical models even more clearly. If the proposed explanation for
behaviour was adequate, it must be possible to build mechanisms 'which will
genuinely manifest the qualities of intelligence, insight and purpose, and
which will in so far be truly psychic'.[16] No closer connection between psychological theory and machine, between explanation and mechanical design is
conceivable. A good psychologist was half an engineer.

As with Tolman, in Hull's case, too, metaphors functioned even outside direct research as an ordering scheme. Good simulations consisted of 'hierarchies of control' in order to direct sub-mechanisms. Scientific theories were constructed as deductive hierarchies of laws, a reflection of the hierarchical structure of reality. Even the social structure which Hull imposed on his own research group seemed to be inspired by the representation of a hierarchical machine.[17] At the top was a select group of theoreticians ('postulate makers'). They passed their work on to a lower echelon of 'deducers' or 'logic-grinders', mathematicians and logicians who had to derive as many hypotheses as possible from the theoretical postulates. The lowest level was that of the 'experimenters', mainly graduate students, who subjected the hypotheses to empirical testing. If with Tolman a scientific researcher still had the dignity of a cartographer, with Hull he was no more than a cogwheel in the hectic machinery of scientific industry.

Hull was not the only researcher to develop mechanical models for psychological processes. Even before the First World War the behaviourist Meyer had recommended the development of mechanical analogies of learning and forgetting as a strategy for a soundly based scientific psychology. He saw in such analogies 'a demonstration of the possibility of an "organism", capable of learning and forgetting, which obeyed no ghost whatsoever, but only the laws of mechanics'.[18] In the 1930s several researchers with neo-behaviouristic tendencies published mechanical models independently of each other.[19] The background to those models was always the same: dislike of mentalistic idiom and a wish to create as close as possible a correspondence between theory and mechanical design.

In this respect the neo-behaviouristic tradition shared two essential characteristics with the computer metaphor which was only to gain influence from the 1950s onwards. And this very fact reveals an apparently anomalous situation: the computer developed into the dominant metaphor for an orientation in psychology which presented itself as the *antithesis* of behaviourism. Why wasn't the computer unceremoniously annexed by behaviourism? After all, this machine had the 'ultra-automaticity' that Hull had dreamed of. The answer to this question requires a few remarks on the historical background of the computer.

The electronic brain

The history of the computer is the history of intimate links between technology and theory, between apparatus and ideas. In the computer two lines of development converge. One leads from the clockmakers of the seventeenth century and the builders of automatons and androids, via innovations in metallurgy and micro-mechanics, through inventors of transmission mechanisms to, in our time, specialists in electronics and micro-physics. The other line leads through the history of mathematics and logic, philosophy and linguistics. Vernon Pratt describes the history of artificial intelligence as a succession of three 'projects' associated with the names of Leibniz, Babbage and Turing – not coincidentally three researchers with a double talent that enabled them to contribute to both technical and conceptual developments.[20]

At the end of the sixteenth century the interest in the application of mathematics increased rapidly. That interest was inspired by practical questions. Overseas trade required reliable navigation methods, and the determination of geographical longitude was especially urgent. Outstanding minds like Napier, Pascal, Leibniz, Boyle, Huygens and Hooke tried to solve the problem, in vain, for only towards the end of the eighteenth century were helmsmen able, thanks to the precision chronometers of Harrison, to navigate with the necessary accuracy. The development of new projection methods in cartography also gave an impetus to mathematics. The intensification of trade relations – with exchange rates, book-keeping, banking and insurance, interest calculations – brought a diversification and proliferation of mathematical tasks. In astronomy, improvements in observation equipment led to an explosion in measurement data that had to be processed. Whether it was a matter of money, distance, cargoes, measures, weights or times, more and more calculations were required. This situation demanded more efficient mathematical methods. In the sixteenth century the Frenchman Vieta introduced the use of letters for both known and unknown quantities. Letters could stand for numbers and geometrical quantities. In this way Vieta gave algebra a decisive *symbolic* character. Other important practical innovations were the decimals of Simon Stevin, introduced in 1585, and Napier's logarithms, published in 1614. One of the first applications of logarithms was, typically, the calculation of compound interest.

The same social need which gave new impetus to mathematics, also accelerated the development of external aids for calculation. Napier constructed his celebrated 'bones', ivory cylinders with figures engraved on them which could be set for multiplication and division. Slide rules were also invented on the basis of Napier's ideas. He himself published logarithm tables for book-keepers, navigators and astronomers. The first attempts to build calculating machines date from this time. The present consensus among historians of science is that it was not Pascal but the German Wilhelm Schickard – a professor of Hebrew and a gifted mathematician – who built the first calculating machine.[21] In a letter to Kepler of 1623 (the year of Pascal's birth), Schickard described his apparatus as a 'calculating clock', and that was what the machine looked like, as regards its inside – six cylinders with figures, variants of Napier's 'bones', moved by cogwheels. The machine could be used to carry out the four elementary mathematical operations. A special facility had been constructed for 'saving' and 'borrowing' in addition and subtraction. Unfortunately the machine itself was lost in a fire in 1624. Compared to Schickard's machine, the *Pascaline* was a fairly clumsy apparatus with which Pascal hoped to ease the laborious calculations of his father (a tax collector). Its cogwheels could turn in only one direction – using addition, in accordance with the principle of the

mileometer – so that cumbersome procedures had to be followed for subtraction. The fact that the machine created a sensation at its first demonstration
and was pirated even before the patent was issued, owed more to the mere idea
that one could now calculate semi-mechanically than to any actual increased
ease of calculation.

Considerably more powerful, in terms of potential, was the calculating
machine designed by Gottfried Leibniz (1646–1716) between 1670 and 1672.
Thanks to a mechanism now known as 'Leibniz's Wheel', the machine could be
used for multiplication. A second novelty was the sliding carriage, like that of
a typewriter, with which each following decimal could be calculated – all this
in principle, because Leibniz's instrument makers were never able to produce
a prototype which worked. In fact no single calculating machine from the
seventeenth or eighteenth century could hold its own against the joint competi-
tion of the slide rule and the book of tables.

If for Leibniz the possibility of mechanical calculation was, in Pratt's words,
little more than 'a gleam in the eye',[22] he made a number of contributions to
the philosophical principles of automatic calculation procedures. The driving
force in Leibniz's theories on the relationship between human and machine
reasoning is that the mathematisation of logic creates the possibility for the
mechanisation of reasoning. Just as a calculating machine manipulates representations of *numbers*, so a calculus of reasoning procedures manipulates the
mechanical representations of *ideas*. This 'calculus ratiocinator' formed, to use
an anachronistic term, a 'programme'. In order to find representations for ideas
and their relations suitable for processing in a calculus, Leibniz attempted to
compile a 'characteristica universalis', a scheme of notation which could serve
as an ideal universal language, purified of the imperfections of natural languages. In this way disagreements could be stated in mathematical terms and
hence, in the view of Leibniz, who was not only a philosopher but also a diplo-
mat, every difference of opinion would be given the status of a calculation and
become resolvable.

Even before Leibniz, but inspired by the same dream of an exact and universal language, the Englishman John Wilkins published a detailed proposal for
an artificial language, in which all technical, scientific and everyday knowledge
was incorporated in an encyclopaedic scheme.[23] In an heroic effort to escape the
curse of Babel, Wilkins began his universal classification of concepts with forty
types, each divided into nine sorts, in turn divided into nine 'differences', such
as colour, weight, etc. Each distinction was given its own letter code. Wilkins's
proposal appeared under the auspices of the Royal Society, which appreciated
the ideal of an unambiguous language. Robert Hooke particularly, the protégé
of Wilkins and himself searching for a 'philosophical algebra', was attracted by
the project: he published a treatise on pocket watches in Wilkins's artificial language.[24] In a letter to Leibniz, Hooke mentioned that he had regularly
exchanged ideas with Wilkins on the idea of a 'universal character'.[25]

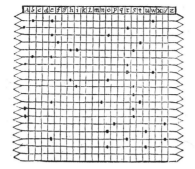

41. Drawing of one of Wilkins's procedures for the encoding and decoding of secret messages. A thread in which knots had been tied, the coded message, had to be stretched across a board by the recipient. The positions of the knots correspond to the letters on the board. This thread contains the message 'Beware of the Bearer, who is sent as a Spy over you.' The procedure is illustrated in J. Wilkins's *Mercury: Or the Secret and Swift Messenger* (London, 1641).

Artificial languages, written in code, followed on from attempts to construct secret languages. As early as 1641 Wilkins wrote a treatise on cryptography (with the subtitle 'Shewing How a Man may with Privacy and Speed communicate his Thoughts to a Friend at any Distance'), in which he presented all kinds of ingenuous procedures for coding and decoding (figure 41).[26] These procedures underlined the fact that content and form of the message were two different things and that the coded message had to be seen as a collection of empty and formal symbols; only the key or interpretation gave it meaning. The distinction between the content of representation and formal shape, between meaning and code, is by definition at its sharpest in cryptography. Seen in this way the cryptography of the seventeenth century was a parallel to Leibniz's ideas on the formalisation of reasoning.

It was not until the nineteenth century that the idea of a formal logic was linked with new techniques for the mechanical processing of symbols. This development is associated with the name of Charles Babbage (1792–1871), Professor of Mathematics at Cambridge, and from 1816, a Fellow of the Royal Society and a true enthusiast for cryptographical projects.

It was Babbage's aspiration to build a machine able 'to combine together general symbols in successions of unlimited variety and extent'. These are the words of Lady Lovelace, Ada Byron, quoted from an article in which she commented on the Analytical Engine of her friend Babbage.[27] The term 'analytical' referred to a new kind of algebra which had been developed in circles around Babbage. This algebra had to be seen as a general system of symbols, in which the rules of logic, mathematics or geometry were specifications. In this way algebra became – again in the words of Lovelace – a 'science of operations'. The Analytical Engine was designed to carry out these operations mechanically.

But in this case the same qualification applied: in principle. Like Leibniz, Babbage did not succeed in having a working prototype of his machine built. For a long time it was assumed that this was due to limitations in nineteenth-century technology, but recently at the London Science Museum, a part of the Difference Engine was built according to the original drawings (a machine which Babbage had designed before the Analytical Engine), making use of the technical means and standards of precision (two thousandths of an inch!) available at the beginning of the nineteenth century.[28] The fact that Babbage himself did not manage to do this was due to a chronic lack of funds (despite astronomical contributions from the government), as well as his difficult nature: he refused to settle for a less than perfect result.

Even if the Analytical Engine only existed in the form of a series of designs, the machine was both conceptually and technically an innovation. Its design had been inspired by the textile industry. The Analytical Engine had a 'mill', a central unit into which the numbers were fed and where they were processed. The results went to a 'storehouse' or warehouse, where they could be referred to in the form of disc positions. For determining the calculating instructions Babbage used perforated cardboard cards which passed through the machine like a kind of barrel-organ card. This procedure was also derived from the textile industry: the Frenchman Jacquard used such cards to drive his weaving machines. In order to demonstrate the potential of his invention, Jacquard had programmed a loom with 2,400 cards, each with a capacity of over 1,000 perforations, in such a way that his own portrait in black-and-white silk was woven (figure 42). Babbage owned such a portrait and was fascinated by the possibility of determining instructions completely mechanically. For his own machine he developed among other things special 'operation cards' for the repetition of an operation (what is now called a 'run') or for carrying out an operation within an operation ('sub-routine'). For Lady Lovelace, Babbage's machine was a mathematical loom: 'The Analytical Engine weaves algebraic patterns just as the Jacquard-loom weaves flowers and leaves.'[29]

The Analytical Engine not only processed numbers but also signs like positive and negative. The essence of the machine lay therefore not in calculation but in the processing of *symbols*. Of all Babbage's contemporaries, it was Lady Lovelace who saw this most clearly. Every domain in which the internal relations can be described in rules, she argued, falls within the scope of the 'science of operations' and is therefore suitable for processing by the Analytical Engine. If once the relationships, say, between musical notes have been described in formal laws, then the Analytical Engine will be capable of composing 'elaborate and scientific pieces of music'.[30]

At the same time that Babbage was working on his designs, developments were taking place in logic which, like the Analytical Engine, were heading in the direction of increasing formalisation. In his *Laws of Thought* the mathe-

42.   Silk portrait of Joseph-Marie Jacquard, inventor of the programmable loom.

matician Boole discussed 'the mathematics of the human intellect', as he stated in the preface, and proposed to interpret algebraic expressions as propositions about sets.[31] The basic idea is that each element may or may not be part of a set. Each proposition in this system therefore has one of two 'truth values' (the term is Frege's): 1 or 0. In this way logic acquired a binary character. According to somewhat different principles but with the same idea of properties and sets, the logician Jevons developed a formalisation of syllogistic logic which was based on the exclusion of invalid conclusions from the set.[32] The mechanisation of this procedure resulted in a machine which Jevons called a 'logical piano'. In 1869 he commissioned a clockmaker to build an apparatus that resembled an upright piano, the keys of which were used to enter the premises. The piano had 'operation keys' with logical operators like *and* and *or*, and 'term keys' for subject and predicate in a proposition.[33] Via an ingenious system of axles all invalid conclusions subsequently turned away from the window strips, so that only the valid conclusions remained visible to the observer (figure 43).

Babbage's Analytical Engine, the mechanical processing of symbols, Boole's binary logic, the formalisation of the syllogism, and Jevons's logical piano – this

43.   Engraving of W. S. Jevons's 'logical piano'. The key for the predicate c has been depressed. The apparatus is illustrated in the frontispiece to Jevons's *The Principles of Science* (London, 1874).

whole Victorian conglomerate of ideas and machines – was an extension of theories that Leibniz had specified two centuries before; it would take almost another century before the machine became available which was to give expression to what had been present in the mind for so long.

After Babbage there followed a period of technical innovation and conceptual stagnation. The counting wheel-like machines of the nineteenth century required long chains of cogwheels and axles, solid but rigid components which set a mechanical limit for the complexity of the machine. In the 1930s, clockwork was finally replaced by an efficient mechanism. In the laboratories of the Bell Telephone Company experiments were conducted with relays which had been in use for some time in the telephone industry. Equipping calculators with electrical switches – originally as a link between the mechanical elements and later in place of them – solved a whole series of technical problems. A fortunate side-effect was the revival of the ideas of Boole: thanks to their on/off switches, calculating machines became binary instruments. These developments increased the calculating capacity of machines very rapidly. At the same time the conceptually crucial insight of Babbage and Lovelace that the machine could process *symbols*, was pushed into the background. However, it was Turing who was not only able to restore this insight to a central position in research thinking, but also gave it a rigorous mathematical formulation.

Alan Mathison Turing (1912–54) studied mathematics in Cambridge. At the age of twenty-five he published an article that at once was to be his first and major work in mathematical logic.[34] In this article he proved that there is a particular class of mathematical problems which cannot be solved by well-defined procedures. This proof was intended as a contribution to the foundations of mathematics and logic, but also contained a component – Turing's definition of a well-defined procedure – that became an essential element in computer theory. Turing linked the proof procedures with the operations of a hypothetical machine. This machine consists of a head – as on a typewriter – through which slides a strip of paper of indeterminate length. The strip is divided into squares. Each square contains a symbol (from a finite set), or is empty. The head 'reads' every square and can then delete a symbol or print one and move the strip one position on, forwards or backwards. Turing proved that with these operations any programme written in a binary code can in principle be executed. This implies that any operation which can be described in a precise step-by-step procedure, is processable by the machine as a series of symbolic instructions. These operations include the operation of the machine itself, which in fact, in Turing's terms, is a 'universal machine', capable of processing the programmes of any specific machine.

Turing's machine, the present-day Turing machine, was a purely hypothetical construct and should certainly not be thought of as a computer in the current sense. Up until after the Second World War the term 'computers' referred to human beings, professional calculators of flesh and blood, working for a university or a company. The monumental power of Turing's imagination allowed him not only to see the abstract possibility of automatic symbol processing machines, but also that the hypothetical existence of such machines had consequences for philosophy and psychology.

The development of computers in today's sense (automatic electronic machines with an internally stored programme for the processing of symbols), underwent an unprecedented acceleration during the Second World War. The armed forces of the Axis powers made use of the so-called Enigma equipment for their communications.[35] With these machines local commanders could decode messages that they received on the radio. Enigma machines were like typewriters, with the difference that the message typed in was transformed electro-mechanically. For this transformation a code was used which changed daily – and later on even every eight hours. At the beginning of the war the British had managed to capture an Enigma machine and in the Government Code and Cipher School at Bletchley Park in Buckinghamshire, a group of mathematicians, logicians and technicians were assembled for the cryptographical project 'Ultra'. They were given the task of breaking the code. Turing was part of this project from the autumn of 1939 onwards.[36]

To this day much of the material produced during the Ultra project remains classified, but it is known that Turing played an important role in the development of a machine which could 'read' two strips of paper photo-electrically and compare them. One strip contained the data, and the other, the patterns which served as a comparison. The machine 'read' 2,000 signs per second and was linked to a teleprinter. Thanks to the matching procedures which were completed at high speed, a large number of possible interpretations of the coded message could be assessed in a short time. A series of these machines was given the name COLOSSUS.[37]

In the same period technicians in America were working feverishly on the development of computers. The impulse did not come, as it did in England, from cryptographic needs, but because of the rapidly increasing demand for fire tables for artillery. The parabola of projectiles depends on factors such as weight, angle and wind speed. These factors can be described in systems of differential equations. For each type of artillery there was a fire table in which these factors were incorporated. When the war broke out hundreds of 'computers' were trained at short notice, mainly female students with a flair for mathematics who were given the task of compiling fire tables. Since demand far exceeded production and the fire tables became increasingly complex (for example, there were tables even for firing sideways from airplanes), the Pentagon decided to support the development of a new electronic computer at the Moore School of Electrical Engineering (Pennsylvania), but on condition that a sister-machine was made available to the war effort. The final result was the Electronic Numerator Integrator Analyser and Computer (ENIAC), a mechanical dinosaur with eighteen thousand radio valves (cooled by an air jet), seventy thousand resistors and six thousand hand-operated switches. The programming of the machine was 'a one-way ticket to the madhouse'.[38] The machine was finished too late to play a role in the Second World War, but shortly afterwards it was used to calculate a mathematical model for a hydrogen bomb explosion.[39]

In 1942 Turing made a journey to America and met the mathematician John Von Neumann there, who was involved as an advisor for the ENIAC. Back in England Turing continued working on the Automatic Computing Engine (ACE) and later on the Manchester Automatic Digital Machine (MADAM). Now that he was surrounded by real computers, his thoughts on the relationship between psychological processes and the operations of these machines began to take shape. For Turing the link between computers and psychology was the human brain, an organ which was being increasingly described as an organic machine.

Since the turn of the century, physiologists had started taking an interest in the processes with which an organism keeps variations in the 'internal environment', such as liquid level and oxygen, within certain limits. Beyond a certain point of abstraction these regulating processes corresponded to the operating mechanisms of complex machines. For the study of the interaction between control mechanisms, the mathematician Norbert Wiener introduced the term cybernetics, from the Greek 'kybernetike', the art of navigation. The parallel between operating mechanisms in organisms and machines emerged, for example, in a cybernetic project of 1945, when Wiener and the physiologist Rosenblueth investigated the control of the heartbeat, making use of the insights of positive and negative feedback which Wiener had gained at the beginning of the war in designing anti-aircraft guns.

In the physiology of the nervous system a link with technology had also been created. Organisms learn to distinguish between stimuli and this selectivity is based on the gradual self-organisation of networks. When the capacity to distinguish increases, the network 'learns' and hence has a memory. In 1943 one of Hull's pupils, the neuro-psychologist Warren McCulloch, published an article on the characteristics of networks; his co-author was an eighteen-year-old mathematician, Walter Pitts.[40] In order to formalise the on/off character of stimulus transfer in the network, they made use of the binary logic of Boole, as Shannon had done in 1938 in his description of switch networks in the telephone industry.[41] A second important line in their article was the comparison between a nerve network and a Turing machine. Their network – in fact an abstract mathematical model of the 'behaviour' of such a network – would like a Turing machine be capable of calculating certain functions. This meant that networks could be conceived of as symbol-processing machines.

Shortly after the war, the developments in cybernetics, theories on nerve networks and the construction of computers, became united in the view that the human brain was a Turing machine (and the computer an electronic brain). Turing, who in the spring of 1947 was visited by Wiener and discussed the principles of cybernetics with him, wrote in September of that year an essay which can be regarded as a preliminary study for his classic *Mind* article 'Computing machinery and intelligence'.[42] Under the title 'Intelligent Machinery' Turing discussed how 'machinery might be made to show intelligent behaviour'. The guiding principle was the analogy with the human brain. Just as the potential latent in the cortex of an infant (in Turing's phrase, 'an unorganised machine') is realised through experience and education, so an appropriate form of education could be designed for computers.

Although it is possible in principle to simulate the behaviour of nerves in electric models, in Turing's view this is not the way that the analogy should be applied: 'It would be rather like putting a lot of work into cars which walked on legs, instead of continuing to use wheels.' The analogy should rather be directed at the level of *information*: 'The electrical circuits which are used in electronic computing machinery seem to have the essential property of nerves. They are able to transmit information from place to place, and also to store it.'[43]

In Babbage's terms, the storing of information still took place in the 'storehouse' of the calculating machine, but for Turing, this now took place in the 'memory' of the computer. First of all, 'memory' appeared as a metaphor, in quotation marks, but later on in his article, the quotation marks disappeared.

Psychology and the computer

Turing's reflections on 'intelligent machines' evoke memories of the 'psychic machines' envisioned by the neo-behaviourist Hull in the 1920s. In fact Turing's thinking is so exactly an extension of that of Hull and like-minded researchers that it would have been perfectly natural for the computer to become the dominant metaphor of behaviourism. That, as has already been said, did not happen, and this requires further explanation.

In many respects Turing was a latter-day Hull (or Hull an early Turing). Both used a behaviourist definition of 'thinking'. The Turing test, proposed in 1950, was based on the idea that if the reactions of a machine in an interview cannot be distinguished from those of a human being, then we have to conclude that the machine 'thinks'.[44] This operational definition of thought based on external reactions fitted into the behaviourist tradition. Turing and Hull also had the same ideas on the relationship between explanation and simulation. Hull maintained the principle that theoretical explanations for behaviour must be converted into mechanical models, and saw in this principle the best guarantee against speculative 'mentalistic' theories; Turing regarded his 'intelligent machines' as a contribution to an exact, anti-mentalistic psychology. A third point of agreement was that both saw the human nervous system and particularly the brain as the link between machine and psychology. Hull felt certain that an exact mechanical copy of the nervous system would produce 'a truly psychic machine'; Turing saw the brain as an organic computer.

But besides agreements there were also differences, and it is those differences that may explain why artificial intelligence did not become the natural successor to behaviourism by other means. In the first place the computer was originally a 'logical' machine. The tradition from which the computer emerged and in which the projects of Leibniz, Babbage and Turing were stages, was dominated by mathematics and mathematical logic, by the formalisation of reasoning. As a result, the computer was associated almost automatically with thought-processes, such as playing chess or proving theorems. These higher psychological processes fell outside the theoretical scope of behaviourism.

A second difference is the level on which Hull and Turing – and by extension behaviourism and artificial intelligence – placed the analogy between brain and machine. For Hull, the mechanical models were analogous to the human nervous system, since external reactions to stimuli showed an identical pattern in both systems; model and organism displayed the same *behaviour*. For Turing, the brain was a machine because the brain was a special Turing machine, a system whose *logical* properties corresponded with those of a computer. The similarity in reactions, for Hull the essence of his 'psychic machines', was for Turing a derivative. It was not coincidental that the latter emphasised the capacity of computers to process and store information. The introduction of the computer metaphor into psychology was mainly due to the usefulness of this notion. And the specific orientation in psychology which was to benefit from this was not behaviourism, but cognitive psychology.

The elementary perceiver and memoriser

In accounts of the rise of cognitive psychology it has been recorded that many theoreticians received their intellectual nourishment from behaviourism and operationalism, and that towards the end of the 1950s they allowed their personal orientation to veer towards a psychology of the higher functions. In the theories explaining these functions the notion of 'information processing' was the central element.[45] According to the AI theoreticians Newell and Simon, psychology between William James and the Second World War had been dominated by 'behaviourism, the nonsense syllable and the rat'.[46] Most theories of memory dealt with 'learning', conceived as the acquisition of discriminating responses. There was little interest among behaviourists in higher memory processes. This was less true in English and continental European memory psychology, but there too much research was focused on learning processes and the functional relationships between stimuli and responses. The move towards more cognitively orientated theories of memory was stimulated by the possibility of imitating memory processes with a computer programme and comparing the effects with the results obtained from psychological experiments.

An early and instructive example of a simulation programme for memory processes is the Elementary Perceiver And Memoriser (EPAM) of Feigenbaum.[47] In the title of Feigenbaum's article, 'The simulation of verbal learning behavior', one hears an echo of behaviouristic learning theories of memory, but the content had a clear cognitive slant; the aim was to present an 'information processing model of elementary human symbolic learning processes'. EPAM was presented as a *psychological* model, without neurological or physiological specifications; the brain was described in general terms as an 'information processor' with 'internal programs for testing, comparing, analysing, rearranging and storing information'. The basic unit, the 'information symbol', was a pattern of bits, corresponding to the representation in the brain of data from the outside world.

The process under examination was the learning by heart of pairs of nonsense syllables. In a simple variant the test subject had to learn the association between a stimulus syllable and a response syllable. Some stable and reproducible phenomena which occur in this type of learning are (a) that clear mistakes are less frequent than the absence of a response; (b) the learning of a second list makes the reproduction of the first list more difficult (retroactive inhibition); (c) correctly reproduced associations are sometimes forgotten but in later trials are nevertheless correctly reproduced (oscillation).

In his simulation programme Feigenbaum tried to reduce the distinguishing, retention and association of syllables to more elementary information-processing processes. After the presentation of a stimulus syllable a perceptual sub-system of EPAM coded the information as an internal syllable which described the separate letters in terms of geometrical properties. For example, the D was given the description 'vertical line/closed loop'. The descriptions stored in the memory were minimal, that is, they were sufficient to distinguish the new syllable from syllables already stored. With each stimulus

syllable a cue or indication was stored which consisted of a minimal description of the associated syllable. The incorrect associations which resulted from
this, for example, because 'vertical line/closed loop' also fits the P, were cor-
rected by expanding the information in the description. As a result of these successive corrections EPAM eventually learned the list perfectly.

EPAM was run on the RAND 7090 and revealed several features which can also
be observed in the learning of nonsense syllables by human test subjects.
During the learning phase the minimal nature of the descriptions (fitting two
or three symbols) occasionally cause incorrect associations. In later trials the
correct syllable *is* reproduced (oscillation). Once the list is stable and has been
learned perfectly, the addition of new material may cause a description previously sufficient for a correct association to yield an incorrect syllable (retroactive inhibition).

Feigenbaum sees EPAM as having two important merits. The first is that some
'behaviours' of the programme can be reduced to elementary processes,
without having been deliberately programmed as such. For example, according
to the theory specified in EPAM, oscillation and retroactive inhibition are the
non-programmed consequences of minimal coding and retrieval specifications.
The second merit is that EPAM suggests an alternative hypothesis for forgetting.
The usual explanations pre-suppose that the memory trace weakens with the
passage of time and disappears, either because of physiological erosion, or by
'the over-writing of old information by new information, as in a computer
memory'.[48] EPAM on the other hand 'forgets' because associations are lost in the
constantly expanding network and become inaccessible for retrieval instructions. Unlike forgetting as a result of decay or 'over-writing' this kind of forgetting is temporary: by changes in the retrieval indications some associations can
nevertheless be reproduced. Hence EPAM explains the apparent paradox of how
forgetting can occur when no information is lost.

The EPAM programme contained precisely the three elements which were to
become the core of later memory simulations. In the first place, the notion of
information was used without any reference to neuro-physiological conditions.
The physical substratum of information-processing played no role at all in the
simulation. In the second place, the manipulations with the information were
represented as transformations of 'symbolic representations'. Analysis,
comparison, testing, storage, reproduction and all other processes between
input and output were carried out on patterns of 'information symbols'. And in
the third place, familiar memory processes (such as retroactive inhibition and
association) were linked with the operations of the programme. Most interest
was taken in 'behaviour' that had not been programmed as such and hence
could be explained as the result of the interaction of processes which had been
programmed.

The approach of which EPAM was the prototype, had the effect of directing
the interest of psychologists towards the role of cognitive strategies, hence dis-

tancing themselves from traditional behaviouristic methods and theories. A characteristic example is the chapter that Miller, Galanter and Pribram devote to memory in their *Plans and the Structure of Behaviour*.[49] They mention in the introduction that they are indebted to the AI projects with which they became acquainted in 1958 ('Newell, Shaw and Simon inspired us by their successes') and in their book apply 'cybernetic ideas to psychology'. Their essay on memory is subsequently devoted to the 'symbolic processes' in the head of the person trying to imprint something on his memory. In their view memory processes are a collection of 'plans', cognitive strategies which are ordered into hierarchies like the routines and sub-routines in a computer programme. The authors contrast this emphasis on the share of mental processes with the sterility of behaviourism, which 'tended to prevent psychologists from speculating about symbolic processes inside the memoriser'.[50]

Statements like these set the tone for the work inspired by the computer metaphor. The fact that the neo-behaviourist Hull had once proclaimed the simulation of thought-processes as a guiding ideal for psychological theory had been relegated to a dark corner of the scientific community's collective memory. It is an ironic twist in the history of psychology that simulations, which for behaviourists were an antidote to mentalism, then became a stimulus for setting up hypotheses about mental processes *underlying* behaviour in the hands of the cognitivists. Thanks to the computer, terms like mind and consciousness returned to the vocabulary of the psychologist.

The computer metaphor

In memory psychology the computer has from the very beginning been more than a simple metaphor. The computer has not only provided specific metaphors like 'over-writing' or 'back-up memory', but is at the same time the background against which such metaphors take on meaning. In the terms of Martin and Harré one can say that the computer represents an extensive 'semantic field', a network of very diverse associations which can be activated by linking them via metaphors with the semantic field of the memory.[51] The heuristic yield of this connection is both philosophical and theoretical.

The computer metaphor has been presented as the solution to two ancient philosophical conundrums linked with the names of Descartes and Hume. The first concerns the relationship between body and mind. Estes writes that the memory can be described on two levels.[52] One level is that of the *physical* processes which are set in motion when a stimulus is presented, processed and stored. This level of the neuronal substratum of memory corresponds to the processes and structures which in the case of a computer are denoted as the 'hardware', the courses of electrical impulses through chips, the magnetising and de-magnetising of molecules, etc. The second level is that of the *psychological* processes involved in the processing of the stimulus, the selection, comparison and reproduction of the information presented. These processes can be regarded as 'computations on symbolical representations'[53] and correspond to the operations of the 'software', such as 'read-in', 'matching' and 'read-out'. This division into two levels of description for memory is in fact a special instance of the thesis defended by Boden and others that mind and brain have a similar relationship to the one between programme and machine. According to Boden, this new perspective on the relationship between body and mind has 'largely solved the old metaphysical problem of Descartes'.[54]

The second philosophical question for which the computer metaphor is said to have provided a solution was christened by Dennett 'Hume's problem' and regards to the status of representations.[55] The representations which Hume used in his theory of knowledge were 'impressions' and 'ideas' and he wisely omitted to postulate alongside these representations a separate 'self'. Such a self would involve a circularity, because the manipulation of representations is a task which itself in turn presupposes representations and so sets in motion a hopeless infinite regression. The consequence was that Hume was now forced to make the representations 'think for themselves', without a supervising agent. He found the solution in the laws of association, the mechanisms through which (in the formulation of Dennett) 'each succeeding idea in the stream of consciousness dragged its successor onto the stage'.[56] But such associations are today no longer seen as a sufficient explanation and this confronts philosophers and psychologists with the dilemma of how one can include representations in theories without being sucked into a regression. This dilemma remained unsolved, writes Dennett, 'until AI and the notion of data-structures came along'. Data-structures are in his view 'if not living, breathing examples, at least clanking, functioning examples of representations that can be said in the requisite sense to understand themselves'.[57]

If a programmer wants to make the computer execute a particular task, for example, play chess, he will try to divide the operation into sub-systems each of which is assigned a component task. Those component tasks can in turn be divided up into simpler tasks, which require proportionately less intelligence for their execution. In an analogous way one can imagine the human mind as a hierarchy of functions which like the routines and sub-routines in a programme are equipped with intelligence in varying degrees. The lowest level of functions Dennett calls an 'army of idiots'.[58] Embodied in simple on/off structures of neurons, which may or may not be firing, this army of simple souls is supposed to have broken the fatal circularity: the whole plays chess, thinks and judges thanks to the activities of structures which themselves presuppose no intelligence. Dennett speaks of homunculi who are gradually further and further unburdened because they delegate their work to less intelligent homunculi.[59]

According to Baars, the notion of representation had fallen into discredit during the reign of the behaviourists because of the threat of circularity. Skinner's image of an 'inner man' who duplicates everything that precisely needs to be explained, depicted in popular drawings of the operation of the brain as the little man in the control room who assesses all incoming information and gives instructions for reactions, was at first sight a convincing *reductio ad absurdum* and discouraged the introduction of representations into psychological theories. Through the advent of the computer this argument is in Baars's view no longer valid: 'The business of representing some part of the world in a computer code has in many instances become so trivial that the homonculus theory has itself become absurd.'[60]

At this philosophical level, the suggested solution to the mind–body problem and the rehabilitation of representations, the computer has had unmistakable heuristic value for psychology in general, and by implication, for psychology of memory. The cognitive revolution has given an enormous boost to memory theory and that raises the question of whether the computer metaphor has also had a heuristic value in specific theoretical terms.

The computer metaphor suggests that in the human memory (an instrument formed by evolution), there should be a programme, the description of which, however, has not been supplied by the *Divine Hacker.* The task of cognitive psychology is to make good for this deficiency. In order to retrieve the architecture of our own memory programme we can seek the assistance of the programmes and systems that we ourselves have devised for storing, manipulating and reproducing data. Computer programmes simulating memory processes can in this view function as theories. 'Within ten years most theories in psychology will take the form of computer programs', predicted Herbert Simon in 1957.[61] Inspection of memory theories ten, fifteen or twenty years later teaches us that this prophecy has not been fulfilled. Reports of memory research in specialist journals have predominantly kept to the traditional fixed format of introduction, experiment, results, discussion, and except within the rather separate circuit of AI theoreticians, the mass of memory psychologists have not stated their theories as simulation programmes. When that did happen, rival theories like that of the analogous or propositional nature of 'mental images', both turned out to be capable of producing convincing simulations, so that no decisive arguments in favour of one or the other could be derived from them. In general, the simulation has remained stuck at the phase of solemn proclamations.

It has become clear that the influence of the computer metaphor asserts itself mainly at the level of theoretical *terms*. Within the metaphor for man-as-an-information-processing-system there emerged in the 1960s an exchange between the vocabularies for the human memory and that of computers. Terms like 'input', 'read-in', 'encoding', 'back-up memory', 'working memory', 'storage', 'address', 'matching', 'over-writing', 'search', 'retrieval', 'read-out' and 'output' acquired a place in a common vocabulary. In psychological theories they referred to hypothetical processes in memory, and in AI theories to mechanisms and structures for information storage in computers. This shared psychological and technical meaning was acquired in an exchange which in general was balanced: over and against the technical influence on psychological jargon, there is at least an equally strong influence of psychology on computer jargon. A term like 'retrieval' was taken by computer science from memory psychology. Terms like 'address' and 'encoding' found their way into psychology from AI. The same applies for the distinction of concepts which emerged in the context of AI – such as that between location-addressable and content-addressable – and had not occurred previously in psychology.[62] In some cases theoretical terms even went back and forth. For example the term 'back-up memory' was derived from computers and was included in memory theories to indicate the temporary storage of information. Conversely the 'memory' in 'back-up memory' derived from psychology, so that psychology had a term which it had lent out, returned to it.

A theoretical renewal often ascribed to the influence of the computer metaphor, is attention to the organisation which memory imposes on the material presented. In the transition from sensory registration to permanent storage the material undergoes transformations which correspond to the coding of input in computers. In previous metaphors, such as photography and the phonograph, writes Estes, people did take into account selective attention, but assumed that the material was stored in the form of unalterable traces (engrams). What is stored in the orientation of the computer metaphor 'are not replicas of experiences, but rather representations encoded in terms of features, that is of values and attributes on various dimensions'.[63] These 'features' are processes which filter and encode the incoming information (again metaphors!) and hence make registrations into representations.

Loftus was also inspired by the metaphor of the computer.[64] In the chapter 'Computerising memory' she projects as many processes and structures as possible from computer memory onto the human memory, in an attempt to present the laws of memory and forgetting in a graphic way. Like Estes she regards the computer as the most adequate metaphor for the flexibility of the memory ('The best and the most sophisticated model of memory's malleable nature.')[65] In a long list of parallels she compares the 'core', a structure where a relatively small quantity of data is available for immediate processing, to the sensory registers, the 'virtual core' to short-term memory, the database on the magnetic disk to long-term memory, the back-ups to the redundant information in memory, the file-structure and the index to the organisational principles of long-term memory, electrically coded information to temporary storage in the working memory, chemical coding with the final storage in long-term memory, the replacement of old files by new versions with the modification of memories, and so on.

Reviewing the literature on memory as a sub-section of an information-processing system, one can observe that the metaphor of the computer has had two functions. In the first place, the computer gave memory psychology a general scheme within which hypothetical processes were assigned a place. The computer provided a skeleton, a 'format' for theory, which invited supplementation. In the second place, the computer metaphor functioned as a supplier of a new series of terms and comparisons, it introduced 'computer-speak' into memory psychology. It gave researchers of various denominations a *lingua franca* with the connotations of exactness and precision, an impression which was further strengthened by the habit borrowed from AI of schematising the processing structures of memory in flow charts.

Both functions have contributed to a general shared orientation in the community of memory researchers. Diverse disciplines and specialisms saw their results included in a common theoretical construction, expressed in a language which showed a certain homogeneity. However, this ecumenical effect should not be overstated. The computer metaphor has also been accused of being too elastic, as if it could accommodate every conceivable finding after 'minor tuning'.[66] Moreover, the computer metaphor admitted many controversies at the level of concrete processes and structures. An example of this is the controversy about the 'sketchpad', the metaphor used by Baddeley for the memory process which enables us to process visual–spatial information.[67] This controversy focused on the question of whether the representations in the 'sketchpad' were predominantly spatial or visual in nature, and led to a series of experiments, including some with blind test subjects, in which an attempt was made to divide the two factors and determine their relative share. The course and results of the debate are not of importance here, but illustrate the fact that within the computer metaphor (the 'sketchpad' is a component of the working memory[68]) more specific controversies can be pointed to (sometimes with their own metaphors), which have only an indirect relationship with the computer.

The low productivity of the computer metaphor as a source of testable hypotheses on specific memory processes, illustrates that the rise in theory-building must be ascribed to other factors. Like cognitive psychology in general, memory psychology appears to have profited mainly from what Baars called 'persuasion by respectable experiment'.[69] From the 1960s onwards, when the interest in higher cognitive processes had recovered from the hegemony of behaviourism, technical and methodological finesse in experimenting quickly increased. The measuring of reaction times and the presentation of stimuli both underwent considerable refinement. Unlike the older 'mental chronometry' the reaction time was used more and more as an indicator of the *nature* (instead of *duration*) of mental processes. Large parts of the theory of memory seem to have profited mainly from methodological and technical ingenuity, such as the hypotheses on sensory registers and the retrieval processes in the short-term memory, the rotation experiments with mental images, and the structure of semantic memory. Estes speaks of 'a confluence of metaphors and methods'.[70] It would, in brief, be misleading to take the computer metaphor as the only, or even the main causal factor in the flourishing of theory in memory psychology.

The computational paradox

Computational principles preceded the computer. That one could conceive of a calculator as an apparatus that processes symbols and that mathematical processes could be described in a logical language with two truth values, are insights which were articulated over a hundred years before the first computers. The essence of the computer as a metaphor for the human mind had already been expressed in the Analytical Engine of Babbage and described by Lady Lovelace. Why then did the cognitive revolution not get underway until the first computers made their entrance? The computational *theory* gained influence only after the development of the *machine*. Why that reversal of the historical order? Or to ask the same question differently: what did the machine offer that theory could not?

The answer is: a demonstration. It is one thing to derive theoretically that following a series of algorithms produces proof of a mathematical proposition, to see a machine *do* this is something of a completely different order. The fact that, by working through a formal programme without human intervention, machines executed tasks previously associated with thought and creativity, had a psychological effect that the computational principles themselves could never achieve.[71] In this respect the first computers were much like the androids, the writing and piano-playing automatons from the eighteenth century: their amazing operations awakened people's curiosity about the theoretical principles which were able to achieve this.

In the 1950s and 1960s the operations of computers were mainly connected with logical–rational tasks. The first successes were achieved in domains like proof theory and chess. Consequently it was almost axiomatic that the 'higher' psychological processes like reasoning and problem solving should be the first to come under the influence of the computer metaphor. The simulations of thought-processes – such as the programmes of Newell and Simon – seemed a point of Archimedes, a place where natural scientific methods could find a hold in their application to the human mind.

In the 1970s the initial enthusiasm for the computer as a psychological metaphor and simulation as a scientific tool gradually gave way to realism. The flood of computer simulations in the early days of AI and cognitive science had an unintended result, quite opposite to that expected. It was established that psychological processes, even the 'higher ones', have a much less rectilinear and rational course than was presupposed in the simulations. Thinking and reasoning turned out to be mosaic-like processes, in which intuitions and suppositions played equal parts as logical deductions and statistically sound deductions. Gardner called this result the 'computational paradox': the intensive attempts to simulate mental processes emphasised the differences rather than the similarities.[72]

This paradox applies in its full extent to memory. The memory of the computer is too good. Its infallibility is its principal short-coming. Human memory is an instrument which, if the need arises, lies and deceives. It distorts, sifts and deforms, takes better care of some things than others. Unlike the computer memory it disobeys commands. It does not bother about instructions to keep one thing and throw something else away, it behaves like the disobedient dog that Cees Nooteboom called it. Whereas circuits in a classical computer are under a central operating system which gives its commands step by step, the human brain seems to be acted upon by scores of impulses at once. Odours, emotions, movements, sounds, perceptions: the memory is a vibrating network of synchronous associations rather than a linear tract of stimulus–storage–reproduction. The computer plays its melodies one key at a time, albeit incomprehensibly fast; the human memory strikes whole chords.

The consequences of the computational paradox have been most clearly highlighted in theories of visual memory. Until the 1980s attempts to construct computer memories in such a way that they 'recognise' images, ended mainly in a series of failures. Computers with a traditional Von Neumann architecture, serial and digital, stored images by converting patterns of light intensity into a digital code. This method of storage required so much memory space that the manipulation of images was an extremely time-consuming process: the comparison of presented images with stored images took so much time to calculate that any resemblance with natural recognition was lost. On the whole, it would be considered quite impolite, if you only recognised someone's face after half an hour in conversation. Moreover, the processing and reproduction of images by computers requires a degree of precision which is absent in human memory. We recognise our son Marius's face even if he holds it cocked to one side or returns badly sunburnt from a sailing trip on the Frisian lakes. In such cases our memory produces the best possible *match*. This capacity for improvisation was lacking in the computers available in the 1970s. When just at that time a new metaphor presented itself, a technique which was able to process large quantities of optical information quickly and efficiently, many memory psychologists looked up from their terminals: their curiosity was aroused.

Notes

1   H. Gardner, *The Mind's New Science. A History of the Cognitive Revolution*, New York, 1985.

2   D. Gentner and J. Grudin, 'The evolution of mental metaphors in psychology: a 90-year perspective', *American Psychologist*, 40 (1985), 181–92.

3   L. D. Smith, 'Metaphors of knowledge and behavior in the behaviorist tradition', in D. E. Leary (ed.), *Metaphors in the History of Psychology*, Cambridge, MA, pp. 239–66.

4   E. C. Tolman, quoted in Smith, 'Metaphors', p. 244.

5   E. C. Tolman, 'Cognitive maps in rats and men,' *Psychological Review*, 55 (1948), 189–208.

6   Smith, 'Metaphors', p. 246.

7   E. C. Tolman, *Purposive Behavior in Animals and Men*, New York, 1932, p. 424.

8   Tolman, 'Cognitive maps', 208.

9   M. Gardner, *Logic Machines, Diagrams and Boolean Algebra*, New York, 1958.

10   Quoted in Smith, 'Metaphors', p. 249.

11   *Ibid.*, p. 250.

12   For a prototype of such an analogy, see C. L. Hull and H. D. Baernstein, 'A mechanical parallel to the conditioned reflex', *Science*, 70 (1929), 14–15.

13   H. D. Baernstein and C. L. Hull, 'a mechanical model of the conditioned reflex', *Journal of General Psychology*, 5 (1931), 99–106 (106).

14   R. G. Krueger and C. L. Hull, 'An electro-chemical parallel to the conditioned reflex', *Journal of General Psychology*, 5 (1931), 262–9 (267).

15   *Ibid.*, 268.

16   C. L. Hull, 'Simple trial-and-error learning: a study in psychological theory', *Psychological Review*, 73 (1930), 241–56.

17   Smith, 'Metaphors', p. 254.

18   M. Meyer, 'The comparative value of various conceptions of nervous function based on mechanical analogies', *American Journal of Psychology*, 24 (1913), 555–63.

19   See for example J. M. Stephens, 'A mechanical explanation of the law of effect', *American Journal of Psychology*, 41 (1929), 422–31; A. Walton, 'Conditioning illustrated by an automatic mechanical device', *American Journal of Psychology*, 42 (1930), 110–11; H. Bradner, 'A new "mechanical learner"', *Journal of General Psychology*, 17 (1937), 414–19.

20   V. Pratt, *Thinking Machines. The Evolution of Artificial Intelligence*, Oxford, 1987.

21   S. Augarten, *Bit by Bit. An Illustrated History of Computers*, London, 1985, p. 15.

22   Pratt, *Thinking Machines*, p. 79.

23   J. Wilkins, *Essay towards a Real Character and a Philosophical Language*, London, 1668. Wilkins's efforts have been discussed by L. J. Cohen, 'On the project of a universal character', *Mind*, 63 (1954), 49–63.

24   M. M. Slaughter, *Universal Languages and Scientific Taxonomy in the Seventeenth Century*, Cambridge, 1982.

25   M. Hesse, 'Hooke's philosophical algebra', *Isis*, 57 (1966), 1, 67–83.

26   J. Wilkins, *Mercury: Or the Secret and Swift Messenger*, London, 1641.

27   Lovelace's article is included in P. and E. Morrison (eds.), *Charles Babbage and his Calculating Engines*, New York, 1961. See also the chapter on the Analytical Engine in Babbage's *Passages from the Life of a Philosopher* (edited with a new introduction by M. Campbell-Kelly), London, 1994, pp. 85–106.

28   D. D. Swade, 'Redeeming Charles Babbage's mechanical computer,' *Scientific American*, February (1993), 62–7.

29   Quoted in Morrison and Morrison, *Charles Babbage*, p. 252.

30   *Ibid.*, p. 249.

31   G. Boole, *An Investigation of the Laws of Thought*, London, 1854.

32   W. S. Jevons, *The Principles of Science*, London, 1874.

33   The 'logical piano' has been discussed by J. C. Kassler, 'Man – a musical instrument: models of the brain and mental functioning before the computer', *History of Science*, 22 (1984), 59–92.

34   A. M. Turing, 'On computable numbers, with an application to the *Entscheidungsproblem*', *Proceedings of the London Mathematical Society*, 42 (1937), Series 2, 230–65.

35   F. H. Hinsley and A. Stripp (eds.), *Codebreakers, the Inside Story of Bletchley Park*, Oxford, 1993.

36   A. Hodges, *Alan Turing. The Enigma of Intelligence*, London, 1983.

37   B. Randell, *The Origin of Digital Computers: Selected Papers*, New York, Berlin, 1973.

38   Augarten, *Bit*, p. 128. The programmer did not type in instructions, but tugged on cables and plugs, moving hundreds of switches for each new task.

39   *Ibid.*, p. 130.

40   W. McCulloch and W. Pitts, 'A logical calculus of the ideas immanent in nervous activity', *Bulletin of Mathematical Biophysics*, 5 (1943), 115–33.

41   C. E. Shannon, 'A symbolic analysis of relay and switching circuits', *Transactions of the American Institute of Electric Engineers*, 57 (1938), 1–11.

42   A. M. Turing, 'Computing machinery and intelligence', *Mind*, 59 (1950), 433–60; the preliminary study 'Intelligent machinery' was later published in B. Meltzer and D. Mitchie (eds.), *Machine Intelligence*, vol. 5, Edinburgh, 1969, 3–23.

43   Turing, 'Intelligent machinery', 13.

44   Turing, 'Computing machinery'; in his previous article (see note 42) Turing gave a much more modest version of what was later to become known as the Turing test: someone plays chess either against a chess machine or against a human chess player. If he is unable to decide from the counter-moves whether he is playing against a human being or a machine, then it is reasonable, Turing believes, to attribute 'intelligence' to the machine. He added that he had once actually carried out this experiment.

45   See for example B. J. Baars, *The Cognitive Revolution in Psychology*, New York, 1986; Gardner, *Mind's New Science*.

46   A. Newell and H. A. Simon, *Human Problem Solving*, Englewood Cliffs, 1972, p. 874.

47   E. A. Feigenbaum, 'The simulation of verbal learning behavior', *Proceedings of the Western Joint Computer Conference*, 19 (1961), 121–32.

48   Note how the writing metaphor reappears in a new technical form (see also chapter 2).

49   G. A. Miller, E. Galanter and K. Pribram, *Plans and the Structure of Behaviour*, New York, 1960.

50   *Ibid.*, p. 126.

51   J. Martin and R. Harré, 'Metaphor in science', in D. C. Miall (ed.), *Metaphor: Problems and Perspectives*, Sussex, 1982, pp. 89–105.

52   W. K. Estes, 'The information-processing approach to cognition: a confluence of metaphors and methods', in W. K. Estes (ed.), *Handbook of Learning and Cognitive Processes*, vol. 5, Hillsdale, NJ, 1978, pp. 1–18.

53   Z. W. Pylyshyn, *Computation and Cognition*, Cambridge, MA, 1984.

54   M. A. Boden, *Artificial Intelligence and Natural Man*, New York, 1977, p. 4.

55   D. C. Dennett, *Brainstorms. Philosophical Essays on Mind and Psychology*, Hassocks, 1978.

56   *Ibid.*, p. 122.

57   *Ibid.*, p. 123.

58   *Ibid.*, p. 124.

59   This suggestion for solving the homunculus questions will be discussed in chapter 9; the same applies to Boden's thesis that the computer metaphor has brought the mind–body problem closer to a solution.

60   Baars, *Cognitive Revolution*, p. 149.

61   Quoted in H. Dreyfus and J. Haugeland, 'The computer as a mistaken model of the mind', in S. C. Brown (ed.), *Philosophy of Psychology*, London, 1974, pp. 247–79.

62   In most computer memories material is stored at an 'address'. Reproduction is possible only through locating the address via an index. Opposed to these location-addressable memories are content-addressable memories, from which material can be retrieved by a direct match between the pattern presented and the pattern stored. (See also chapters 7 and 8.)

63   Estes, 'Confluence', p. 8.

64   E. F. Loftus, *Memory*, Reading, MA, 1980.

65   *Ibid.*, p. 171.

66   M. J. Watkins, 'Human memory and the information-processing metaphor', *Cognition*, 10 (1981), 331–6.

67   A. D. Baddeley, *Human Memory. Theory and Practice*, Hillsdale, NJ, 1990.

68   *Ibid.*, p. 113.

69   Baars, *Cognitive Revolution*, p. 157.

70   Estes, 'Confluence', p. 1.

71   When asked whether he could have developed his computational theory of the human mind if no computers had existed, Marvin Minsky replied, 'In theory, yes. But no one would have believed me.' (Personal communication, 21 October 1989.)

72   Gardner, *Mind's New Science*, pp. 384–8.

7   The holographic memory

On first acquaintance a hologram has a disconcerting effect. From a distance
you see a greyish-looking picture hanging up against the wall. Coming closer,
you suddenly see depth behind the surface. With a good hologram you tend to
want to look behind the picture: it is as though you are looking into an illuminated alcove and seeing the image floating in it. This image can be observed
from various points of view: as your visual angle changes you see the perspective in the image change, as though there were a three-dimensional object
actually floating there. Holography has, almost literally, added a new dimen-
sion to photography. The stereoscope also gives an illusion of depth, but that is
created by the difference in perspective between two ordinary photos and the
effect of depth occurs only when those photographs are viewed from a specific
distance. If one's focus changes, foreground and background move along with
it: one cannot view the illustration from various angles and at the same time
see depth. In the case of holograms one can. Observing the visitors to a hologram exhibition, one can see that the effect is literally jaw-dropping: people
gape at holograms in the same way as they must have looked at the first photographs in the nineteenth century. Because of the 'impossible' impression of
three dimensions in a flat plane, a hologram resembles a window into an astral
reality, constructed of light instead of matter. The effect is magical and enchanting.

Photographing with laser light
In 1948, the British physicist Dennis Gabor published an article in *Nature* on a
method of increasing the resolution of photographs taken with an electron
microscope.[1] He demonstrated that the image of an object can be reconstructed
from the interference pattern of two beams of light. The behaviour of light can
be described by using a model of wave movements – the effects of interference
between light waves are in many respects identical to those between waves in
water. When two waves with the same wavelength converge, the wave movements will either reinforce or neutralise each other, depending on the

44.   Enlarged photograph of the interference pattern on a holographic plate.

combination of peak–peak, trough–trough or peak–trough. From this pattern of interference the original pattern of the separate wave movements can be derived. A frequently used analogy is that of a pond into which a handful of pebbles have been thrown: if a moment later the surface were frozen from one instant to the next, one could calculate the structure of the whole surface from part of that surface (figure 44).

Gabor made use of this effect by causing interference between two light beams. These are the reference beam, the light conducted straight to the film, and the object beam, the light reflected by the object to be photographed. In ordinary photography a one-to-one representation of the distribution of light reflected by the photographed object appears on the photographic plate; in holography the information is distributed over the film in the form of an inter-ference pattern (figure 45). Gabor called this kind of film a *hologram*, from the Greek 'holos', whole: the pattern stored contains all the information necessary for the reconstruction of the whole image. In 1971 he was awarded the Nobel Prize for his discovery.

Producing a good reference beam requires a source which emits light that is monochromatic (of one particular wavelength) and coherent (uninterrupted trains of the same wavelength). In his first experiment Gabor himself made do with a high-pressure mercury lamp which sent its light through an aperture measuring ³⁄₁₀₀₀mm (figure 46). Only small, unfocused holograms could be pro-duced in this way. It was not until the invention of the laser in 1960 and the improvements in technology introduced by the physicists Leith and Upatnieks in 1963, that it became possible to produce a powerful reference beam. The first convincing holograms, with clear, three-dimensional images made their appearance in 1964. The simplest method of constructing a hologram (see figure 47) uses a laser beam which is split in two by a diffractor: one beam goes

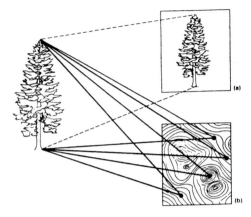

45.   Drawing showing the difference between a photograph (a) and a hologram
       (b). On a photograph, each point of the object is represented by a specific
       point in the image. On a holographic plate, each point of the object is repre-
       sented in various locations.

directly to the plate and a second beam reaches the plate via the object to be
recorded.

Nowadays there are countless ways of making holograms. Not all the
methods are of importance here: theory of memory was linked mainly with the
holographic techniques of the 1960s and 1970s. Holograms from that period
have the following qualities in common: (1) Because of its distributed storage
the holographic plate is relatively insensitive to damage. Using a part of the
hologram, the whole image can be reconstructed, although the sharpness of
detail and variation in points of view decreases with the size of the plate. (2) An
extraordinary amount of information can be stored in a hologram. By using
different reference beams, thousands of images can be stored on a single plate
which reappear when illuminated with their 'own' reference beam. Relatively
little 'white noise' occurs (information theory originates from the science of
sound (acoustics)).

Specific variants of holography possess the following additional properties:
(3) If two objects are photographed simultaneously either of the two object
beams can function as the reference beam for the other. In this case illumination with one object evokes a 'ghost image': a slightly vaguer and more transparent image of the other object. (4) If one object is a particular word, for
example AUTOMAT, and the other object is a bright spot of light, illumination
with AUTOMAT results in a spot of light.[2] Illumination with a page of text then
produces spots of light in corresponding positions for each occurrence of the
word AUTOMAT. Holograms provoked the same mixture of astonishment and
awe which Boyle reported in 1677 when he saw the word DOMINI glowing in the
dark.

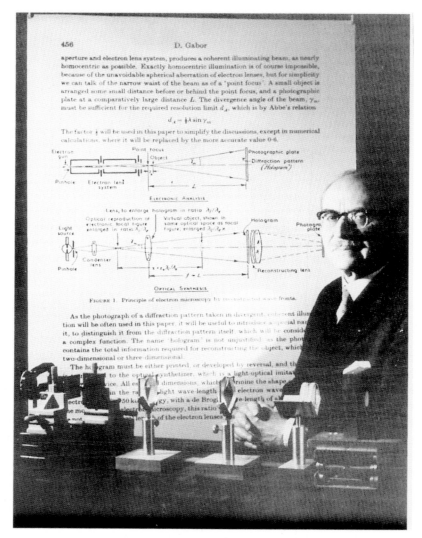

46.   Photograph of the physicist Dennis Gabor, the inventor of holography, in front of an enlarged page from one of his first publications on holography. In the foreground is the experimental apparatus described on that page.

The hologram as a metaphor

In 1963 the Dutch physicist Van Heerden did what Hooke and Draper had done in 1682 and 1856 respectively: he presented the most recent technology for the manipulation and registration of light stimuli as an analogy for the operation of human memory. After phosphorescence and photography, holography now became a metaphor for visual memory.

Pieter Jacobus Van Heerden gained his doctorate in 1945 on a topic in nuclear

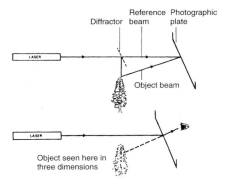

47.   Diagram showing the making of a hologram (above). Light reflected from an
object interferes with light conducted straight to the plate (the reference
beam). The interference pattern is recorded. Diagram showing the reconstruction of a hologram (below). When the developed plate is illuminated
with the reference beam a three-dimensional image appears where the
object originally stood.

physics.[3] Through the agency of the physicist Nico Bloembergen, the later Nobel
Prize winner, Van Heerden was invited to the Harvard Physics Department.[4] He
stayed there for five years and left in 1953 to take up a research post with
General Electric. In 1962 he joined Polaroid Research Laboratories in
Cambridge. Van Heerden did research for Polaroid into the optical properties of
crystals and remained there until his retirement in 1982.

The years at Harvard were extremely stimulating ones for Van Heerden. He
attended lectures on artificial intelligence and information theory. The papers
given by John Von Neumann, Donald MacKay and Claude Shannon especially
made a deep impression on him. Von Neumann had been involved in the
construction of the ENIAC (see chapter 6). He saw the computer as an 'electronic
brain', an information-processing system which in principle could simulate all
the processes in the human nervous system. The development of this theory
appeared posthumously.[5] MacKay, originally from the UK, had worked on the
development of radar during World War II. Having come to the United States on
a Rockefeller Scholarship in 1951, he published an article in that same year on
'Mind-like behaviour in artefacts'.[6] Finally, Shannon, as an information theorist,
had used the principles of binary logic shortly before the war in his description
of switching networks in the telephone industry (see chapter 6). The influence of
each of these three theorists is discernible in Van Heerden's hologram analogy.

From Von Neumann and MacKay, Van Heerden took the notion that intelligence can be embodied by artificial information-processing systems. The behaviour of these systems could be described in accordance with the binary
principles specified by Shannon. But because of his background in optics, Van
Heerden did not automatically think of the computer as the best analogy. His

research into the storage and reproduction of light stimuli suggested an analogy which up until then, had been left out of accounts of artificial intelligence.

Van Heerden focused the analogy with holography on two properties which make the human memory such an efficient tool, certainly compared with artificial memories: the virtually instantaneous association and the large storage capacity.[7] With holography, Van Heerden showed, one can construct an *associative* memory. Associative memories are of importance in cases where the information cannot be ordered in an index. This happens, for example, in the storage of optical patterns. Van Heerden deduced theoretically that the presentation of a stored pattern automatically evokes a 'ghost image' of the information stored simultaneously with that pattern. No index is required for such a search procedure. Van Heerden went on to point out that his theory on three-dimensional storage applies to every phenomenon in which interference occurs between waves, and as a function of these waves permanent changes occur in the reproductive medium. This consideration opens the possibility of applying holographic principles to the brain. To the extent that electric impulses reproduce themselves in the neuronal networks of the brain and the structure of those networks is changed as a result of those impulses, it could be argued that storage of information in the brain corresponds with the optical storage in a hologram. Van Heerden maintained that his analogy lent support to the hypothesis previously advanced by Beurle that information storage in the brain is based on interactions between waves of brain activity.[8]

The hologram might offer an analogy for the huge storage capacity of the human brain, as well as for association. If in the course of our life, Van Heerden calculated, we were to store one bit per second, the quantity of stored information would correspond approximately to the number of brain cells, $c.$ 10^9. An artificial system equivalent to the human brain would therefore have to process new information – which has to be constantly compared with previously stored information – at a rate of approx. 3×10^{10} binary operations per second. This seemed to rule out the construction of an artificial system as technically unfeasible: 'For all practical applications, it looked like the end of a trail. If that sort of thing was going on in our brain, it was incomprehensible! Certainly, it would not be possible to realise it in machines.'[9] The hologram metaphor, Van Heerden writes with hindsight, provided an unexpected solution to this paradox. Once the parallel with holography had presented itself, 'it gradually became clear to me that optical storage and processing of information can provide a way of accomplishing this "impossible" operation demanded by the theory of intelligence. In fact, it seems quite possible that the operation of the brain is physically quite analogous to optical processing. It becomes even necessary to consider this hypothesis of brain action very seriously, since no other method is known, or likely to exist, which can accomplish these feats.'[10]

Eclipse

The journal in which Van Heerden published his two articles on the hologram, *Applied Optics*, was a prestigious but specialist forum. It lay outside the citation circuits of AI theoreticians and psychologists. Where Van Heerden himself expected an explosion of interest from psychologists, for a long time there was no reaction at all. When almost ten years later the first sporadic references to his pioneering work appeared, it was due to the fact that the hologram analogy had meanwhile been introduced into memory psychology by another author.

The article on the hologram analogy which *did* manage to attract the attention of psychologists appeared in the *Scientific American* in 1969 and was written by Karl Pribram.[11] Pribram was at the time attached as a neurosurgeon to Stanford University School of Medicine, where he was conducting a number of experiments with monkeys. Pribram recorded their brain activity while they were learning a visual recognition task. In his article Pribram pointed to the brain's impressive resistance to damage. In neurological clinics portions of brain tissue are sometimes removed without far-reaching effects on behaviour. An incision in the *corpus callosum*, the connection between the two halves of the brain, has no perceptible effect: only in relatively complicated experimental set-ups, such as split-brain experiments, are there demonstrable differences with intact brains. This points to the existence of substantial spare capacity. This reserve in its turn is supposedly based on information stored in a distributed way in the brain. But how can that scattered information be reconstructed?

'A possible clue to the puzzle', wrote Pribram, 'came from an optical artefact, the hologram, which was then being made for the first time with the help of coherent laser light.' Referring to an article in the *Scientific American* on laser holograms,[12] Pribram presented the hologram as a model for the distributed storage and reproduction of information.[13] He described how the activation spreading through the neuronal structures could produce interference patterns analysable with the same mathematics as those of holographic interference, how holograms are resistant to damage, how the synaptic changes as the result of learning can be regarded as codes, etc. The hologram, in short, was the obvious analogy for a hypothesis which was supported by the knowledge of the neuronal substratum and at the same time could be experimentally tested. Pribram's own experiments had been a beginning.

Looking back, it is not difficult to see why Pribram's article eclipsed the earlier contributions by Van Heerden. First of all, the findings were linked to a longstanding neuro-psychological controversy – the localisation of memory traces – which since the 1920s had prompted an uninterrupted series of experiments. While the analogy of the hologram might be a new element in it, the terms in which Pribram posed the problem were familiar to the psychological community. He referred to concrete behaviour, to learning effects, reactions to lesions, synaptic changes, EEG records, neuronal links, visual projection areas, inhibitions and activations, all of them topics which helped psychologists assimilate the hologram into a pre-existing corpus of knowledge. Whereas Van Heerden had presented the hologram in the context of *information theory* – but found no audience among information theorists – Pribram gave the hologram a *neurological* slant.

In rhetorical respects too Pribram had more to offer to the psychological community than Van Heerden. His article was accompanied by twelve illustrations: schematic drawings of the experiments with monkeys, maps of the brain, drawings of neuronal tracts, etc. The combination of text and illustrations created a public far wider than the specialised field of neuro-psychology. That public was also informed that in the meantime, the hologram analogy had been included in a research programme that had been running for years and was on the point of producing important new insights. Added to the suggestion that the neuro-physiology of memory was now linked to the 'most sophisticated principle of information storage yet known' (Pribram), the article must have created the impression of coming from the cutting edge of science, where experiments are conducted with the most advanced resources and where developments are very rapid.

The brain as a Fourier hologram

Pribram followed up his own article in a way that facilitated the introduction of the hologram analogy into memory psychology. In a short space of time he wrote a long series of articles and chapters, with a large number of co-authors in a wide variety of journals.[14] It was mainly Fourier holography that was important for the analogy with a neuronal network. In this type of holography, a convex lens carries out a Fourier transformation on a pattern of optical stimuli in the input plane. This transformation is also known as convolution. The resulting pattern lies in the transformation plane and is in turn Fourier-transformed by a second convex lens into a pattern in the output plane (correlation). The transformation plane corresponds to the memory: the patterns in this plane 'are the "memories" of the optical system'.[15] Pribram argued that in the brain there are structures which carry out a Fourier transformation on the incoming nerve impulses and hence form the neuronal equivalent of the first lens in holography. The result of this transformation is stored in neuronal structures which correspond with the holographic film. A second Fourier transformation processes this storage into an image at the output level. If the incoming pattern resembles one of the stored patterns, a bright spot appears in the optical system of the hologram. In the brain, recognition will produce a small burst of firing neurons. The artificial system may 'recognise' patterns, for example fingerprints or signatures; according to Pribram, the neuronal system recognises, 'literally'.[16]

The analogy presupposes that more or less permanent changes take place in the brain as a result of incoming stimuli. According to Pribram the sensitivity level of a neuron will change as a function of the net quantity of activation. This neuronal parallel of 'exposure' raises the chances of conduction of a stimulus. This facilitating effect depends on the similarity between the pattern presented and the original patterns that have led to this particular distribution of sensitivity levels. Changes occur in the membranes of the receiving neurons which are consistent with the holographic interpretation of brain processes. For example, it has been established from intracellular measurements of the activity in the neuron of invertebrates that cells which are repeatedly given pairs of input patterns eventually exhibit identical output patterns whenever only one of the two patterns is presented. This can lead to one input imitating the effects of the other input, as if the latter were present. The comparison of the cortex of rats brought up in a deprived or enriched environment indicated that neuronal structures may change as a result of experience: in the case of rats brought up in the enriched environment, a characteristic pattern of thickening in the post-synaptic membranes appears in the course of time in the initially homogeneous brain mass.

In holography there are two phases of 'photography'. The first is that of the recording ('exposure'), the second that of the reconstruction of the image ('illumination'). In Pribram's view the neuronal parallel to this latter form of exposure stems from the association areas in the cortex. He claimed that the required anatomical connections and neuronal functions had already been pinpointed experimentally.[17] In a hologram the reconstructed images are projected into a space *outside* the storage medium; one sees the image in front of or behind the holographic plate. In the neuronal hologram an analogous form of projection takes place – Pribram speaks of 'extrajection' – and this process, he argues, explains how it is possible for us to experience our perceptual or memory images as though they are situated outside our brains. Holography therefore explained 'how a brain process can give rise to an image which is experienced as remote from the representational mechanism and even the receptor surface which is involved in the construction of the image'.[18] In the reconstruction of auditory patterns something comparable occurs, writes Pribram, because with well-adjusted loudspeakers the sound seems to issue from a point halfway between the two speakers. Besides Pribram, Longuet-Higgins, Westlake and Cavanagh have tried to specify neuronal scope for holographic processes.[19]

In search of the engram

Various findings from memory research for which holography offered a suggestive parallel are often adduced in support of the holograph metaphor. The most important of these is the distributed storage of memory traces. Reference is generally made to Lashley's enthusiastic search for the engram.[20] Lashley taught rats the way through a maze, then removed part of their cortex and after they had recovered from the operation again made the animals negotiate the maze. The difficulty which the rat experienced in finding the route was roughly proportional to the *quantity* of cortex removed – a link that is known as the 'law of mass action' – but bore no relation to specific damage *sites*. In 1950, after a long career in the neuro-physiology of remembering, Lashley was forced to admit that he had not succeeded in finding anything like an engram: whatever part of the brain he removed, the rats retained access to what they had learned before the operation. Findings from other extirpation experiments pointed in the same direction. In rats, 80 per cent of the visual cortex may be damaged without this affecting the capacity to react to visual patterns; in cats, 98 per cent of the optical pathways can be severed without serious consequences for perception. Even the *combination* of these two procedures had little effect on 'visual recognition behaviour'.[21] In humans, too, fairly large-scale brain damage can occur which leaves the memory intact. Some lesions cause at most a certain blurring of outlines in the visual field. This resistance to damage is currently known as 'graceful degradation' and is generally considered to be an indication of the distributed storage of memory traces.

However, Lashley was not to have the final word on the localisation of memory traces. In the 1950s the neurosurgeon Penfield developed a new technique for brain research. He allowed his patients to remain conscious during their operation. After a local anaesthetic – the brain itself has no sensation – the cranium was opened and the surface of the brain stimulated with an electrode. Patients were asked to describe their sensations. When Penfield stimulated the hippocampus with his electrode, some of his patients reported unusually detailed memories or 'flashbacks', as if they were reliving some previous experience. An example: 'Oh, a familiar memory – in an office somewhere. I can see the desks. I was there and someone was calling to me – a man leaning on a desk with a pencil in his hand.'[22] Findings like these introduced a problem into neurology. Lashley's results seemed to suggest that memories are stored in a distributed way over the brain and for that reason cannot be removed with a simple excision of the lancet. But Penfield's experiments suggested that memories can be activated by the very fine tip of an electrode and thus must have a specific, very localised neuronal substratum.

The hologram metaphor makes it possible to give a measure of credence to both hypotheses. If the structure of the memory is similar to that of a hologram, then the information can be both global and local. With memory traces distributed over parts of the brain as interference patterns, the stimulation of a fragment can activate the whole image (Penfield), while conversely the removal of a portion of the traces does not affect the ability to reconstruct the whole image (Lashley). According to Rose the neurological community embraced the new metaphor 'with an almost audible sigh of relief'.[23]

A notion closely connected with distributed storage is the compound nature of memory traces. This means that different memory traces might have a common neuronal substratum. On the basis of holographic processes Cavanagh explained that it is possible 'to superimpose many interference patterns on the same group of neurons'.[24] Those overlapping memory traces result in a large storage capacity. The information density in turn makes the problem of efficient access particularly pressing. But for this, too, the hologram metaphor suggests an appropriate mechanism. Van Heerden already indicated that the hologram can be seen as an associative memory, a storage system without a catalogue or an index. The situation is also described – using a pair of concepts borrowed from computer science – in terms of content-addressable (as opposed to location-addressable) memories. In the human memory there are innumerable elements which cannot be assumed to be ordered in an index. The very capacity to recognise or summon up at will thousands of faces, suggests that the visual memory is content-addressable in nature. The analogy with holography in which the presentation of a pattern automatically evokes other patterns, would in that case be more appropriate than that with the location-addressable computer memory. Pribram pointed out that we generally remember more details the more contextual information we have. If we visit a neighbourhood where we once lived, memories surface which seemed to have disappeared forever: 'What better mechanisms can be operating than the associative recall provided by the holographic process?'[25]

Holography has also been associated with the experience when, not quite being able to find a word causes the sensation in one that the 'outline' of the word *is* available. This occurs in the TOT phenomenon: a word is on the tip of your tongue, but just cannot quite be reproduced. In 1890 William James gave a vivid description of the introspective experience evoked by such a semi-present word:

> Suppose we try to recall a forgotten name. The state of our consciousness is peculiar. There is a gap therein; but no mere gap. It is a gap that is intensely active. A sort of wraith of the name is in it, beckoning us in a given direction, making us at moments tingle with the sense of our closeness, and then letting us sink back without the longed-for term. If wrong names are proposed to us, this singularly definite gap acts immediately so as to negate them. They do not fit into its mould and the gap of one word does not feel like the gap of another, all empty of content as both might seem necessarily to be when described as gaps. When I vainly try to recall the name of Spalding, my consciousness is far removed from what it is when I vainly try to recall the name of Bowles.[26]

Research into TOT states – artificially provoked with definitions of unfamiliar words – shows that test subjects are generally capable of providing partial information about the word being sought, such as the number of syllables, the sound or the initial letter.[27] Metcalfe and Murdock have suggested that this latter phenomenon is based on the partial activation of a distributed trace.[28] The portion activated presents the information which is available, the sound or an initial letter, and hence forms the silhouette of the word sought. In their

48. Diagram illustrating the holographic hypothesis for explaining the déjà-vu experience. In the visualisation of this hypothesis c1 and c2 represent the holograms of a present perception and a memory image respectively; according to the hypothesis, the perception of a1 results via the resemblance of c1 and c2 in the activation of memory image a2, thus producing the illusory effect of déjà-vu.

view this process has an analogy in holography: partial activation provokes a 'ghost image' of the object sought. This parallel is tempting, certainly if one considers that a 'ghost image' would then correspond to the beckoning phantom which William James detected in his consciousness.

A similar hypothesis inspired by holography explains that equally fleeting mental phenomenon, the déjà-vu experience. During a déjà-vu experience the perception of a situation is experienced as a repetition of a previous situation, while one is aware at the same time that one has not previously experienced the present situation. As long ago as 1904, the Dutch psychologist Heymans speculated that déjà-vu experiences occur because a present perception is not properly associated with the content of the memory and hence evokes the impression of a vague memory image.[29] Recently Sno and Linszen have advanced the hypothesis that this illusion is the result of too great a similarity between the holographically coded information of the present perception and the holographic information of a previous experience (figure 48).[30]

Holography and heuristics

Objections to the hologram metaphor are as diverse as its applications. Some authors have simply denied that there are neuronal equivalents of holographic processes. For example, the perception psychologist Gregory argued that the hologram metaphor encounters insurmountable objections because the eye does not have access to phase information.[31] Rose wrote that no-one had succeeded in specifying the neuronal structures which can process the information in a holograph-like way and that 'this particular excursion into memory modelling' must be provisionally regarded as over.[32] Other authors were equally dismissive. Lindsay and Norman devoted no more than a footnote to the observation that hologram metaphors could only explain the 'law of mass action' and that apart from that, they had not been applied to sufficient phenomena of memory for their merits to be judged.[33]

This sample of objections also illustrates the fact that various authors have a wide variety of views on the level at which the analogy between holography and memory should be located. The student who asked Pribram during a lecture whether all those laser beams were not dangerous to brain cells was taking the metaphor rather too literally.[34] It is true that optical processes occur in the eye but the visual stimulus is not processed *as light*. Beyond the retina, the optical stimulus changes into a pattern of electrical impulses. Where the similarities between the hologram and brain *were* to be sought in that case, remained unclear. Van Heerden focused the analogy on the wave-like character that light beams and neuronal processes supposedly have in common and which can be described with one and the same mathematics. Eich followed him in this: 'It is not the image-like characteristics of holograms that define the holographic hypothesis; rather, it is the formal operations of convolution and correlation that are important.'[35] She accordingly classified holography among the mathematical models.

However, other authors saw the common mathematics as a subordinate point. For Arbib, for example, the only thing that mattered was that neuronal and holographic processes have certain *effects* in common. For him it was not the physical or mathematical parallels that counted, but the similarities in the results, such as the distributed storage of traces and the resistance to damage. The convolutions and correlations on which these results were based, he argued, are irrelevant. For Arbib the hologram was expressly a metaphor: 'To profit from the metaphor, we must avoid too literal use of it.'[36] In all probability he would not have accepted Gregory's criticism – that the light entering the eye is not phased – as a cogent objection to the hologram metaphor.

Metaphors may serve as a proof of the fact that the hypothetical processes described by the theory are empirically possible. As we have seen, this is a time-honoured use of metaphors. The references to phosphorescence in Hooke's theory of the visual memory were intended to demonstrate that matter is capable of storing light stimuli. The photography metaphors of the nineteenth century were intended to familiarise the reader with the notion that the brain can store latent visual images and later reproduce them. The link between holography and visual memory also fits into this tradition. For example, Van Heerden arrived at a theoretical estimate of the quantity of information in the human memory which was so high that its processing by the brain appeared to be an 'impossible operation'.[37] But now that holography could prove that the storage and reproduction of so much information was technically possible, it became more credible that the brain was also capable of storing information in a distributed way. Murdock reasoned along the same lines.[38] He wrote that in a distributed memory no single element has a separate trace – yet every individual element can be retrieved. Holographic models proved that it is possible to store information in compound traces without the danger of interference.

The criticisms of the hologram metaphor also have parallels in nineteenth-century theories concerning memory and photography. That applies, for example, to the accusation that the hologram metaphor leads to an infinite regress. In holography the stored image is 'read out' by illumination with an appropriate beam and projected in a quasi-space in front of or behind the storage medium. Subsequently the viewer observes this projection. Pribram's holographic memory theory states that the stored images are projected outside the storage medium (the brain) and from there absorbed into consciousness. Various authors have pointed to the risk of a regression in this procedure: how can the memory perceive the projected images without duplicating the whole procedure? Human consciousness as a reading-out of the hologram in the head, Arbib wrote, may lead to the homunculus fallacy: 'For if memory reconstructs the visual input we may be back to "explaining" perception in terms of a little man sitting in a control room inside the head, monitoring neural messages from the periphery, and starting an infinite regress of smaller and smaller homunculi.'[39]

A discussion of this question will be postponed until the chapter on the homunculus (see chapter 9); but here we can already point out that the photographic metaphors of the nineteenth century raised the same fear of regression. Huber, for example, argued in 1878 that 'impressions cannot see themselves' and that images reproduced by the brain have to be perceived by consciousness actually in order to produce a visual memory (see chapter 5). He judged that photographic metaphors contributed nothing to theories of memory precisely because the central question, the absorption of experience into the consciousness, remained unsolved. Some present-day authors believe that the hologram metaphor has the same flaw.

The hologram metaphor evokes memories of nineteenth-century concepts in heuristic respects, too. An inspection of older memory theories teaches us that various notions which we are used to linking with the hologram metaphor were already articulated in the nineteenth century. For example, the hypothesis of distribution is relatively old and, logically speaking, not dependent on 'interference'; distribution could also occur because several copies are stored in various parts of the brain. This theory has been defended by the biologist Richard Semon.[40] This same idea of redundancy, in evolutionary terms so useful for survival, has been expressed in our age in terms of *back-ups*. The idea that various memory elements have a common neuronal substratum ('composite traces') was also introduced into memory psychology over a century ago, as we saw, by Galton and his 'compound photography'. Even the notion that every individual element in a certain sense contains the whole is older than the holo-gram metaphor. The following passage was written without the mathematical background of holography, since it dates from 1891: 'Each element [of the nervous system] – speaking figuratively – may be considered as a minute area intersected by an indefinite number of curves of different directions and orders. Thus a molecular commotion in any such area may run into the system along any one of innumerable curves. In every such small fragment "the whole curve slumbers".'[41]

These references to nineteenth-century memory theories make it clear that concepts such as interference, distribution, reconstruction or composite traces were not originated by the hologram metaphor. One might retort that the merit of the hologram metaphor lay not in the *introduction* of these terms but in their

…ited in a graphic way how distribution …cesses; how the common neuronal sub-…acity; how presentation of a part of the …and how this latter mechanism in turn …sable character to memory. But the fact …ot be ascribed to the hologram is proved …en already referred. In this article, Beurle …r the way in which excitation processes …i through a neuron complex. This model …l features of the *later* holographic model: …in sensitivity levels as a function of that …imilarities are very striking. Beurle main-…ices it is possible for a separate wave with …ige the medium in which the wave move-…subsequent occasion, Wa alone is capable …his is almost literally the holographic pro-…nd yet there is not a single reference in the …matter existed only as mathematical enti-…ie that many of the key notions associated …without the hologram metaphor.[43]

…ion might also be that holography provides …model. What value did holography have in …e argued that the usable elements in the …tions of convolution and correlation. But …iented in models totally disconnected with …have summarised various 'metaphors for …as the filtering of bundles of light rays in …of colours which are stored in those beams. …metaphors.[44] Kohonen wrote that none of the holographic principles demonstrated so far is really necessary for the implementation of an associative memory and that data in an associative memory are also accessible without reference beams and similar aids.[45] Willshaw constructed an alternative model for distributed associative memories 'the correlograph', which describes the 'essentials of the holographic memory' without laborious Fourier transformations. He concludes that there is nothing remarkable about holographic models and that they are, if anything, too complex in relation to the calculations involved.[46] Holography, one can conclude, was only one of the possible models for associative memory and probably not the best.

Compared with the enthusiasm with which the first advocates introduced the hologram metaphor into psychology, the benefits were a disappointment. The most refined visual metaphor available did not lead to new findings or even new research questions either in neurology or in psychology. The neurological results cited in favour of the hologram metaphor had been found independently of that metaphor. Moreover, those findings had in many cases only a limited supportive value. That physical changes occur as a result of experience is, strictly speaking, part of the *logic* of any materialistic theory of memory. The fact that a pattern of membrane thickenings (or whatever kind of physical pattern) emerges in the initially homogeneous brain of rats, is a common prediction for all materialistic memory theories and does not lend support to the specific claim that memory processes can be described holographically. Such results show at most that holographic principles do not conflict with what is already known about brain processes.

In psychology, it is equally impossible to point to empirical results which have been taken directly from the metaphor or suggested by it. Holographic principles have been associated with numerous findings, such as the facilitating influence of contextual information on visual memory or the partial reproducibility of words which are on the tip of your tongue, but these phenomena have not been placed in a different theoretical perspective by the hologram metaphor, nor do they owe their discovery to it. The same applies to the holographically inspired hypothesis for the déjà-vu experience. The hypothesis that déjà-vus are based on partial correspondence between the patterns of present experience and a memory image was stated as long ago as the nineteenth century and even then was also linked to the notion that memories are stored in neuronal patterns that partly overlap.[47] That this coding can now be described in holographic terms is a minor point in relation to the cognitive core of the explanation – that the experience is the effect of partial identity.

To summarise, the phenomena which have been linked with holographic theories were already known and can also be explained by non-holographic theories. Theoretical notions like distribution, interference and composite traces already occur in nineteenth-century memory theories. The fact that it is possible to order the separate processes into a coherent whole without holography was proved by Beurle. Finally, as a mathematical model, holography has been replaced meanwhile by more economical models. In fact, the hologram metaphor marked a clear advance only as an 'existence proof': holography was able to represent more complex hypothetical mechanisms. This was particularly true for the processing of very large quantities of information and the possibility of combined, but non-interfering information storage. At the same time it must be emphasised that this is an indirect form of support: the objection raised in the nineteenth century by Ribot to photographic metaphors – what use is it to know how a photograph 'retains' when we do not know how the *brain* retains memories – similarly applies to holography.

Stagnation?

The view, however, that only the mathematical aspects played a (short-lived) role in the construction of theory and that physical holograms were entirely insignificant is far too sceptical: after all the *mathematics* of holography was available from as early as 1948, while this technology was only introduced as a metaphor from the moment when the first *physical* holograms were made with lasers. Obviously mathematics alone was insufficiently spectacular to influence theories of the visual memory. To set the historical record straight: the fascinating properties of physical holograms awakened interest in the mathematics of holography. Later it turned out that these mathematical properties could be captured in simpler models. In this sense the hologram has definitely had heuristic value. The very fact that Willshaw classified his correlograph under the heading 'non-holographic models' says something about the origin of his model.[48]

The initial attraction of the hologram metaphor in the 1970s seems to be connected with gaps in the computer metaphor which were emerging precisely at that time. The attempts to make computers process optical information and provide them with an efficient visual memory had come to nothing. The traditional serial computer had to convert light stimuli into a formal code and then carry out calculations on that code. For most 'human' tasks, such as the recognition of faces, this procedure is too slow and too inaccurate to be a really good model for the way in which the human brain works. The hologram metaphor, on the other hand, offered the success of a rapid and associative memory without an index.

Anyone drawing up a balance of literature on holography and memory around 1980, would have noted a certain stagnation. The episode of the hologram seemed to be an isolated bend of a river, cut off and filled with stagnant water and detritus. A number of scientometric criteria can be adduced for that impression of stagnation. In the first place there was a citation circuit of very limited scope. One can also see this occurring in the case of a specialised area of science, but then references are usually very recent. This did not apply to the hologram metaphor. In the second place, there has been a rapid increase in the number of self-references ('self-kick') in Pribram's articles. Self-kick rose within eight years, from a few per cent to over 25 per cent. There has to be more behind the steep curve than simply vanity. One has the impression that the self-references were borne largely out of necessity. From the early 1960s onwards there appeared, on average, two articles a year on holography and memory. Apparently there was scarcely a 'body of literature' for Pribram to draw from, except for the articles which he himself had written. Holography was mainly a metaphor of distribution, yet its traces in the scientific community around 1980 were very localised. If someone had erased the contributions of Pribram to the literature on visual memory, he would have wiped out a large part of the memory of holography.

But in the years *after* 1980 things changed. In theory-building on 'parallel distributed processing' and connectionism various concepts associated with the hologram metaphor enjoyed a renaissance. In a very different technical and historical context, that of research into neural networks, terms such as content-addressability, graceful degradation, parallel processing and distributed representation were assigned a central role in theories of memory. And this time the scientific community *did* allow itself to be convinced.

Notes

1   D. Gabor, 'A new microscopic principle', *Nature*, 161 (1948), 777–8.
2   M. A. Arbib, *The Metaphorical Brain*, New York, 1972, p. 186.
3   P. J. Van Heerden, *The Crystalcounter. A New Instrument in Nuclear Physics*, Amsterdam, 1945.
4   Biographical information taken from two letters from Van Heerden to the author (20 September 1993 and 19 October 1995).
5   J. Von Neumann, *The Computer and the Brain*, New Haven, 1958.
6   D. MacKay, 'Mindlike behaviour in artefacts', *British Journal for the Philosophy of Science*, 2 (1951), 105–21.
7   P. J. Van Heerden, 'A new optical method of storing and retrieving information', *Applied Optics*, 2 (1963), 387–92; 'Theory of optical information storage in solids', *Applied Optics*, 2 (1963), 393–400. Both articles are included in P. J. Van Heerden, *The Foundation of Empirical Knowledge*, Wassenaar, 1968.
8   R. L. Beurle, 'Properties of a mass of cells capable of regenerating pulses', *Philosophical Transactions of the Royal Society of London; Ser. B*, 240 (1956), 55–94.
9   Van Heerden, *Foundation*, p. 29.
10   *Ibid.*
11   K. R. Pribram, 'The neurophysiology of remembering', *Scientific American*, 220 (1969), 73–86.
12   E. N. Leith and J. Upatnieks, 'Photography by laser', *Scientific American*, 212 (1965), 24.
13   Pribram first used the hologram metaphor in 'Some dimensions of remembering: steps towards a neuropsychological model of memory', in J. Gaito

(ed.), *Macromolecules and Behavior*, New York, 1966. It is unclear whether Pribram knew the work of Van Heerden in 1966 or 1969. He did refer to Van Heerden a few times in later publications.

14   In representing Pribram's holographic theory of memory I have drawn mainly on K. Pribram, M. Nuwer and R. J. Baron, 'The holographic hypothesis of memory structure in brain function and perception', in D. H. Krantz, R. C. Atkinson, R. D. Luce and P. Suppes (eds.), *Contemporary Developments in Mathematical Psychology*, vol. 2, San Francisco, 1974, pp. 416–57. Acccessible information on the hologram metaphor can be found in D. Goleman, 'Holographic memory: interview with Karl Pribram', *Psychology Today* (February 1979), 71–84.

15   Pribram, Nuwer and Baron, *ibid.*, p. 428.

16   *Ibid.*, p. 444.

17   K. R. Pribram, 'Mind, brain and consciousness: the organization of competence and conduct', in J. M. Davidson and R. J. Davidson (eds.), *The Psychology of Consciousness*, New York, 1980, pp. 47–63.

18   Pribram, *ibid.*, p. 59.

19   H. C. Longuet-Higgins, 'Holographic model of temporal recall', *Nature*, 217 (1968), 104; P. R. Westlake, 'The possibilities of neural holographic processes within the brain', *Kybernetik*, 7 (1970), 129–53; J. P. Cavanagh, 'Two classes of holographic processes realizable in the neural realm', *Lecture Notes in Computer Science*, 22 (1975), 14–40.

20   K. S. Lashley, 'In search of the engram', *Society for Experimental Biology (Great Britain). Physiological Mechanisms in Animal Behavior*, New York, 1950.

21   Pribram, Nuwer and Baron, 'Holographic hypothesis', p. 417.

22   W. Penfield and L. Roberts, *Speech and Brain Mechanisms*, Princeton, NJ, 1959, p. 45.

23   S. Rose, *The Conscious Brain*, Harmondsworth, 1976, p. 253.

24   J. P. Cavanagh, 'Holographic and trace strength models of rehearsal effects in the item recognition task', *Memory and Cognition*, 4 (1976) 2, 186–99.

25   K. R. Pribram, *Languages of the Brain*, Englewood Cliffs, NJ, 1971, p. 162.

26   W. James, *The Principles of Psychology*, New York, 1890. Quoted from *Principles*, New York edn, 1981, p. 243.

27   R. Brown and D. McNeill, 'The tip of the tongue phenomenon', *Journal of Verbal Learning and Verbal Behavior*, 5 (1966), 235–7.

28   J. Metcalfe and B. B. Murdock, 'An encoding and retrieval model of single-trial free recall', *Journal of Verbal Learning and Verbal Behavior*, 20 (1981), 161–89.

29   G. Heymans, 'Eine Enquête über Depersonalisation und Fausse Reconnaissance', *Zeitschrift für Psychologie*, 36 (1904), 321–43; Heymans's research was re-analysed by H. N. Sno and D. Draaisma, 'An early Dutch study of déjà vu experiences', *Psychological Medicine*, 23 (1993), 17–26.

30   H. N. Sno and D. H. Linszen, 'The déjà vu experience: remembrance of things past?', *American Journal of Psychiatry*, 12 (1990), 1587–95.

31   R. L. Gregory, *Mind in Science*, London, 1981, p. 376.

32   Rose, *Conscious Brain*, p. 253.

33   P. H. Lindsay and D. A. Norman, *Human Information Processing*, New York, 1977, p. 440.

34   Arbib, *Metaphorical Brain*, p. 186.

35   J. M. Eich, 'A composite holographic associative recall model', *Psychological Review*, 89 (1982) 6, 627–61.

36   Arbib, *Metaphorical Brain*, p. 187.

37   Van Heerden, *Foundation*, p. 29.

38   B. B. Murdock, 'Convolution and correlation in perception and memory', in L.-G. Nilsson (ed.), *Perspectives on Memory Research*, Hillsdale, NJ, 1979, pp. 105–20.

39   Arbib, *Metaphorical Brain*, p. 187.

40   R. Semon, *Die Mneme als erhaltendes Prinzip im Wechsel des organischen Geschehens*, Leipzig, 1904.

41   G. T. Ladd, *Physiological Psychology*, London (1887) 1891, pp. 423–4.

42   Beurle, 'Properties', 81.

43   This is subject to the following reservation: it is possible that Beurle, a physicist like Gabor, drew his inspiration from the mathematical model of holography, but in his final article removed anything reminiscent of holography. For that matter, Beurle is an enigmatic figure in the (pre-)history of the hologram metaphor. His publication in the *Proceedings* mentions him as working at the Radar Research Establishment, Great Malvern, but not much else could be discovered about him. The reprints sent to him by Van Heerden were 'returned to sender' (letter from Van Heerden to the author, 20 September 1993).

44   Metcalfe and Murdock, 'Encoding', pp. 162ff.

45   T. Kohonen, *Associative Memory*, Berlin, New York, 1977.

46   D. Willshaw, 'Holography, associative memory, and inductive generalization', in G. Hinton and J. Anderson (eds.), *Parallel Models of Associative Memory*, Hillsdale, NJ, 1981, pp. 83–104.

47   See also E. Boirac, 'Correspondance', *Revue Philosophique*, 1 (1876), 430–1.

48   Willshaw, 'Holography', 93.

8   An enchanted loom

Our brains are encased in curved, resilient sections of bone joined by zig-zag seams. Inside, between the skull wall and the brain, are three membranes. The outermost membrane is inelastic and tough and protects the brain against injury from bone splinters, while the innermost membrane is soft and follows every convolution and groove in the brain's surface. Between these two is the arachnoid mater, which is linked to the inner membrane by thin ribs of tissue. The space between the membranes is filled with a crystal-clear liquid which has a shock-dampening effect. The human brain is the jewel in the crown of evolution, and is locked in a vault with multiple security systems. All our thoughts, actions and movements are governed by the 1,400 grams of nerve tissue lying motionless in our cranium. In the dark, silent folds of this Unmoved Mover resides the capacity to imagine a sun-drenched beach or to remember music. From the seclusion of its bony casing the brain allows us to smell, feel and taste the world. The instrument that enables us to reflect on the infinity of the firmament itself occupies no more space than two clenched fists held side by side.

Measured on a different scale, the brain is majestically proportioned, containing an estimated one hundred billion cells, as many as the number of stars in the Milky Way. This microcosm emerged from an authentic Big Bang: the embryonic brain grows at the rate of a quarter of a million cells a minute. In maturity this universe contracts again, albeit slowly, since we lose ten thousand or so cells a day, as many as were created every two seconds in the embryonic phase.

Neurology and psychology

The nineteenth-century physiologist Dubois-Reymond tried to establish what he called a 'molecular astronomy of the brain', but in his day the instruments required for such a science were inadequate. The state of technology did not permit any investigation of the more refined anatomical structures of the brain. Neurologists showed ingenuity in measuring volume or weight, but these

49.   The neurologist Paul Flechsig (1847–1929), surrounded by aids for exploring
the brain. In front of him are ultra-thin sections of brain tissue held between
glass plates. Stoppered bottles containing chemicals for preparing and
colouring the sections are shown on the right: colouring techniques made
it possible to specify the morphology of various types of brain cells. Behind
Flechsig hangs a map of the brain with part of the temporal lobe cut away.
By the end of the century, the combination of microscopic and chemical
tissue research resulted in a relatively accurate charting of the brain.

measurements proved either indirect or irrelevant. Scope for recording separate functions in the brain was limited. Contemporary instrumentation did not match the scale on which the brain is built, so that the nineteenth-century neurologist gave the impression of someone trying to inspect the inside of a pocket watch with carpenter's tools.

The knowledge gathered within these technical limitations related mainly to the localisation of functions and was mostly the result of lesion research. Observations of function loss were connected with neurological damage, often established at post-mortem or in some other way. The first maps of the brain that could lay any claim to accuracy were drawn towards the end of the nineteenth century, showing sensory projection and association areas and 'centres' for speech and verbal memory.

This newly acquired topographical knowledge did not lead to any greater insight into the microstructure of the brain. It had been known since the days of Bell and Magendie that neurons conducted electrical impulses as a result of chemical processes, but the specification of the various functions of neurons was not given real impetus until improvements were made in histological research methods.[1] Using Sartorius's brain microtome, extremely thin sections could be made. Achromatic microscopes – less subject to distortion by illumination – raised the standards of research into brain tissue. These instruments, added to the chemical colour techniques which were developed towards the end of the century, led to an exciting series of neurological discoveries (figure 49). In

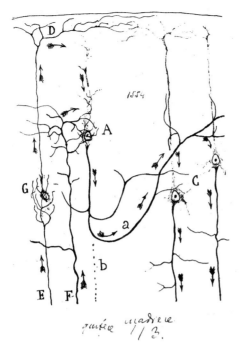

50.   The Spanish neurologist Ramón y Cajal (1852–1934) excelled in histological research and identified many different types of neurons. This is his schematic representation of possible neural pathways in the cortex.

1878 Bevan Lewis was the first to describe the pyramid cells in the cortex. In the 1890s Meynert identified different layers of human cortical tissue. At the turn of the century Ramón y Cajal was able to pinpoint various distinct types of neurons and describe their most important functional structures (figure 50). He also succeeded in following sensory nerve pathways on their route through the brain. At the same time, Sherrington identified the mechanisms of stimulus conduction in the peripheral nervous system. The knowledge available in the first decades of the twentieth century gave greater precision to a representation of the brain that had been familiar in outline for at least half a century. The pathways of the impulses could be followed better than ever before and the interaction between the various types of neurons could also be more accurately identified, but as an organ, instrumentally, the brain still functioned as an electric switchboard between stimuli and responses, the neuronal equivalent of a telegraph network or telephone exchange (figure 51).

In psychology, this interpretation of the brain sufficed for a long period of time. The first generation of behaviourists had little interest in the neuronal substratum of associations between stimulus and response and, moreover, did not think it needed this knowledge to understand their relationship.

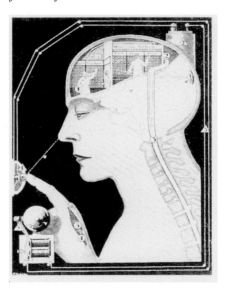

51.   Drawing of the brain as an electrical switching device between stimulus and response. The visual stimulus of the bell reaches the forebrain via the eye and the optical centre in the hindbrain (d). In the forebrain – the seat of the will – the decision is taken to ring the bell (1). This impulse is transferred to the motor centre in the hindbrain (2) and from there transmitted via the spinal cord (3) to the muscles of the hand (4 and 5): the finger presses the bell.

Psychology started and finished with observable behaviour and one could only speculate on the hidden intervening processes. The inaccessibility of the brain was not regarded as a shortcoming. For behaviourists, the function of the brain could be adequately summarised in the metaphor of the telephone exchange. There was no need for further specification. The neo-behaviourists found the telephone exchange too limited a metaphor (one may recall Tolman's remark that the brain was more like a 'map control room' than 'an old fashioned telephone exchange'), but they too refused to look for neuronal parallels for their metaphors.

The cognitive revolution of the 1950s was in many respects a break with the aspirations or methods of behaviourism. Cognitivists trying to clarify the nature of the processes between stimulus and response, freely referred to representations and brought about a change in focus from 'behaviour' to 'information'. But the replacement of the telephone exchange by the computer did not awaken greater interest in the operation of the brain. The background to this continuing neglect of neurology lay in what was seen as the essence of the computer metaphor. When Sherrington compared the brain to an 'enchanted loom', in which millions of bobbins flash back and forth, weaving an endless alternation of patterns, he was using virtually the same metaphor employed half a century before by Lady Lovelace to describe the proto-computer designed by Babbage ('the Analytic Engine weaves algebraic patterns just as the Jacquard loom weaves flowers and leaves'). There was, however, one difference, small but essential, implicit in the adjective 'algebraic': Babbage's machine operated with *symbols* and that property became the starting point of the computer metaphor. Computers and the brain are in this view similar systems because their operation can be described in terms of algorithms, mathematical rules for the manipulation of symbols.

This supposedly took the enchantment out of the loom. Those few pounds of nervous tissue in our cranium had, it was claimed, become subject to calculation, and the thoughts, perceptions and memories laid down in that tissue related to the brain in the same way as the programme of the computer relates to the mechanism of chips and currents. Conversely, given the relevant algorithms, a computer could produce conscious processes. The latter is indeed the view of the radical wing of AI: consciousness is woven out of the flashing back and forth of millions of calculations.[2]

The view of psychological processes as a set of operations on symbols failed to generate curiosity about the neuronal substratum of those operations, partly as a result of the spate of technological innovations that transformed computer technology from the 1940s onwards. In the rapid succession of generations, with their switches, valves, transistors and chips, the symbol-processing functions were executed by a wide variety of physical processes. Moreover, various programmes could be run on the same machine. Nothing could be deduced from the programme about the structure of the hardware or vice versa and to some extent this gave the relationship between programme and machine an arbitrary character. Linked with the computer metaphor was a suggestion that the human brain was only one of the possible embodiments of an 'information-processing system'. The precise structure – the *hardware* of the computer or the *wet ware* of the brain – was of only indirect importance for the execution of the 'cognitive programme'.

Yet in the early years of AI it looked for a moment as if theory would be able to link up with the properties of neurons and their ordering into networks. In the classic article by McCulloch and Pitts 'nerve-nets' were compared to a Turing machine and the authors maintained that Boolean binary logic could describe both the electric switches in an artificial system and the stimulus transfer between neurons.[3] Later AI authors mainly saw the *logical* aspects of this connection between the brain and the Turing machine – the fact that, conversely, the mathematical representation of the 'nerve-net' might inspire a more *neurologically* orientated theory, went virtually unnoticed. It is true that in 1951 Marvin Minsky wrote a doctoral thesis on a 'learning machine' modelled on a neuronal network, but he too was lured away by the apparently much greater potential of digital computers and abandoned this line of research.[4]

Of the few attempts to build artificial systems with a brain-like architecture, that of the psychologist Frank Rosenblatt was the most energetic. Rosenblatt produced a 'perceptron', a machine with a grid of 400 photo cells, ordered like the cells of the retina, linked with a layer of 512 neuron-like elements.[5] The presentation of optical patterns activated neurons. This activation signalled another group of neurons to set a matching process in motion. By manipulating the strength of the connections Rosenblatt was able to make his network 'recognise' all the letters of the alphabet. This achievement led to optimism, in the first instance in Rosenblatt himself: 'The perceptron has established, beyond doubt, the feasibility and principle of non-human systems which may embody human cognitive functions at a level far beyond that which can be achieved through present-day automatons.'[6]

Ten years later this branch of research was abandoned prematurely. In *Perceptrons* Minsky and Papert presented a mathematical analysis in which they listed the fundamental limitations of network models.[7] Their criticism discouraged further research along these lines.[8] The effect of *Perceptrons* rapidly became noticeable to Rosenblatt and like-minded scientists: they looked on disgruntled as within a few years the funding for their work flowed back into the mainstream of AI research.

To summarise, neither the behaviourists, nor the cognitivists, nor the leading theorists from the AI community believed that they could borrow any useful insights from neurology. The brain was viewed either as a switching device or as a Turing machine; in both cases the precise structure of the machinery was irrelevant. Between the study of the behaviour of neurons on the one hand and research into higher psychological functions like thinking, judging or problem-solving on the other, lay an extensive no-man's-land. And for a long time no one believed that anything of value would be found there.

The brain metaphor

This split into two research domains, separated by a no-man's-land, possibly damaged the development of psychology. The absence of a level of theory and research situated *between* the behaviour of neurons and that of people was to lead to an unnecessary restriction of the 'search area'. Allman compares it to an attempt to discover the operation of a television set by first studying the wiring diagrams and subsequently watching TV for a while.[9] From the beginning of the 1980s onwards initiatives were taken on various sides to reduce the gap between neurology and psychology.

In 1982 an article appeared in the *Proceedings* of the American Academy of Science that marks the beginning of the 'connectionist revolution'.[10] The author, John Hopfield, a theoretical physicist, had a shared appointment at the California Institute of Technology ('Cal Tech') and Bell Laboratories, where he studied the formal properties of networks. Perhaps the relevance for psychology is not immediately apparent from the title of his article, 'Neural networks and physical systems with emergent collective computational abilities', but the five key words with which the content was categorised for the benefit of auto-matic literature retrieval, indicate the points of contact between artificial and natural memories: 'associative memory/parallel processing/categorisa-tion/content-addressable memory/fail-soft devices'. In his article Hopfield opts for a level of analysis which is neurologically more realistic than the traditional architecture of computers, but on the other hand simplifies the properties of actual neuronal networks to such an extent that they fall within the range of mathematical description. The components in Hopfield's network (neurons) may be in a state of 'firing' (1) or 'non-firing' (0). A neuron fires only after exceed-ing its threshold value. Unlike a perceptron, where all the impulses went in a 'forward' direction, the Hopfield network operates with impulses in both direc-tions (A activates B, but B can also activate A). A second difference is that the per-ceptron was based on neurons working synchronically, as in a conventional digital computer, whereas in a Hopfield network there is no question of a (neurologically unrealistic) global synchronism. These two differences, Hopfield explains, give his network interesting new properties.

The mathematical structure of the Hopfield network is too technical to go into briefly. What is important for connectionist theory, is that Hopfield proves that in a network of simple homogeneous elements relatively permanent pat-terns of equilibrium are created, which can function as a physical substratum for the storage of information. Hopfield refers to the 'learning rule', stated by Hebb as long ago as 1949, that if two adjacent neurons A and B are repeatedly active simultaneously, the synaptic resistance between A and B decreases and hence the likelihood increases that the activity of A will also lead to the activ-ity of B.[11] Because B in turn has links with following neurons and these links become more accessible through stimulation, chains of activity are created, a process that has been compared to the carving out of a river bed. Hopfield pos-tulates that the pattern of synaptic resistances or current links can be viewed as an artificial memory. The Hopfield network has the following properties. (1) It works in a content-addressable way: presentation of a pattern activates the corresponding stored pattern without the intervention of an index or the checking of a list of addresses. (2) Presentation of a part of the pattern never-theless activates the whole stored pattern, so that the network has to a certain extent a correcting capacity. (3) In the case of ambiguous patterns the most probable statistical match is sought. (4) Patterns which display a high degree of similarity merge into a common pattern, which gives the system the capacity for generalisation and categorisation. (5) The switching-off of individual ele-ments has only a gradual adverse effect ('fail-soft') on its performance.

The impact of Hopfield's article was not only a theoretical one. The impres-sive mathematical apparatus, the publication in a leading scientific magazine and the connection with advanced technical models conferred prestige on a kind of research which had not as yet secured any institutional position. Within the community of AI theoreticians and cognitive psychologists the hegemony

of the computer metaphor was non-controversial and the more neuronally orientated theorists had only limited access to research funds. With his article
Hopfield brought about a sea-change which was received by other pioneers of
research into neural networks at once with gratitude and astonishment. One of
them, Jim Anderson, made the following confession in an interview: 'Neural
networks have been around a long time, but Hopfield is a big-name physicist at
Cal Tech and big-name physicists have a media access that you wouldn't believe.
So all of a sudden neural networks started getting a lot of attention – it's been
the greatest thing that could ever happen to the field.'[12]

In the mid-1980s the growth of connectionism exploded. As in an embryonic
brain a finely branched network of connections was formed in an extremely
short time – theoretical, technical, social. The self-organising capacity of this
network manifested itself in new magazines with names like *Neural Networks*
(1988) or *Neural Computation* (1989), in voluminous textbooks, a separate circuit
of conferences and societies of its own. Since then, the first histories of the
connectionist revolution have appeared and courses on neural networks now
form part of the standard curriculum in cognitive science.[13]

The move towards theories inspired by the structure of brain tissue has been
called the replacement of the computer metaphor by the brain metaphor.[14]
Although the concept of metaphor has been stretched to breaking-point here –
perhaps it should be called a model – the term, brain metaphor, aptly illustrates
the continuity with older metaphors like the hologram or the computer.
Connectionists project the properties of neuronal tissues, whether or not in a
stylised form, onto the theories of cognitive functioning and try to derive testable hypotheses from the differences and similarities which emerge in this
'double image'.

The rhetoric that accompanies the connectionist revolution parallels that of
the cognitive revolution of the 1960s down to the last apocalyptic detail. Once
more we are on the eve of a Copernican revolution in thinking about the
human mind, all existing views of our mental architecture will have to be radically reviewed, and the ultimate mysteries of the brain and consciousness
solved again. Connectionist models, Smolensky assures us, 'will offer the most
significant progress of the past several millennia on the mind/body problem'.[15]
This then has remained the same: the consistent use of the future tense.

But just as on closer inspection the cognitive revolution has turned out in
some respects to be a continuation of ideas previously specified by the
behaviourists, similarly, the connectionist revolution is only partly a break
with cognitivism. Nor was connectionism a creation *ex nihilo*: on the contrary,
at least three lines of research converge in it. In the first place there were individuals, widely scattered across time and place, who during the hegemony of
the computer metaphor secretly maintained confidence in the potential of
neural networks. Among these 'keepers of the flame', as Allman calls them,[16]

are Grossberg, who as far back as the beginning of the 1970s published articles on neural networks, Cooper and Kohonen.[17] Hinton and Anderson also published at an early stage on associative memories modelled on neural structures.[18]

A second and more recent area of research supporting connectionism concerns 'spin glasses'.[19] Spin glasses are synthetic materials, in which 'spin' refers to the quantum mechanical rotation which causes a magnetic effect. At different temperatures spin glasses have different states of equilibrium, which consist of patterns of magnetic orientation. These patterns can be described with the same mathematical models as the Hopfield network.[20] Because the 'behaviour' of spin glasses resembles that of neural networks, techniques for the analysis of spin glasses can be used on neural networks. A third historical line of research into connectionism is the theory in the 1960s and 1970s that was inspired by the hologram metaphor. The continuity between the holographic memory and neural networks will be discussed later.

However, the convergence of these three historical lines of research could only lead to such a sudden acceleration in the development of connectionism because a vital technical condition had been met. That condition was, ironically, the rapidly increasing power of the conventional computer. Hopfield simulated his parallel network on a serial computer and a majority of connectionists followed him. Because of their higher computational speed and the greater memory capacity, conventional computers are capable of calculating the parallelism of neural networks sequentially. Attempts have been made to build computers with parallel processors, but these machines are still at an experimental stage. Parallel machines require splits in the programmes in order to drive the various processors and that has proved difficult to achieve for the moment. The bulk of neural networks are represented in traditional computer memories.

Like cognitivism during the rise of the computer metaphor, connectionism quickly gained status through striking technical successes. From institutes like AT&T Bell Laboratories, Texas Instruments, IBM, General Electric and NASA a flood of research projects began, partly with military applications (again just as in traditional AI). For example, Gorman and Sejnowski designed a neural network for the recognition of mines from sonar signals and Farhat constructed a network that identified vehicles through an analysis of radar signals.[21] Cruise missiles are equipped with neural networks which compare patterns in the landscape with patterns stored in the memory and in this way give information about direction and height. In the meantime, ample commercial uses have been found. There are neural networks for the recognition of signatures, fingerprints, faces and voices.

Of course not all these applications are relevant to psychology. Just as in AI, one must distinguish between simulations of products and simulations of processes. In the case of *product* simulations it is a matter of imitating the final result, for example the answer to a sum or the assessment of a chess position. With simulations of this type one can make free use of what Dennett has called 'cognitive wheels', technical discoveries and design tricks which may not occur in nature, but do produce a quick solution (like wheels for transport).[22] *Process* simulations on the other hand are intended to imitate not only the result but also the mechanisms which lead to that result. Every simulation of a neural network takes its place in the continuum between product and process simulation, depending on whether the simulation takes more or less account of what we think we know about actual neuronal processes. Product simulations in neural networks may make use of processes which do not occur in the brain. An example of this is 'backward error propagation'.[23] In this technique, the desired pattern at the level of execution is taken as the starting point and the strength connections between the elements are modified 'backwards'. This procedure is repeated until the input produces the desired output without further intervention. This neural equivalent of a cognitive wheel is an efficient aid for constructing networks, but at the same time it is neurologically unrealistic, since the transmission mechanism of a neuron, the axon, cannot function as a receiver.[24] Moreover, this form of learning presupposes an intervention by the constructor ('supervised learning'), while the brain learns without outside help.[25] Although many neural networks are therefore of only indirect importance to psychology, connectionism is beginning to exert an influence on theory, particularly in the area of (pattern) recognition, learning and memory.

The networks in the memory

Those prepared to take a broad view can call any neural network a memory. Networks change structure as a function of experience. The configuration of connections and their strengths can be seen as the recording of those experiences, which becomes visible in the greater ease with which certain patterns are processed and reproduced. Neural networks 'take on' aspects of the patterns which they have previously processed. This broad definition of memory corresponds with the interpretation which Ewald Hering gave to memory in his classic essay of 1870.[26] Experience involves facilitation processes which simplify the reproduction of certain patterns and 'retain' these patterns in the form of a predisposition. In Hering's view, human memory, laid down in the brain, is a special instance of a general property of organic matter.

This interpretation of memory is not without complications (which will be discussed later), but shows that neural networks, 'organised matter' *par excellence*, have a strong intrinsic connection with learning and memory. Much of the research is focused on the development of learning rules which specify how the network organises itself. Three types of functional layers are generally distinguished: the input level, which receives the stimuli from the environment in the form of an activation pattern: the execution level, that indicates the response; and one or more 'hidden' layers, which provide for the connection between the input and output level. Just like neurons, the elements in the network have both a weight and a threshold: not every cell is equally important and cells vary in the ease with which they can be activated. The weight strengthens or weakens the signal, depending on the positive or negative value of the weight. What matters in a neural network is not the individual element, but the pattern of strength connections between the elements. In a neural network representations are stored in a distributed way.

Two properties, which according to connectionists give neural networks a high degree of psychological realism, were identified by Block more than two decades before the connectionist revolution.[27] Those properties are 'resistance to noise' and 'graceful degradation'. In a discussion of a perceptron that was trained to distinguish an x from an E, Block showed that the introduction of 'visual white noise' (either by activating at input level 30 per cent of incorrect elements along with the correct ones, or by giving a one-in-three incorrect feedback) only had a minor influence on the pattern recognition of the network. He also showed that damaging the system, by turning off elements, had a gradual effect proportional to the amount of damage, a property which Hopfield dubbed 'fail-soft' and for which 'graceful degradation' has now become the standard term. Both the tolerance of inconsistencies and the insensitivity to interference, form a sharp contrast with the processing of information by conventional computers.

A third property of neural networks underlines the contrast with the computer further. A neural network functions as a content-addressable memory. The pattern of input automatically activates the associated pattern, without the intervention of an index or list of locations which have to be consulted in a location-addressable memory. In traditional AI the relationship between input and location of storage is arbitrary and hence the address has to be separately coded. Content-addressable memories operate on a time scale which is psychologically more realistic.[28]

In recent years, neural networks have been linked with a whole series of topics from the psychology of memory. For example, there are networks for associative learning and for the simulation of the processes in the working memory. Another well-known instance is the network for the forming of prototypes which Jay McClelland and David Rumelhart presented in 1985.

The general dog

The capacity to process patterns instead of discrete packages of information has been used by various authors of the connectionist persuasion to simulate the human capacity for seeing the same thing in different things. In our Heraclitic existence nothing repeats itself in identical form and in order to learn from experience it is necessary to lay down general categories of sameness. How those categories form themselves in our mind and how they are related to the reality of concrete objects and events, has been the object of philosophical reflection since the time of Plato. Recently, neural networks have been constructed in which the forming of categories, so the designers maintain, is a natural consequence of the distributed storage of patterns.[29]

Objects or concepts can virtually never be defined on the basis of defining characteristics which can be summed up in a list. In most cases such a list is of indeterminate length or the properties are insufficient to decide about inclusion or exclusion. Wittgenstein illustrated this on the basis of the concept 'game', but even an apparently simple category like 'bird' highlights this problem. The ability to fly, for example, is not adequate as a criterion: not all birds can fly (ostrich) and not everything that flies is necessarily a bird (bat). With such criteria as having feathers (what about a plucked chicken, for example) or laying eggs (a platypus is not a bird), there are inevitably similar problems. Yet we form categories in our memory by somehow or other bypassing the complications of definitions and criteria.

Research into the structure of semantic networks has suggested that *prototypes* play a part in this. Reaction-time experiments show that the question 'is x a bird?' can be answered affirmatively more quickly, the more bird-like x is. These experiments indicate that canaries and blackbirds seem more bird-like than penguins or ostriches. The 'birdness' of a bird is obviously already present in our memory as a prototype and functions as a standard with which we compare birds.

McClelland and Rumelhart designed a neural network capable of forming prototypes. They first set a series of activation values of pluses and minuses with twenty-four positions. The purpose of this series was to represent a 'general dog'. The first eight positions defined the name of the dog, and the last sixteen, the properties. Subsequently, fifty 'specific' dogs were presented to the network by varying one property each time. Once these fifty dogs, each with a different name, had been stored, a fragment of the prototype was inputted. The various names then cancelled each other out and the network reproduced the complete prototype. This general dog had never been presented as such to the memory, but nevertheless emerged from it. 'Plato scholars will envy the system's ability to see the true form of doghood on the basis of the distorted shadows on the wall of the cave', writes Clark.[30]

Broadly speaking, neuronally inspired theories on the forming of the categories have the form of the network just described.[31] As soon as the overlap of the physical substratum of the stored patterns exceeds a critical limit there is a stronger and stronger deposit of the common elements in the patterns, until eventually a prototype forms which does not necessarily correspond to any of the patterns presented. This ability to generalise is naturally linked with its opposite: discrimination – after all, if the overlap between the prototype and a new set of presented patterns remains below the threshold, *other* categories will form and be stored in the same network.

One can assert that the prototype network learns according to completely different principles from the computer. Firstly, the forming of prototypes is not programmed separately as a task, but follows as an automatic consequence of storage. The fact that rules, definitions and criteria are generally lacking in natural contexts is not an objection if they do not have to be programmed. Secondly, in the view of the connectionists the re-evoking of a pattern corresponds more closely to what appears to happen in the human memory. A fragment of the pattern is often sufficient for recognition, as in the case of a partially covered face, unlike the all-or-nothing reproduction from a computer memory.

Claparède's drawing-pin

As with cognitive processes like learning, categorising and discriminating, neural networks have been associated with various forms of retention. An example is CALM, the Categorizing And Learning Module of Wolters and Phaf.[32] This network simulates the performance of patients with anterograde amnesia and is intended to shed light on the distinction between implicit and explicit memory.[33] An implicit memory is one which is inaccessible to consciousness, but one in which experience is stored. It was only when dealing with amnesic patients that it became obvious that the implicit memory really existed. A century ago the Russian neurologist Korsakoff discovered that patients who had developed serious memory problems as the result of alcohol addiction, sometimes retained certain experiences, although they were not conscious of remembering. Korsakoff recorded the case of a patient who had been given electric shock treatment, and who no longer remembered anything about it, but surprisingly, when the patient saw the box of electric shock equipment, he nevertheless asked him anxiously, 'I expect you're coming to electrocute me?'[34] A similar case was reported in 1911 by the Swiss psychiatrist Claparède.[35] While doing his rounds on the wards, Claparède would usually shake hands with his patients. One morning he secretly put a drawing-pin on his palm when he shook hands with a female Korsakoff patient with complete anterograde amnesia. The following day he put his hand out again, but this time the woman refused to shake hands with him. She wasn't capable of explaining why she refused, she did not even know that she had met Claparède before, and yet the memory of the painful pinprick was clearly stored and the record of this had an influence on her behaviour a day later. From more systematic experiments with three amnesic patients, carried out by Schneider, it emerged that the recognition of a whole picture on the basis of seeing only a fragment of it gradually improved from day to day, even though the patients would swear blind that they had never seen the pictures before.[36]

The irony of the situation is that the observations of Korsakoff and Claparède and the findings of Schneider regarding what remains intact in the case of memory loss were forgotten in psychology itself. Only in 1968 was the relative imperturbability of what came to be known as the 'implicit memory' rediscovered. A case study of Henry M., who since an unsuccessful brain operation in 1953 had suffered from a serious form of anterograde amnesia, showed that the capacity to learn simple motor tasks remained unaffected.[37] In experiments with other patients, skills like the recognition of pictures and word completion proved to be intact.[38] Korsakoff's box and Claparède's drawing-pin were rediscovered in the 1980s, and are now a regular part of review articles on the distinction between implicit and explicit memory.[39] In a long series of experiments it has been established that patients with memory loss can learn motor and perceptual tasks almost as fast as people who still have intact memories.[40] For example, mirror drawing, reading mirror writing, the learning of the route through a drawn maze, or the solving of spatial puzzles, are mastered by patients with memory loss just as quickly as others (figure 52) They forget *that* they have learned something – and introduce themselves to the person conducting the experiment every morning – but do not forget what they have actually learned. In this way, their performance of the task constantly improves. In the case of memory loss the implicit memory is spared.[41]

In the case of memory tasks which appeal to the explicit memory, the test subject has an active, conscious memory, both of what he learned and of the context of learning. Clues taken from that context have a favourable effect on the reproduction of what has been learned. In the case of implicit memory tasks this contextual effect is lacking and the learning is only expressed in a gradually improved performance. If patients are asked to remember a series of word pairs and to practise them daily, they will, in the end, be able to reproduce more and more words correctly – especially if the patients are prompted with the initial letters of the words. In spite of this, however, the patients will have no conscious memory either of the actual words or of having learned them. Anterograde amnesia obviously has a different effect on the explicit and implicit forms of memory. The CALM network was designed to simulate this difference in effect.

As an explicit memory task, the designers chose the free reproduction of words, with the learning context as a clue. The implicit memory was measured by word completion, with two or three initial letters as clues. The heart of the network consisted of two modules for words and contexts respectively. Wolters and Phaf created twelve artificial test subjects by filling the empty network with a basic lexicon of twenty words, learned in six different contexts. The 'lesion' responsible for the occurrence of anterograde amnesia was simulated by artificially lowering the rate of learning, so that no associations between new words and contexts could be formed. Subsequently, they presented new words both to the amnesic and the intact part of the network. In the case of the amnesic network there was a drastic deterioration in free reproduction, whilst reproduction with the initial letters as a prompt was unaffected and indeed

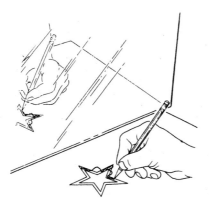

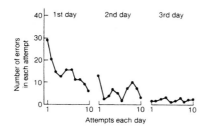

52.   Diagram illustrating a test where a subject has to trace the shape of the star while looking in the mirror and without straying outside the original lines. Because of the reversal of right and left this is initially a tricky task, but with practice, his performance improves rapidly: twenty attempts are made over two days and then on the next day the test subject is able to follow the outline of the star almost perfectly (see graph). Patients with severe memory loss master this task as quickly as test subjects who do not suffer from any memory loss. The processes that remain intact in memory loss are part of the 'implicit memory'.

even improved somewhat (possibly because of reduced interference). Thus the network simulated the different sensitivity of the explicit and implicit memory to an impairment in storage.

Neural networks, computers and holograms
It is still too early for a balanced judgement on the heuristic value of the brain metaphor. Neural networks have been linked with virtually the whole spectrum of memory, but the bulk of these networks simulates some or other well-known phenomenon from memory psychology. However useful such simulations may be, ultimately the heuristic merits of connectionism will have to be expressed in predictions on 'new' phenomena, phenomena which cannot be deduced from existing theories and can be tested in experiments. Like many computer simulations in classical cognitivism, neural networks provide a duplication of

the phenomenon rather than the explanation. In specialist journals and text-books on memory, even the most recent ones, connectionism is consequently presented as a promise, not as a set of results.[42]

For a comparative judgement of the merits of the brain metaphor for memory psychology it is useful to involve two rival metaphors in the discussion, the first of which, the computer, is frequently mentioned in literature on connectionism and the second, the hologram, virtually never. What is the relationship of these two technical metaphors to the brain metaphor? And why are they treated so differently?

The literature on connectionism is dominated by the relationship to the computer metaphor. In the rhetoric surrounding the connectionist revolution, the computer is presented as a misleading metaphor which is now being replaced by the much more vital connectionism. Classical cognitivists are treated as representatives of an *ancien régime* which allowed theory to stagnate badly, an attitude which is not so very different from the cognitivists' attitude to the behaviourists a generation earlier. Sterile, limited and irrelevant are again the adjectives used to characterise old-style theory: sterile because the computer metaphor is supposed not to have helped theory progress; limited because cognitivism was focused solely on 'higher processes' like language and problem-solving, ignoring pattern recognition or learning; irrelevant because an explanation in terms of operational symbols did not clarify how those processes are represented in the brain. Connectionism, on the other hand, produces neural networks which recognise faces or which assimilate the pronunciation of new words in a short time and in the future, after further refinements, will suggest new theories across the whole field of the human mind.

This comparison, so unfavourable for classical cognitivism, is extended by some to the domain of philosophy. For example, Thagard maintains that 'natural intelligence', as it has emerged in the course of evolution, presupposes reactions on a timescale with limits which are not respected by conventional computers but are respected by networks.[43] He therefore expects that neural networks will contribute more to the solution of the mind–body problem than functionalism, the theory which was inspired by the computer metaphor. In this way, Thagard links a philosophical point of view on the relationship between body and mind, with differences between computers and neural networks, differences which in the first place are connected with the present state of simulation techniques. An opinion like Thagard's does illustrate the extent to which, at the cost of the computer metaphor, connectionism has succeeded in capturing people's imaginations.

Some connectionist authors contrast the computer metaphor unfavourably with the brain metaphor on spurious grounds. Within the computer metaphor, they argue, memory is an all-or-nothing process, what is being sought is either in the memory or it is not and accordingly it is reproduced as a whole or not at all.[44] They argue that connectionism allows for various forms of forgetting and partial reproduction. This argument is misleading. The EPAM memory simulation (see chapter 6) was programmed precisely to imitate a kind of forgetting – the temporary unavailability of information through inadequate retrieval indications – which does *not* have this all-or-nothing character. Process simulations like this support the computer metaphor. Conversely, no support can be derived for the brain metaphor from the performance of an advanced but neurologically unrealistic network. The level of comparison between the computer and brain metaphors should be that of process simulations.

The bulk of connectionist theories relates to subjects like learning, association and pattern recognition while the computer metaphor mainly affected theories on 'higher' processes like problem solving and reasoning. This difference in orientation makes a detailed comparison between the two metaphors difficult. As an argument for the superiority of 'brain-style' simulations over classical computer simulations, connectionists often appeal to principles of a more general nature, such as the greater neurological or psychological reality content of neural networks. But this too needs qualification. In reality the parallels between neuronal tissue and neural networks are so minimal or superficial that it is doubtful whether the relationship should be seen in terms of similarities. Neurons exhibit great mutual differences in construction and function. Some neurons are no more than simple switches, links in a long chain. Other neurons, such as the pyramid cells, have hundreds of connections that integrate the impulses of large groups of cells. Neurons are ordered in the most varied layers, courses and circuits. Their activity is modulated by chemical processes under hormonal control. None of these properties can be found in neural networks, which as a rule consist of homogeneous elements, ordered in a limited number of levels. The computer switches in the neural network operate a hundred thousand times faster than the neurons they are simulating. The established practice of calling neural networks 'idealisations' is misleading: the differences between model and reality are simply too great. This helps to explain the apparent paradox that practitioners of the neurosciences have great reservations about connectionism.

But the *psychological* reality content of neural networks is also relatively insignificant. In the case of animals and humans, it has been established that there is an enormous selectivity involved in the forging of associative links. Associations between food and nausea, for example, are created much faster and are also more stubborn than associations between stimuli which have no organic link. The same difference occurs in the acquisition of elementary cognitive skills. Toddlers quickly learn that objects which are no longer visible, such as a rattle under a cushion, do continue to exist ('object permanence'). Animals which have to pursue their prey even when it is temporarily invisible, such as foxes, develop object permanence, whereas animals whose food remains immobile, like herbivores, do not.[45] Neuronal tissue is to a great extent 'pre-wired', accessible to some associations, recalcitrant or closed to others. In neural networks this difference does not exist: all associations are equally easy or equally difficult to establish, irrespective of the meaning of what is associated. Neural networks, as far as the latter property is concerned, are more like the memory of a computer than a human memory.

Ecumenically inclined authors tend to see classical cognitivism and connectionism as each other's complements rather than their rivals and accordingly have published conciliatory proposals. For example, Baddeley views the classical programme as a theory on the *organisation* of mental processes, while connectionism specifies how the details of those processes are learned by neural structures.[46] Estes believes that a theory on the forming of categories can have both a connectionist and a cognitive 'layer'.[47] Clark maintains that the varied brain structures and the coordination between them require processes which are all viewable as 'computations', but can be described sometimes more simply with connectionist rather than cognitivist principles.[48] Finally, Vroon believes that in the federative empire that constitutes our brain there is room for a wide variety of learning principles.[49] The brain metaphor, one can conclude, is not diametrically opposed to the computer metaphor, as was sometimes suggested in the early days of connectionism. As regards the psychology of memory, both metaphors provide inspiration for two research programmes which have each retained their own progression and direction up until now.

Various connectionist authors were inspired at the outset of their careers by the hologram metaphor. For example, in the early 1970s, Cooper read the article in *Nature* in which Longuet-Higgins compared the brain to a hologram. He was intrigued by the property of 'graceful degradation' which the hologram seemed to share with the brain. Finding holograms unconvincing as biological systems, he asked one of his graduate students 'to cook up a more physiologically acceptable model'.[50] The student subsequently discovered the neural networks of Anderson. Another connectionist of the first hour, Hinton, also stated that he was brought to the idea of neural networks by holograms: 'I was thinking about neural nets when I was sixteen. I had just found out about holograms, and it seemed to me to be an obvious metaphor for the mind.'[51]

More convincing is the link between holography and networks at the level of theory. The most important theoretical notions at present associated with neural networks were first specified in the literature on the hologram metaphor. Holographic memories are *content-addressable*. The information is stored in the form of *distributed* representations, which results in low sensitivity to information loss in the event of damage (*graceful degradation*). Patterns are stored and reproduced according to *parallel* principles. In short, holograms share with neural networks precisely those properties which are presented as merits of connectionism.

However, there are hardly any references to holograms in the literature on neural networks. The most important propagandist of the hologram metaphor, Karl Pribram, is rarely quoted.[52] In the indexes of the connectionists' textbooks there is an absence of references to the publications of Van Heerden, who presented associative models for memory as early as 1963. Why did the hologram metaphor disappear from view, when its properties matched those of neural networks so well?

Part of the explanation can be distilled from the collection of essays edited by Hinton and Anderson on parallel models for memory.[53] This collection, by now a classic of connectionist literature, contains a separate chapter by Willshaw on the link between holography and associative memory.[54] In it he describes how between 1967 and 1972 he and Longuet-Higgins attempted to construct a distributed memory. These models were inspired by the holograms which were then becoming available thanks to developments in laser technology. The performance of holography as a metaphor of memory was disappointing in relation to their mathematical–physical complexity and both researchers tried to find a method which would reduce that complexity. The second phase of their research led to the development of several 'non-holographic' models, including the 'correlograph'. This model made use of mathematical operations which derived from the analysis of holography, but lacked the other complex operations which information undergoes in a real hologram. The 'correlograph' simulated the essence of holography by storing and reproducing distributed patterns. Willshaw then went on to describe how the operations of the 'correlograph' could be lodged in an associative network.

The chronology of their research efforts reflects the following development. The properties of physical holograms as a medium for the storage of information aroused the interest of neurologists and neuro-psychologists. The interpretation of the hologram as an artificial memory led to models which stayed as close as possible to the properties of holograms. At a later stage, theoreticians gained a better insight into the physical–mathematical properties of holograms which were essential for memory function and they developed models which were technically and formally simpler. In the last phase it turned out that the relevant processes could also be accommodated in network-like structures and the theory of the holographic memory merged with connectionism. Once this point had been reached the references to the holograms of the 1960s and 1970s were no longer important: the useful elements in holography could be couched in the theoretical terms of neural networks more simply and convincingly.

This last point does not mean that the hologram was an irrelevant detour in memory psychology. For a long time holograms were the only parallels to the human brain with an ounce of plausibility. The hologram was the only artificial memory that was content-addressable, which stored distributed information and proved resistant to damage. Precisely these somewhat magical properties, embodied in an optical system, aroused interest in their mathematical under-pinnings. These, in turn, were simulated in neural networks. The hologram metaphor provided the thermal current on which connectionist ideas have soared upwards.

The line of least resistance

A neural network is the formalisation of the line of least resistance. The route taken by a pattern through the network is determined by the thresholds and strength connections, the mathematical equivalents of the grooves which pre-vious patterns have worn in the network. It is this configuration of grooves that contains the record of experience which has been processed by the network and which is denoted in connectionist literature as 'memory'.

If one overlooks their mathematical form for a moment one finds in neural networks the time-honoured concept of *facilitation*, the easier conduction of an impulse the more often the associated elements are activated.[55] In the seven-teenth century Descartes, following the physiology of his time, looked for the physical substratum of facilitation in the dilation of pores in the brain as a result of the more frequent flow of the gas-like substance in the nervous system. For Hartley, a century later, the nervous system was a buzzing sound box in which experience was preserved in the form of vibrations and resonances. In the nine-teenth century, it was thought that if electrical resistance was diminished, then the conduction of impulses would therefore become easier, and as a conse-quence, experience would gradually carve out a stabilising pattern of neural pathways. In the twentieth century the most diverse mechanisms for facilita-tion have been suggested: the forming of new synapses, the sensibilisation of dendrites, larger quantities of neuro-transmitter, etc. One idea which has been repeatedly expressed in a variety of ways derived from current physiology is that memory is based on the selective accessibility of certain routes, pathways, tracts, chains, circuits, connections. Much-used metaphors for these routes which are also found in the literature on neural networks, are 'grooves', and 'beds'.

In the nineteenth century 'mental physiologists' like Ladd and Maudsley were guided in their theories of memory by assumptions about the processes in the brain. In their view retention was based on circuits of sensitised nerve cells. When these circuits were activated by stimuli from outside, they spoke of recognition; activation from within resulted in memory. In 1880 William James described how psychological laws of association could be traced back to the 'physical fact that nerve currents propagate themselves easiest through those tracts of conduction which have been already most in use'.[56] He specified a 'law' which contained the core of Hebb's learning rule: 'When two elementary brain-processes have been active together or in immediate succession, one of them, on reoccurring, tends to propagate its excitement into the other.'[57] James also described a process of association ('redintegration') with diagrams which

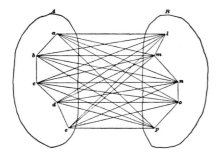

53.   William James's diagram of associative pathways in the memory. A is the set
      of neural pathways a, b, c, d and e, activated at the end of a dinner party; B
      is the set of neural pathways that were active during the walk home through
      the bright, freezing-cold night. The reactivation of any arbitrary element in
      A will activate the elements of B, just as conversely, the elements of B will
      activate A. The interactions between the 'discharges' in 'pathways' carve the
      associations between A and B more and more deeply, until ultimately A
      cannot be conceived without B and vice versa. If part of the link is lost, each
      element will still remain accessible.

display what would now be called, complete connectivity, content-addressability and 'graceful degradation' (figure 53).

   Neuronally inspired explanations were suggested for higher cognitive processes too. Galton's theory on the forming of prototypes is a case in point. He
maintained that nerve elements which have once processed a particular
pattern of sensory information become 'tender', 'liable to be easily thrown
again into a similar state of excitement'.[58] Processing of similar stimuli results
through repeated activation of the same elements in 'blended memories', in
which the common element is reduced to a prototypical representation. This
mechanism was suggested by the metaphor of the 'average portraits' and could
be physically simulated thanks to the 'compound photography' developed by
Galton himself. In this technique the differences in exposure, in favour of what
is repeated, had the same effect as repeated activity in nerve tissue: an optical
pattern of grooves was carved into the photographic plate. The analogy between
the compound portraits and the prototype network is so persuasive that one
could include phrases from Galton's articles in the analysis of McClelland and
Rumelhart without any fear of discovery. A compound portrait, wrote Galton in
1879, is the photographic equivalent of generalised memory images 'that are
not copies of any individual, but represent the characteristic features of
classes'.[59] This is precisely what the prototype network does: the storage of
specific patterns leads to the appearance of a pattern which shows the properties of the class as a whole.

   If one sets the work of James or Galton alongside that of the connectionists
one notices both similarities and differences. In the neural networks one finds

a revival of classical 'mental physiology'. The mechanisms responsible for the forming of associations, are still based on facilitation processes. As before, the emphasis is on learning and habituation. Connectionist hypotheses of specific memory processes, like the forming of categories and prototypes, also have parallels with older theories; Galton's prototypical murderer was produced by essentially the same process of reduction of variation as the prototypical dog of Rumelhart and McClelland. Memory traces are preserved in the strength or accessibility of the connections. Representations have a distributed character. Memory is a gradual process. Reproduction is based on the reactivation of the neuronal circuits involved. The present-day connectionists have much in common with the classical tradition, particularly on points which they consider prominent contributions to memory psychology. Reading about their neural networks may even provoke an occasional sensation of déjà-vu.

But there are also differences, and they are equally essential. Neural networks are specifications of hypothetical mechanisms, the operation of which can be empirically tested. The diagrams of James and others might be convincing or otherwise in the light of what was known about the operation of the memory, but they were not experimentally accessible. With neural networks one can experiment freely. Various types of learning rules, thresholds and weights, veto cells and feedback, signal/interference ratios, modules and circuits can all be tested for their effects by simulating the network on the computer. Moreover, these neural networks are mathematically analysable. The diagrams in the literature of 'mental physiology' were schematic and informal, neural networks are formalised as fully as possible and, apart from the 'hidden layers', mathematically transparent. This property has enabled connectionism to link up with theories of signal detection and pattern recognition. Their experimental accessibility and mathematical analysability in addition to the technical requirement that they must actually function ensure that neural networks are more than simply a new form of associationism.

For the moment, the heuristic value of neural networks seems to lie at the conceptual level. Connectionists explore a different 'search area' to that of the cognitivists, making use of different explanatory principles and with at least half an eye on neurological reality. Their models are a correction of the kind of psychology dominated by the computer metaphor. The fact that the human brain does not operate as a location-addressable device, does not run through indexes, and does not form categories on the basis of explicit criteria, only comes as a surprise to theoreticians who had accepted the computer metaphor too subserviently, William James would not have been shocked. Neural networks cancel out steps which were inspired by the computer metaphor and perhaps should not have ever been taken. An example is that the computer metaphor interprets the memory as a set of compartments, analogous to the design of programmes ordered in flow charts, and with a distinction between processing and storage, while in connectionism, processing and storage are part of one and the same system. Wolters and Phaf are of the opinion that in this respect the brain metaphor rectifies the computer metaphor: 'The dropping of the distinction between processor and memory in connectionist systems is a step which was made long ago in psychology, but which because of the computer metaphor had temporarily fallen into disuse.'[60] The computer caused an eclipse (to borrow Robert Hooke's metaphor) in the collective memory of psychology and temporarily removed something from the sight which is now visible again in all its clarity.

Besides merits, connectionism has shortcomings at the conceptual level too – this is certainly the case compared with the analyses of memory which appeared in the nineteenth century. In connectionist theory, neural networks are called memory systems and stored patterns, memories. Whether the reactivation of the neuronal tract of a particular representation is actually a memory or simply a repetition of experience, in other words, whether reactivation is one of the necessary conditions rather than a full explanation, is a question that one sees raised seldom if at all, in connectionist literature. In this respect, the work of nineteenth-century psychologists showed much more finesse.

In his *Principles of Psychology* William James devoted a section to a precise definition of 'remembering'. A memory, he argued, not only relates to the past, but must also be experienced *as* past, more specifically as belonging to *my* past. A memory must have the quality of 'warmth and intimacy' that makes it into a personal experience. These properties cannot be based on a simple reactivation of neuronal tracts. In this case we would just be duplicating the original experience. Remembering is precisely reliving something, *plus* the consciousness that the experience can be located in one's personal past. Memory, writes James, 'is a *psychophysical* phenomenon, with a bodily and a mental side. The bodily side is the functional excitement of the tracts and paths in question; the mental side is the conscious vision of the past occurrence, and the belief that we experienced it before.'[61] Subsequently James wonders how the physiology of the carving out of associations could explain this conscious side of memory, and then he makes an observation which over a hundred years later is still relevant especially to neural networks:

> The two excitations are simply two excitations, their consciousnesses are two consciousnesses, they have nothing to do with each other. And a vague 'modification' supposed to be left behind by the first excitation, helps us not a whit. For, according to all analogy, such a modification can only result in making the next excitation more smooth and rapid. This might make it less *conscious*, perhaps, but it could not endow it with any reference to the past. The gutter is worn deeper by each successive shower, but not for that reason brought into contact with previous showers.[62]

James does not deny that the carving out of patterns is a crucial element in the theory of memory, he simply believes that these physiological processes are only part of the explanation.

James himself was uncertain as to how exactly that theory of memory was to be completed. In a concluding discussion of what he calls the 'metaphysics involved in remembering', he writes that this conceptual problem is part of the 'one great mystery' of how brain processes are linked with psychological processes: 'It is surely no different mystery to *feel* myself by means of one brain-process writing at this table now, and by means of a different process a year hence to *remember* myself writing.'[63]

It is not fair to reproach connectionists with not having succeeded in solving this 'one great mystery'. But by calling neural networks memory systems, and the stored patterns, memories, they give the impression of not even seeing the mystery.

Notes

1   M. A. B. Brazier, *A History of Neurophysiology in the Nineteenth Century*, New York, 1988.

2   The distinction between 'strong' and 'weak' AI is significant here. Weak AI argues that computer simulations are important for increasing the precision of hypotheses on psychological processes and for testing them. Strong AI is the more radical view that simulations duplicate psychological processes and are hence themselves psychological processes.

3   W. McCulloch and W. Pitts, 'A logical calculus of the ideas immanent in nervous activity', *Bulletin of Mathematical Biophysics*, 5 (1943), 115–33.

4   The machine simulated the behaviour of rats learning the route through a maze and consisted of forty elements, the values of which changed as a function of reinforcement.

5   F. Rosenblatt, 'The perceptron: a probabilistic model for information storage and organization in the brain', *Psychological Review*, 65 (1958), 386–408.

6   Quoted in W. F. Allman, *Apprentices of Wonder. Inside the Neural Network Revolution*, New York, 1989, p. 104.

7   M. Minsky and S. Papert, *Perceptrons: An Introduction to Computational Geometry*, Cambridge, MA, 1969.

8   Allman, *Apprentices*, p. 105.

9   *Ibid.*, p. 6.

10   J. J. Hopfield, 'Neural networks and physical systems with emergent collective computational abilities', *Proceedings of the National Academy of Science*, 79 (April, 1982), 2554–8.

11   D. O. Hebb, *The Organization of Behavior*, New York, 1949.

12   Allman, *Apprentices*, p. 135.

13   In addition to *ibid.*, G. Johnson's *In the Palaces of Memory*, New York, 1991, also provides a good insight into the connectionist change of direction.

14   See also C. Brown, P. Hagoort and Th. Meijering, *Vensters op de geest. Cognitie op het snijvlak van filosofie en psychologie*, Utrecht, 1989, p. 17; G. Wolters and R. H. Phaf, 'Connectionisme: een nieuwe uitdaging voor de psychologie', *De psycholoog*, 7/8 (1988), 361–9.

15   P. Smolensky, 'On the proper treatment of connectionism', *Behavioral and Brain Sciences*, 11 (1988), 1–74.

16   Allman, *Apprentices*, p. 111.

17   Collected in S. Grossberg, *Studies of Mind and Brain*, Dordrecht, 1982. An early connectionist article by Cooper is L. N. Cooper, 'A possible organization of animal memory and learning', *Nobel Symposium*, 24 (1973), 252–64. Kohonen's major work is T. Kohonen, *Associative Memory*, Berlin, New York, 1977.

18   G. Hinton and J. Anderson (eds.), *Parallel Models of Associative Memory*, Hillsdale, NJ, 1981.

19   D. J. Amit, G. Gutfreund and H. Sompolinsky, 'Spin-glass models of neural networks', *Physical Review A*, 32 (1985), 1007–18.

20   D. L. Stein, 'Spin glasses', *Scientific American* (July, 1989), 36–42. In 1982, Hopfield himself referred to a special class of spin glasses, the Ising spins.

21   Allman, *Apprentices*, p. 136.

22   D. C. Dennett, 'Cognitive wheels: the frame problem of AI', in C. Hookway (ed.), *Minds, Machines and Evolution*, Cambridge, 1984, pp. 129–51.

23   This technique was developed by D. Rumelhart, J. McClelland and R. J. Williams, 'Learning representations by back propagating errors', *Nature*, 323 (1986), 533–6.

24   This argument was put forward by G. Hinton, 'Connectionist learning procedures', *Artificial Intelligence*, 40 (1989), 185–234; it was opposed by C. F. Stevens, 'Strengthening the synaps', *Nature*, 338 (1989), 460–1.

25   Another example of a cognitive wheel in neural networks is the 'veto cell', a single dogmatic neuron that can counteract the combined efforts of a group of neurons by blocking the impulse.

26   E. Hering, *Über das Gedächtnis als eine allgemeine Funktion der organisierten Materie*, Vienna, 1870.

27   H. D. Block, 'The perceptron: a model for brain functioning, 1', *Reviews of Modern Physics*, 34 (1962), 123–35.

28   P. T. Quinlan, *Connectionism and Psychology*, Chicago, 1991.

29   J. McClelland, D. Rumelhart and the PDP Research Group, *Parallel Distributed Processing: Explorations in the Microstructure of Cognition, vol 1*, Cambridge, MA, 1986.

30   A. Clark, *Microcognition: Philosophy, Cognitive Science, and Parallel Distributed Processing*, Cambridge, MA, 1989, p. 99.

31   See also A. G. Knapp and J. A. Anderson, 'Theory of categorization based on distributed memory storage', *Journal of Experimental Psychology: Learning, Memory, and Cognition*, 10 (1984) 4, 616–37.

32   G. Wolters and R. H. Phaf, 'Implicit and explicit memory: implications for the symbol-manipulation versus connectionism controversy', *Psychological Research*, 52 (1990), 137–44.

33 Anterograde amnesia is loss of memory for events following some trauma; in retrograde amnesia, part of the material stored *before* the trauma can no longer be reproduced. The dichotomy between explicit and implicit memory has also been described in terms of declarative versus procedural memory. A. Baddeley, *Human Memory. Theory and Practice*, Hillsdale, NJ, 1990, p. 207.

34 S. S. Korsakoff, 'Etude médico-psychologique sur une forme des maladies de la mémoire', *Revue philosophique*, 28 (1889), 501–30. Current thinking sees memory loss in Korsakoff's syndrome as caused not by alcohol but by neurological damage resulting from nutritional deficiencies.

35 Claparède's story can be found in D. L. Schacter's review article, 'Implicit memory: history and current status', *Journal of Experimental Psychology: Learning, Memory, and Cognition*, 13 (1987) 3, 501–18.

36 K. Schneider, 'Über einige klinisch-pathologische Untersuchungsmethoden und ihre Ergebnisse. Zugleich ein Beitrag zur Psychopathologie der Korsakowschen Psychose', *Zeitschrift für Neurologische Psychiatrie*, 8 (1912), 553–616.

37 S. Corkin, 'Acquisition of motor skill after bilateral medial temporal lobe-excision', *Neuropsychologia*, 6 (1968), 255–65. Henry M. suffered from a severe form of epilepsy; the operation was designed to reduce the frequency of fits.

38 E. K. Warrington and L. Weiskrantz, 'New method of testing long-term retention with special reference to amnesic patients', *Nature*, 217 (1968), 972–4.

39 D. L. Schacter, M. P. McAndrews and M. Moscovitch, 'Access to consciousness: dissociation between implicit and explicit knowledge in neuropsychological syndromes', in L. Weiskrantz (ed.), *Thought without Language*, Oxford, 1988, p. 244.

40 P. Graf, L. R. Squire and G. Mandler, 'The information that amnesic patients do not forget', *Journal of Experimental Psychology: Learning, Memory, and Cognition*, 10 (1984) 1, 164–78.

41 Schacter, 'Implicit memory'.

42 See also Baddeley, *Human Memory*, pp. 357ff.

43 P. Thagard, 'Parallel computation and the mind–body problem', *Cognitive Science*, 10 (1986), 301–18.

44 Wolters and Phaf, 'Connectionisme', 369.

45 D. A. Oakley and H. C. Plotkin (eds.), *Brain, Behaviour and Evolution*, London, 1979.

46 Baddeley, *Human Memory*, p. 378.

47 W. K. Estes, 'Toward a framework for combining connectionist and symbol-processing models', *Journal of Memory and Language*, 27 (1988), 196–212.

48 Clark, *Microcognition*, p. 161.

49 P. A. Vroon, *Tranen van de krokodil*, Baarn, 1989.

50 Quoted in Johnson, *Palaces*, p. 151. Cooper was referring to H. C. Longuet-Higgins, 'Holographic model of temporary recall', *Nature* (6 January, 1968), 104.

51 Quoted in Allman, *Apprentices*, p. 119.

52 Pribram himself, though, did point to the continuity between holography and connectionism: K. H. Pribram, 'From metaphors to models: the use of

analogy in neuropsychology', in D. E. Leary (ed.), *Metaphors in the History of Psychology*, Cambridge, MA, 1990, pp. 79–103.

53   Hinton and Anderson, *Parallel Models*.

54   D. Willshaw, 'Holography, associative memory and inductive generalization', in Hinton and Anderson, *Parallel Models*, pp. 83–104.

55   B. R. Gomulicki, 'The development and present status of the trace theory of memory', *The British Journal of Psychology. Monograph Supplements*, xxix (1953).

56   James's essay appeared in the *Popular Science Monthly* in March 1880 and was later included in a slightly modified form as the chapter on 'Association' in *Principles of Psychology*, New York, 1890. Quoted from W. James, *Principles of Psychology*, Cambridge edn, MA, 1983, p. 531.

57   *Ibid.*, p. 534.

58   F. Galton, 'On generic images', *Proceedings of the Royal Institution*, 9 (1879), 161–70.

59   *Ibid.*, 162.

60   Wolters and Phaf, 'Connectionisme', 368.

61   James, *Principles*, p. 617.

62   *Ibid.*, p. 618.

63   *Ibid.*, p. 649.

9   The homunculus

The alchemists' boldest vision was not the discovery of the Philosopher's Stone or the art of making gold, but the creation of an artificial human being, a *homunculus*. For the alchemists, the homunculus represented the dream of 'nature through art', the act of creation repeated by human means. Allegorical drawings showed the divine blessing being sought for this daring project, with the homunculus in a glass globe, as if in a retort, the product of human intellect and the labours in an alchemical laboratory (figure 54).

The theme of the homunculus continued to fascinate people through the centuries. From the Jewish 'golem' stories down to the Frankenstein novels, the creation of artificial life has haunted the imagination like one of those projects at the limits of human ability which may perhaps one day become reality.

In our day and age Artificial Intelligence has presented itself as the science capable of realising the aspirations of the alchemists. The creation of a new thinking being with the resources of the laboratory, would be a fitting culmination to the attempts to manufacture a replica of man's own intellect, a contemporary example of 'nature through art', perhaps less occult than the projects of alchemy, but certainly just as ambitious.

In the three or four centuries since the alchemists the *term* homunculus took on a different meaning. In psychology and AI the homunculus is the designation of a specific theoretical problem. A theory contains a homunculus as soon as the explanation of a psychological process appeals to the same process which requires explanation. The logical term is 'petitio principii' – assuming what has to be proved. Because this argument can be expanded *ad infinitum*, the homunculus is often equated with infinite regress.

Like the homunculus of alchemy the homunculus in psychology has its own iconography. In popular-scientific representations of the human brain, the homunculus is depicted as a little man who observes incoming sensory information, evaluates it and subsequently acts on it. This iconography is time-bound, just as the representations of the brain itself; the homunculus is surrounded by a technology which is constantly renewing itself (figures 55 and 56).

54.   Engraving of the alchemical homunculus as a dream of 'nature through art'.

At the end of the nineteenth century he found himself in a kind of telegraph office, full of panels of switches with lines coming in and going out, busy with wires and plugs. In the 1920s the homunculi used the latest techniques for registering and reproducing information: film cameras, screens and projectors.

Nowadays in representations of the brain one can see the monitors and computers which are found in offices and industry, but they are still operated by homunculi. A fully automated brain, with empty control rooms, is not found

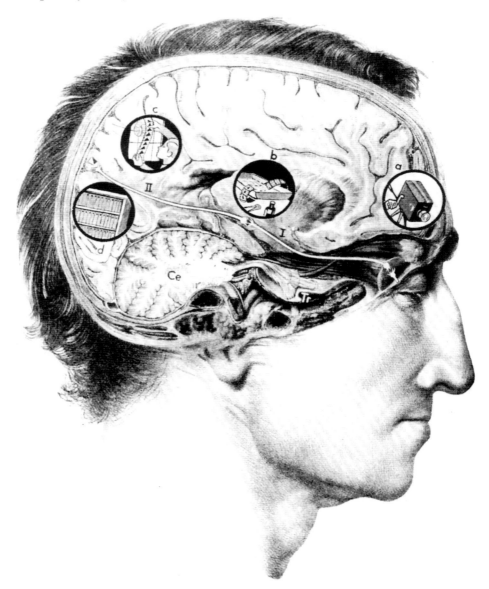

55.   In this cinematographic metaphor of the visual memory (1929), presented by F. Kahn in *Das Leben des Menschen*, a film camera operated with a crank functions as the eye. The images on the film are developed and passed on to the visual projection area at the back of the brain. There they are examined by a little man and stored in what the caption calls the 'optical memory centre', represented as a film archive. The whole process is automatic, apart from the activities of the film archivist.

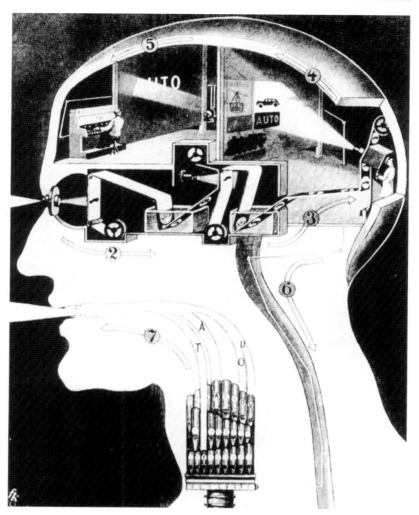

56.   Fritz Kahn's illustration entitled 'What goes on in our head when we see a
      car and say "auto"', appeared in a later edition of *Das Leben des Menschen*. The
      process of perception, registration and reaction is now much more detailed.
      The (automatic) film camera of the eye takes the picture of a car. The film
      passes through various developing baths and reaches the visual projection
      area. There an operator projects the image of the car onto a screen and at
      the same time puts the word AUTO underneath. Those letters are passed to a
      following screen, which is read by the little man at the 'speech organ'. The
      latter presses the keys for A, U, T and O on his keyboard, whereupon the organ
      pipes of the speech apparatus produce the required sounds. The course of
      this whole process, the text states, 'shows in its astonishing speed a striking
      similarity to television and radio technology'.

57.   Engraving of Descartes's explanation of the reflex. The heat of the fire forces the *spiritus animales* in the nerve B into the brain. The pressure forces the pores in the brain to open, including the entrance to the cranial cavity F. The *spiritus animales* contained in it flow into nerve B, make the muscles swell and cause the leg to be withdrawn. Descartes pointed out that we perform this action 'comme une machine' ('mechanically'): the soul has no effect on it.

in popular-scientific depictions. There is obviously something in our intuition which resists the thought that our brain can do its work without the supervision of a thinking, evaluating consciousness. The explanation for this resistance may be connected with introspective experiences.

All the abilities and processes that our brain contains fall between two concepts which indicate the extremes of our functioning, *reflex* and *reflection*. Like the body, the mental apparatus of our memory has reflexes, purely automatic reactions, using fixed circuitry, and executed by an innate mechanism. This compartment of our memory is inaccessible to consciousness. As Von Hartmann put it in the last century, we have access to the *results* of those processes, not to the processes themselves. The activities which take place there are also impossible to influence. This cognitive impenetrability has been described for such phenomena as our perception of optical illusions. However often we experiment with optical illusions, however much insight we have into the mechanisms responsible for the illusion effect, our sensitivity to the illusion remains intact; obviously susceptibility to optical illusions is laid down in a part of our software that cannot be modified.

The opposite to these reflex processes is reflection, which is linked with voluntary memory and provides us with the introspective experience that we can supervise what goes on in our memory. Part of our memory *is* accessible to our consciousness, we are perhaps not lord and master in it but we can imagine what is found there as we please, evoke it in our mind's eye and consider it.

Ironically these extremes, reflex and reflection, have the same etymological origin: they both have to do with mirroring. Reflex, because in the seventeenth century it was assumed that violent sensory stimuli requiring a quick reaction were immediately 'bounced back' by the brain into a motor movement (figure 57). Reflection, because thoughts and representations in memory were supposed to be 'mirrored' in consciousness (which is preserved in the figurative meaning of reflection) thus creating that strange duplication which probably only human beings have: thinking and knowing that you are thinking, remembering and being aware that you are remembering something.

The same duplication is expressed in an almost irresistible tendency to represent the act of remembering as a person who enters the memory and starts searching there. The writer Rudy Kousbroek talks of a restless archivist, a monomaniac who is constantly kept active: 'As soon as he has an idle moment, he goes to the archive and takes out all kinds of cases which have long ago been dealt with, which he reintroduces unnoticed into the administration. Invoices that were settled years ago appear in the accounts, long since signed letters are again presented for signature.' He spends his evening hours in the cellar, leafing 'through files whose existence everyone in the organisation had forgotten'.[1] The novelist W. F. Hermans writes that our recollection sometimes behaves 'like a drunken servant, who is able to retrieve only cobwebs, slivers of glass and stories about ghosts from a cellar where the most precious wines are stored'.[2] Such homunculi are the verbal equivalents of the industrious employees who in the drawings of exposed brains are busy recording, developing and filing sensory information.

Who looks at the hologram?

In memory psychology the homunculus is an infamous heresy. A theory of memory contains a homunculus as soon as it assumes a capacity which 'remembers' where material is stored or which 'recognises' material, after all, remembering and recognising presuppose a memory. The homunculus is an extra problem instead of a solution.

In all the metaphors dealt with so far, a homunculus has appeared sooner or later. Hooke's metaphor of the microcosm contained a homunculus of the pontifical kind. From the centre of the microcosm the soul assigned all impressions a form and a place, introduced associations, 'recognised' certain impressions as corresponding with stored impressions and hence duplicated precisely those processes which a theory of memory ought to explain. In Hooke's microcosm the soul was a memory-within-a-memory.

Similar problems arose in the nineteenth century with the metaphors borrowed from photography and the phonograph. Reacting to the photographic metaphors of his age (see chapter 5) Huber argued that the preservation of visual impressions in the brain is not itself a memory; only the presence of a consciousness that can absorb those impressions makes it a true memory. Without consciousness the traces are 'blind'. Guyau chose virtually the same words in the commentary on his phonograph metaphor. The needle engraves a record of the sound stimuli on the phonographic disc, he explained, but as long as the consciousness does not absorb the sound vibrations as they are played, this trace remains 'deaf to itself'. Whether it be visual or auditory stimuli that are stored, reproduction in the memory presupposes a consciousness which uses those traces.

An identical problem occurs with the much more modern metaphor of the hologram. In a hologram the stored image is 'read out' by illumination with a laser beam. This illumination projects the image into a virtual space outside the storage medium where it can be perceived. In Pribram's holographic theory of memory it is assumed that the stored images are projected outside the storage medium – the brain – and are hence absorbed into consciousness. Various authors have pointed out the awkward presence of a homunculus in this theory.[3] If consciousness is able to 'observe' images, this act presupposes a repetition of the problem: an agent would also be required to observe images in the homunculus. The perception of projected images creates an infinite series of homunculi, a procession of ever-smaller dwarves.

'Who observes the hologram?', a question which appears so simple, actually introduces an awkward dilemma. On the one hand, something essential seems to be lacking in a theory in which images are recorded and stored, but are not reproduced in the consciousness; the images remain unperceived, unnoticed. On the other hand, a theory in which the consciousness 'observes' images is conceptually deficient: a consciousness which looks at memory images like an observer at his monitor is homuncular. This leads to a discouraging dilemma. In the words of Dennett: 'Therefore, psychology *without* homunculi is impossible. But psychology *with* homunculi is doomed to circularity or infinite regress, so psychology is impossible.'[4]

In this dilemma one can discern the outlines of an ancient philosophical problem linked with the name of Descartes and which surfaced in the latter's theory of memory. A discussion of Descartes's theory of memory will enable us to analyse the philosophical questions at issue in the homunculus problem and which have received such graphic expression in memory metaphors.

Descartes on memory

Descartes's theory of memory has to be reconstructed from the scattered passages which he devoted to remembrance in his books and correspondence. Human memory, he argued, can be divided into a 'corporeal' and 'spiritual' memory. Of spiritual memory, Descartes said little more than that it exists and that its operation is based on 'traces' which intellectual experience leaves behind in the soul. The operation of corporeal memory was described by Descartes in his *Traité de l'homme*. The human nervous system, he maintained, consists of thin hollow tubes, filled with a gaseous substance, the *spiritus animales*. These animal spirits, 'a very gentle wind, or rather a kind of very pure and very fierce flame', also fill the pores in the brain. When an object is perceived, the animal spirits in the sensory nerves are activated, are forced into the brain and so stretch a part of the pores. The perception of other objects in turn causes other patterns of stretched pores and in this way every object perceived leaves a trace. The physics of those traces is reminiscent of the erosion of a bed. The more often a trace is used, the deeper it becomes. This purely physical mechanism underlies a type of memory which Descartes described in a letter to Father Mersenne and which one would now call 'muscle memory': 'a lute player, for instance, has a part of his memory in his hands: for the ease of bending and positioning his fingers in various ways, which he has acquired by practice, helps him to remember the passages which need these positions when they are played'.[5] In a subsequent letter to Mersenne, possibly in response to an objection from his correspondent, he discussed the assumption that it is precisely events from our childhood that we remember best. At first sight that is difficult to reconcile with the theory of memory traces because traces become blurred the older they get. In his reply, Descartes describes the process which corresponds to the present-day hypothesis of *trace consolidation*: that we remember the events of our youth so well is mainly due to the fact that 'we have done the same things again and renewed the impressions by remembering the events over and over from time to time'.[6] Old people who recall a scene from their childhood, are not remembering their childhood, but a *memory* of their childhood.

A phenomenon like association also fitted in with the theory of memory traces. To clarify this Descartes drew on a physical analogy depicted in the *Traité de l'homme* (figure 58). If thorns are pressed into a cloth, holes will be created. By repeating this action, some of these holes will become wider until finally they will stay permanently open. If on another occasion only some of the holes are pressed, then some of the old and new holes will open together. The holes in the cloth are the pores in the brain, the thorns, the animal spirits which are forced into the pores by sensory stimuli. If the stimuli exhibit a pattern, such as in the perception of a face, part of that pattern, perhaps the nose and two eyes, may evoke the rest of the pattern by association: even without thorns the holes open a little wider.[7]

In Descartes's view a comparable mechanism was used when training animals. If one were to quieten a hunting dog whenever it were to see a partridge flying out of its cover, the natural association between stimulus and reaction would be replaced by a new association mechanically: the existing trace, the natural groove engrained by the animal spirits, would silt up and such training would create a new groove.[8] Descartes considered animals to be *automata* and suggested that training a dog was nothing more than recalibrating a machine for a different task. Descartes viewed the physical memory of animals as the cogwheels between incoming stimuli and outgoing reactions. Associations in this type of memory came automatically. To the extent that the human memory is material in nature, the same applies to the associations in human memory. To a large extent we learn without the involvement of the soul.

But *subsequently* there is a difference. Unlike animals, human beings are capable of voluntary memory. Descartes discusses this topic in the *Passions de*

58.   Engraving of Descartes's physical analogy for association.

l'âme, under the heading: 'How we find in the memory the things we wish to remember.'[9] When the soul wants to recall something, this volition causes the pineal gland (epiphysis) to incline successively in different directions. The animal spirits are in this way forced into various parts of the brain until they reach the place where the traces are to be found which were left by the object sought. The ease with which the animal spirits flow to this pattern of stretched pores, causes a certain movement in the pineal gland. Finally the soul recognises this as the memory of the object sought.

The attraction of Descartes's theory is its coherent explanation of quite diverse phenomena: the training of animals, the automatic responses of trained musicians, the fact that memories of events from long ago are still clear in our minds, the creation of associations between stimuli, and the voluntary memory. But a price is paid for that comprehensiveness. In the first place, it remains unexplained how the soul, as a non-spatial, non-material substance, can take cognisance of what occurs in the material memory, or, conversely, how an event in the material memory can lead to a representation in the soul. This is the problem of *interaction*, a problem which is acutely present in the pineal gland and also occurs in Descartes's theory of perception. It is simply a familiar conceptual scar which has become intertwined with Cartesian dualism. The second problem relates to the *circularity* in the theory of voluntary memory. The keystone of the Cartesian explanation is the movement of the pineal gland which is *recognised* by the soul as that of the object sought. But recognition is a process that presupposes a memory and hence cannot play any part in an explanation of remembering. A soul which recognises does not represent the solution, but is a duplication of the problem.

These two conceptual questions, interaction and circularity, are intertwined in the notion of 'trace'. Descartes used the term 'vestige'. He compared traces to folds in a piece of paper: the traces in the brain cause a predisposition to a particular movement, just as one can easily fold a sheet of paper once it has already been folded. These traces are purely physical in nature. The traces in the brains of animals form the material deposit of previous stimuli and reactions and if the animal appears to learn from experience it is because the traces predispose it mechanically towards certain reactions. The traces in human memory are partly identical. The physical changes in the brain make reactions possible, such as the rapid finger movements of a lutanist, movements which previously could only be executed with great effort. Philosophical complications only arise with a second aspect of the memory trace. In voluntary memory the soul can recognise a particular movement of the pineal gland as the memory that is being sought, due to the fact that movement is a *representation* of the object which the soul wishes to recall. The movement of the pineal gland 'represents that same object to the soul'.[10] It is precisely this representational character of the memory trace that summarises the problem of interaction and circularity: (1) How can a physical situation be connected with a non-physical abstraction like 'representation'? (2) How can the soul remember which movement represents which object without in turn assuming that there is a memory present in the soul?

In Descartes's theory of memory the two main problems of Cartesian dualism are repeated in miniature form. The question is now whether more recent theories and metaphors for memory have been able to solve those problems.

Homunculus and the computer

The metaphors with which Guyau, Luys and other theoreticians from the tradition of 'mental physiology' described the physical substratum of a memory, were derived from artificial memories which did not yet exist at the time of Descartes. Nevertheless one can clearly recognise the essential mechanisms of Descartes's theory of memory in them. Through the phonograph and the photographs Guyau and Luys illustrated that sensory experience left traces in the brain. In both cases the traces have a latent character: they are activated only when sensory perceptions are reproduced in the memory. The nerve currents of Guyau follow courses which have been worn out by experience. Thus the stretched pores of Descartes reappear. Unfortunately the complications of Cartesian memory theory are repeated as well: the traces in Guyau's auditory memory remain 'deaf to themselves', the visual impressions in Luys's theory remain 'invisible to themselves'. None of the authors specify the way in which the consciousness absorbs the traces. Both Guyau and Luys observed *that* there is a connection between physical traces and conscious memory, but it is precisely that point, the *how* of that connection, that remains a mystery.

Anyone who states a problem surrounding the physical substratum of memory in these terms – and at first sight it seems a very natural way of describing it – will be sceptical about the possibility that technical progress will eventually provide the metaphor which deals with these conceptual problems. If the consciousness is assigned the role of observer (after all we are conscious of remembered images and sounds) the question keeps arising of how physical storage can lead to conscious experience. It is as if *every* memory theory in which experiences leave traces is sooner or later haunted by the ghost of Descartes. The problem of the homunculus seems inherent in the use of representations.

In the view of some authors, the computer metaphor has solved two related questions and thus it has solved the homunculus problem at the same time. One question is designated by Dennett as 'Hume's problem', and relates to the status of representations.[11] According to Dennett's analysis, the computer metaphor has proved that representations do not presuppose an interpreting or supervising agency, since the functions in the programme which use representations can be divided into ever simpler component tasks which, at the lowest level, no longer presuppose intelligence.[12] Since the lowest level is no more than an 'army of idiots', there is no question of circularity. The only task of those 'idiots', wrote Dennett, 'is to remember whether to say yes or no when asked'.[13] In a recent version of this analysis, Dennett explicitly linked his solution with the status of representations: 'The subsystems don't individually reproduce all of the talents of the whole. That would lead you to an infinite regress. Instead you have each subsystem doing a part, so that each homuncular subsystem is less intelligent, knows less, believes less. The representations are themselves, as it were, less representational.'[14] The advent of the computer has, he believes, stripped the notion of representation of its homuncular character.

The second question to which the computer metaphor suggests a solution is the 'problem' of Descartes. The computer, it is argued, is the first machine to enable us to have a coherent perspective of the relationship between spirit and body. Because of the new meaning that the computer has given to the notion 'machine', wrote Boden, the old metaphysical problem of the connection between body and soul has been 'largely solved'.[15] Computational insights, she argues, make it clear 'how it is possible for the mind to act on the body during purposive action and voluntary choice'.[16] Translated to the memory these are precisely the two mysteries from Cartesian memory theory: the interaction between body and soul and the operation of voluntary remembering. A metaphor which has solved these mysteries, even if only 'largely', is, of course, worth closer investigation.

What theorists who use the computer metaphor have in common despite all their differences, is the central position they assign to the intentional character of mental states. The psychological terms in daily usage, knowing, thinking, remembering, refer to something in the outside world or something in an inner experience, but always something that lies outside the act of knowing, thinking or remembering – I know that it's raining, I think John is lying, or I remember that I read a book yesterday. It is these intentional notions, writes Boden, that give human consciousness its subjective, interpretive character and an acceptable theory of mind will have to do justice to that character.[17] The theory inspired by the computer metaphor of mind appeals to 'mental representations', in which, at a symbolic or semantic level, knowledge is established about the outside world and our inner experience. Because of this referential element, representations link up with intentional states: our consciousness gives *meaning* to the world and is able to do so because of the semantic character of mental representations. What makes the computer such a plausible metaphor for the human mind is the combination of meaningful processes and what are in themselves meaningless physical processes in the mechanism of the computer. The mechanism corresponds to the human nervous system, the programme to the psychological processes. In this way, the computer metaphor gives us the best of both worlds: it recognises both the existence of mental states and the existence of a physical substratum. Thanks to the computer, it is argued, the scar of an impossible interaction has disappeared from dualism.

Before analysing this solution to the mind–body problem more closely, it will be useful to present a concrete application of the computer metaphor to a memory process: pattern recognition by 'optical neural computers'.

Optical neural computers

Children who are not even three are capable of recognising a variety of clockwork mechanisms – tower clocks, alarm clocks, car clocks, watches, pendulum clocks – and refer to them all as 'tick-tocks'. This means that they possess the ability to solve *random problems*, even though they are unable to recognise this themselves. These kinds of problems arise through the practical impossibility of defining a recognisable pattern, for example a tree, in all its possible variants (figure 59).[18] Since the operations of conventional computers are precisely based on explicit definitions and instructions, mechanical pattern recognition has been a laborious process up until now. Without a complete list of defining characteristics, a computer runs the risk of supposing that a telephone pole is a tree, a mistake which even three-year-olds do not make.

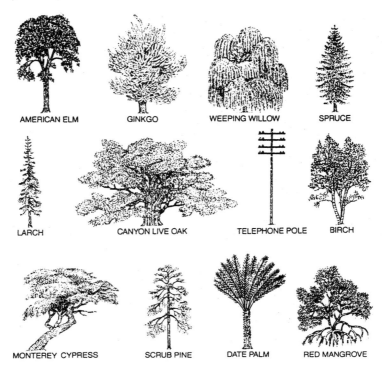

AMERICAN ELM   GINKGO   WEEPING WILLOW   SPRUCE

LARCH   CANYON LIVE OAK   TELEPHONE POLE   BIRCH

MONTEREY CYPRESS   SCRUB PINE   DATE PALM   RED MANGROVE

59.   Drawing illustrating the visualisation of a *random problem*. Even without an exhaustive list of all the variants on trees, a child of three is capable of deciding fairly accurately what belongs in the category 'tree'. A specification of the pattern suitable for conventional computers (for example, in terms of 'trunk' and 'side branches') might lead to the incorrect inclusion of the telephone pole.

In the 1980s, ideas have been developed about a computer architecture which is better adapted to pattern recognition.[19] Because this alternative architecture tries to imitate the anatomical structure of a neural network and processes part of the information with light rays, it is called an optical neural computer. Computers of this type work with several processors, which process the information in parallel via a large number of connections. The large number of connections make it necessary to use optical means. Light beams can intersect without interference and are therefore also practical in three-dimensional structures. The light beams are converted in an optical neural computer by memory elements into one of two states: 0 or 1, and in this way, like traditional computers, can be used for the storage and reproduction of information.

But a comprehensive memory, whether or not created optically, is in itself not capable of solving *random problems*: a sequential search through such a memory will take a long time. The only efficient alternative is a direct association between information presented and information stored without the

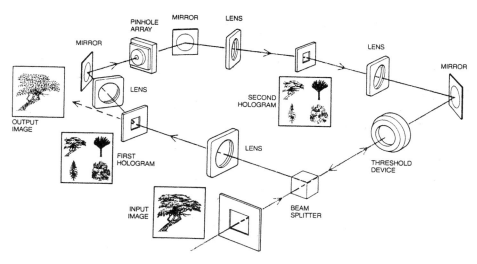

60.   Scheme of a pattern-recognition system developed at the California Institute of Technology by Y. S. Abu-Mostafa and D. Psaltis. The optical image of a cypress (bottom centre) is conducted through a hologram which functions as the memory and in which the patterns of four trees are stored. The interaction between the pattern presented and the stored patterns then passes to a second hologram, which chooses from the four patterns the one which corresponds most closely to the pattern initially presented. The cycle is repeated until the best possible match is obtained. The latter finally appears as an output image (left).

requirement of complete resemblance. Such an association process is the most important property of human memory: a familiar face evokes a whole pattern of connected information, the name, our feelings about that person, the last time we spoke to him, and in all probability this process does not have the step-by-step structure of an algorithm. This raises the question of whether the anatomical structure of the brain can suggest an organising principle for such associations.

Computers in which the processing elements are ordered like the neurons in the brain can be made to solve *random problems* by using the connections between those elements as storage mechanisms. Such a machine would 'learn spontaneously' because associations are created between presented problems and stored solutions. Recognition of a tree would be possible through association between the pattern of the tree which is presented and previously stored patterns of trees. In the prototype of an optical neural computer developed by Abu-Mostafa and Psaltis, a hologram functions as the memory (figure 60). In a flat plane 10,000 neurons are simulated by a number of elements. Reflexivity changes depending on the intensity of the light stimulus applied to the back. In this way, a change is simulated in the threshold value of the neurons.

Patterns which are presented are compared with stored patterns in a number of repeating cycles, with a match becoming ever more exact. When the similarity is sufficient the relevant stored pattern is presented as the output: the computer has 'recognised' the pattern.

Mnemosyne's gift

Within the metaphor of the optical neural computer, the notion of memory trace has two aspects. From a purely physical point of view, the configurations of the altered threshold values form a whole series of inert traces, a dead labyrinth of switches, silent and invisible to itself. At the same time, these traces have a referential or symbolic character: they represent the pattern of a tree. They have *meaning*, and it is that meaning which is recognised by the computer. In this respect there is no fundamental difference at all between the classical computer, with explicitly programmed representations, and the connectionist theories in which the representation consists of patterns of strength connections in neural networks. In both cases there is a memory trace that can be interpreted in both a physical and symbolic way.

Has this interpretation of the memory trace actually solved the mind–body problem, insofar as it relates to memory? Does the computer metaphor really show us how the interaction between a physical substratum and consciousness is possible? How it is possible to speak of the choice of a trace without regress? How the homunculus has been ousted? In short, is the optical neural computer really a more appropriate metaphor for human memory than, say, the phonograph?

If one considers the homunculus problem as an incentive which encourages us to explain as many memory processes as possible in a regression-free way, then the optical neural computer is a more productive metaphor than the phonograph. In the case of a phonograph various interventions are necessary for the reproduction of the stored material, while the pattern-recognising computer deals with reproduction completely autonomously. In the case of the phonograph, reproduction is only possible at the price of a regress: the choice of a trace requires an agent who has to remember what information is stored in what trace. The activation of a phonographic trace therefore presupposes a memory, namely of the person who is using the apparatus and wants to listen to a particular piece of music. In the case of the optical neural computer the choice of a trace is made completely automatically. The pattern presented evokes the associated trace without further intervention. No memory is needed to use this computer memory.

Hence in practical and methodological respects, the computer metaphor is indeed a step in the direction of a regress-free theory. But to the solution of the *fundamental* homunculus problem (how the physical configurations, however represented, with whatever they are compared, are absorbed into consciousness), the computer metaphor contributes just as much (or as little) as older metaphors like the phonograph or even Plato's wax tablet. Both mysteries of Descartes, the connection between body and soul and the circularity of voluntary memory, are left unsolved in the computer metaphor. The first problem, interaction, would be solved only if the information – the level that corresponds to 'mind' – were to influence the mechanism, in terms of *information*. And that is not the case. However natural it may be to describe a particular input pattern as the drawing of a tree, however natural it is to see a tree in the reproduced patterns, the fact that both patterns *represent* something (or are even 'patterns' at all) is simply due to human attribution. The same applies to the representations in the memory of the computer: the patterns of changed threshold values convey visual information only 'in the eye of the beholder'. To say that representations 'affect' the physical processes in a computer is a misleading expression: the only thing that affects the physical processes are the preceding physical processes. The computer interpretation of the memory trace does not provide a solution to the problem of interaction, but rather a radicalisation of it: a strict parallelism of physical and representational processes.

Dennett's strategy for solving the regress problem by dividing up homunculi of the pontifical kind into teams of less intelligent homunculi, who only have to remember 'whether to say yes or no when asked', does not help us. Even less intelligent homunculi still use representations which are only representations because they have been assigned meaning from outside. Even at the lowest level of homunculi, that of the simplest souls, as long as information is still processed, the regress has not been broken.[20] Representations of the most stupid homunculi may be 'less representational', as Dennett argued, but this does not mean that they cease to be representations. The crucial argument has been emphasised by Haldane: 'The philosophical problem of meaning and intentionality is not one of explaining how things can have so *much* of them, but rather one of explaining how they can have them *at all*.'[21]

This removes the basis of the view that computational insights make it clear 'how it is possible for the mind to act on the body during purposive action and voluntary choice', as Boden put it, because it is not the representations themselves that affect the body, but their physical correlates. The computer does not recognise *meaning*, so there is no recognition at all. The conclusion must be that none of the theories discussed so far, including those which have been inspired by computational metaphors, escape the complications of the mind–body problem.

The gist of this analysis is that the homunculus comes in two versions which are insufficiently distinguished in the literature. The first one is methodological in nature and states the requirement that theories must be as free as possible from regress. In this variant, the homunculus problem allows a gradual solution and one metaphor can approach the ideal of a regression-free explanation better than another. The other version of the homunculus problem is philosophical in nature and is connected with the relationship between body and mind. This second homunculus is summed up in the mystery of how physical events in the brain come into our consciousness and how material changes in neuronal connections can have a conscious aspect in the phenomena of personal memory. These two homunculi are closely related, perhaps even twins, but not identical ones: the 'methodological' homunculus may be ousted without the 'Cartesian homunculus' being expelled. At least present-day theories of memory, have not succeeded in doing the latter whichever metaphor they are inspired by.

It is arguable whether this conclusion says anything detrimental to these theories. The mass of memory theories is tailored to what has been called a 'third-person' psychology. Other people's memory is not subjectively accessible and we only become aware of someone's memories when they are expressed in observable behaviour. In the practice of memory research this behaviour is the reproduction of material or learning by experience. This external point of view is opposed to the 'first-person' psychology, in which a personal consciousness is presupposed which is introspectively accessible. Voluntary memory and other subjective memory phenomena are part of 'first-person' psychology. This is a shift of vital importance. Descartes placed a philosophical caesura between human consciousness and the physical part of reality. For memory, this meant: the human memory against the processing of physical stimuli in the brain. But in psychology the caesura is rather between the personal memory and the memory of others. This last caesura is methodological in nature and is connected with the means of access: introspection or observable behaviour.

The distinction between first and third-person perspective may also clarify why present-day psychologists do not worry too much about conceptual problems concerning voluntary memory or other subjective phenomena. In human memory as dealt with in recent theory, the 'listening to', or 'selection' of a trace by consciousness plays no role because in a 'third-person' psychology it is not necessary to presuppose a consciousness. The memory has approximately the status which Descartes assigned to the memory of animals: a mechanism in which stimuli leave 'traces' in the form of associations, an automated switching system without a supervising consciousness. There is no question of interaction between body and mind in an inanimate mechanism and nor is there of voluntary memory. Quite simply there *is* no consciousness that is aware of recollection. From the 'third-person' perspective, memories are summaries of externally perceived behaviours. One cannot say that the computer metaphor of memory has solved the mind–body problem precisely for that reason. It is true that in normal parlance a computer has a memory, but the intuitive hesitation that we feel when we say that this memory contains recollections or that a computer can remember something, is quite natural.

Mnemosyne has not given the same gifts to everyone. The memory that she gave to you and others is subject to external investigation. The memory that she gave me has a subjective, personal access, a secret door from inside. The price of that privileged access is a stubborn mystery: I do not know how my personal, introspective experience is linked to the observable processes in my brain. In my memory I cherish an intimate but unfathomable possession.

Notes

1   R. Kousbroek, *Een kuil om snikkend in te vallen*, Amsterdam, 1971, p. 49.

2   W. F. Hermans, *Boze brieven van Bijkaart*, Amsterdam, 1977.

3   See also chapter 7.

4   D. C. Dennett, *Brainstorms. Philosophical Essays on Mind and Psychology*, Hassocks, 1978, p. 122.

5   Letter to Mersenne (1 April 1640). In R. Descartes, *The Philosophical Writings of Descartes (Vol. III: The Correspondence)*, trans. by J. Cottingham, R. Stoothoff, D. Murdoch and A. Kenny, Cambridge, 1991, p. 146.

6   Letter to Mersenne (6 August 1640). *Ibid.*, p. 151.

7   R. Descartes, *The Philosophical Writings of Descartes (Vol. I)*, trans. J. Cottingham, R. Stoothoff and D. Murdoch, Cambridge, 1985, p. 107.

8   R. Descartes, *Descartes' Philosophical Writings*, trans. N. Kemp Smith, London, 1952, p. 305.

9   *Ibid.*, pp. 298–9.

10 *Ibid.*, p. 299.

11 See also chapter 6.

12 Dennett's analysis was anticipated by F. Attneave, 'In defense of homunculi', in W. A. Rosenblith (ed.) *Sensory Communication*, Cambridge, 1961.

13 Dennett, *Brainstorms*, p. 124. The same theory is developed further in D. C. Dennett, *Consciousness Explained*, London, 1991.

14 D. C. Dennett, 'Artificial intelligence and the strategies of psychological investigation, in J. Miller (ed.), *States of Mind*, London, 1983, pp. 66–81.

15 M. A. Boden, *Artificial Intelligence and Natural Man*, New York, 1977, p. 4.

16 M. A. Boden, *Minds and Mechanisms: Philosophical Psychology and Computational Models*, Brighton, 1981, p. 31.

17 *Ibid.*, p. 38.

18 A similar problem arises in the forming of categories (see chapter 8).

19 Y. S. Abu-Mostafa and D. Psaltis, 'Optical neural computers', *Scientific American* (April 1987), 66–73.

20 For analyses with a similar gist: J. Margolis, 'The trouble with homunculus theories', *Philosophy of Science*, 47 (1980), 244–59; D. Draaisma, 'De angst van de homunculus voor het scheermes', *Kennis en methode*, 8 (1984) 3, 225–39.

21 J. Haldane, 'Psychoanalysis, cognitive psychology and self consciousness', in C. Wright and P. Clark (eds.), *Mind, Psychoanalysis and Science*, Oxford, 1988, pp. 113–39.

Epilogue

The churnings of the metaphor mill have projected constantly changing images of our representations of memory. Memory was once a wax tablet, codex or magic slate, then again an abbey or theatre, sometimes a forest in which our recollection hunted for the trail of hidden game, or on other occasions a treasure chest, aviary or warehouse. When writers on memory have used their own metaphors, they have quite innocently recorded whatever preoccupied them or surrounded them. Augustine's imagery for memory describes the fields and caves around Carthage. In Thomas Aquinas's metaphors one senses medieval respect for traditionally sacred texts. Robert Fludd's graphic image of the memory as a theatre reflects a microcosm of occult arts and a waning of Hermeticism. Robert Hooke portrayed himself in his metaphors as a mechanistic thinker, an experimenter and an expert microscopist. Through the centuries metaphors have had a preserving quality and in that way gained an almost museum-like power.

At the same time, metaphors have given shape to views and interpretations of memory. In a playful metaphor like that of Plato's aviary, the memory does not have the same meaning as in the representation of the memory as the light-sensitive plate of a photographic camera, exposed to sensory stimuli. One metaphor turns our recollections into fluttering birds which we can only catch at the risk of grabbing the wrong one, the next one reduces memories to static and latent traces. Anyone who, like Carus, thinks of memory as a labyrinth or as a mysterious, incomprehensibly rapid loom, has a different memory in mind than Van Heerden or Pribram, who describe storage and reproduction in the formal terms of holography. With each new metaphor we place a different filter in front of our perception of memory.

Working chronologically from Plato up until the present-day researchers of neural networks, these metaphors acquire an increasingly technical character. Where for centuries the artificial memory of writing or the printing of a stamp in wax seemed sufficient imagery for philosophers, in the seventeenth century more complicated metaphors appeared, derived from mechanical analogies.

After the Romantic period, from the middle of the nineteenth century onwards, it became the new artificial memories, photography, the phonograph and cinematography, which dominated theory. Acoustic, visual and other sensory impressions leave their traces in the neuronal register of the brain. Neuronal processes become telegraphic codes, the brain a switchboard between incoming and outgoing lines. After the turn of the century, the neo-behaviourists developed mechanical models with which learning behaviour could be simulated. The electro-mechanical 'psychic machines' of Hull were attempts to uncover the processes between stimulus and reaction. After the Second World War the computer became the dominant metaphor for the human mind, a machine which it was claimed processed symbols and could do justice to the situation that much of what is in our memory has meaning. In the 1970s the hologram focused attention on qualities such as 'graceful degradation', content-addressability and distributed storage. Reflected in theory, the memory came to look like the technologies it was modelled on.

This slow metamorphosis was welcomed rather than lamented in psychology – the science which declared memory its lawful domain. From Robert Hooke down to the supporters of neural networks, memory metaphors have been linked to a certain excitement about the existence of artificial systems which can 'remember' something purely in a physical way. What remained constant throughout the metamorphosis of metaphors is the enthusiasm with which these artificial memories were presented. Whether one reads Draper on the first photographic procedures, Guyau and Delbœuf on the auditory memory of the phonograph, Galton on the 'compound photography', Hull on his 'psychic machines', Turing on the 'electronic brain', Van Heerden and Pribram on the hologram or Rumelhart and McClelland on their neural networks, all the time there is the enthusiasm surrounding techniques or apparatuses with which memory processes could be duplicated. This enthusiasm partly arose out of personal involvement – Hooke, Draper, Galton, Hull, Turing and Van Heerden developed the techniques which were later to return in their work as metaphors – but it was also connected with the awe surrounding simulations of psychological properties. Artificial memories seemed to prove the viability of a material explanation for human memory, without reference to something as ethereal as mind or consciousness.

The natural consequence was that the psychology of memory obtained a close connection with technological developments and also derived status from it. The Académie des Sciences where Daguerre revealed his procedure in 1839 and where in 1878 the phonograph was demonstrated, the Royal Institution where Maxwell (1861) and Galton (1878) gave their lectures on photography, the workshops of inventors like Edison and Bell, the technical institutes where the first computers were designed and built, the Polaroid laboratory where Van Heerden worked on holographic systems, the laboratories of Cal Tech, MIT, NASA and Texas Instruments where neural networks were developed – in all these places the prestige of technology illuminated memory psychology. In western culture where psychology after all arose, this association has always been appreciated.

It seems that neural networks are the artificial memories which in our age are most compatible with the qualities of natural memory. These prostheses are exceptionally powerful, particularly at the level of learning, association and recognition. As a formalisation of the path of least resistance they offer an artificial parallel of what the 'mental physiology' at the end of the last century specified as a substratum of memory: memory rests on the carving out of activational patterns into neuronal tissue. The correspondence between connectionism and 'mental physiology' is fairly compelling and in this way it seems as if the metaphor mill has come round full circle, as if it were projecting through current interpretations of memory the same image as a century ago. That would be putting it too strongly. In its time 'mental physiology' tried to give a neuronal specification to laws of association which originated in the reflective traditions of philosophy. The 'nerve-nets' of McCulloch from the 1940s had a background in Boolean logic, switch theory and information theory. The neural networks of today are formalisations of neuronal connections which can be simulated on computers. These three episodes from the history of memory each have their own background and domain, their own standards of precision and design, their own criteria for testability. The history of memory is Heraclitic: no single metaphor or theory repeats itself in an identical shape.

Yet the similarities in these three projections are sufficient to see repetition too. In attempting to explain memory in terms of neuronal processes, a specific and typical orientation in memory research repeats itself and hypotheses which were already present in the older theories are once more introduced into the psychology of memory.

There is also repetition at the level of specific memory metaphors. In psychology one can see the same theoretical notions returning in constantly changing metaphorical forms. This applies, for example, to the mechanism specified by Galton for the construction of prototypical representations, a mechanism which was repeated rather than refined in the prototype networks of McClelland and Rumelhart. This applies even more to the notion of facilitation. For all the enormous variety of physiological processes which have been pointed to as a substratum for the engraving of traces, the core has remained the same. The Cartesian pores in the brain and the 'vibrations' of Hartley, the nerve circuits and associative pathways of mental physiology, the 'nerve-nets' of McCulloch, the Hopfield networks and the spinglasses – each of these theories and models expresses the notion of facilitation. The activation of neural tracts facilitates its own repetition and this disposition to activation serves as the representation of experience. The general conclusion must be that the continual variation of terms and metaphors suggests more change than there actually is. Our conceptions of memory are always mixed with the technologies used as metaphors and appear to change completely with each successive image. But after a while, the familiar features show through again, and the similarities are recognised.

Let us consider one final question. What metaphor, of all those that have been discussed, best describes the memory of psychology itself? Without a doubt, the answer should be Freud's magic slate, that miraculous instrument that preserves everything without ever filling up. Like the magic slate, psychology seems to have two memories. The celluloid sheet on the surface receives stimuli and can easily be wiped clean. It is always available for new notes. Everything that is written on that celluloid sheet finds its way into a deeper layer of wax, but this layer is very difficult to access. Permanent traces can only be consulted by removing the outer layer. In the corpus of monographs, textbooks and journal articles, psychology possesses an infallible collective memory, written in wax. But the older these recorded insights are the less influence they have. It seems as if periodically a hand appears, to carry on Freud's metaphor, that removes the outermost sheet of the wax layer, and so wipes the surface clean. The text is preserved within, but it is a text that is no longer read, which is also a form of oblivion. Unless we consult those deeper registers more frequently, texts will continue to appear on the ever receptive celluloid surface, repeating what has long been present.

Index of names

Index of subjects